The Creative Arts:
On Practice, Making
& Meaning

The Creative Arts:
On Practice, Making
& Meaning

edited by
Sally Ann Murray and Michèle Betty

The Creative Arts: On Practice, Making & Meaning

Dryad Press (Pty) Ltd
Postnet Suite 281, Private Bag X16, Constantia, 7848,
Cape Town, South Africa
www.dryadpress.co.za/business@dryadpress.co.za

Copyright © Dryad Press
Text copyright © Individual Authors
All rights reserved

No part of this book may be reproduced or transmitted in any form or by any electronic or mechanical means, including photocopying and recording, or any other information storage or retrieval system, without prior written permission from the publisher or copyright holder.

Cover design & typography: Stephen Symons
Copy Editor: Helena Janisch
Proof Reader: Adri Marais
Set in 9.5/14pt Palatino Linotype
Cover Image: Henrietta Scholtz: *On Humankind i*. Walnut ink and charcoal on paper, 54 cm x 37 cm, 2018

First published in Cape Town by Dryad Press (Pty) Ltd, 2024
ISBN 978-0-7961-1310-8

Visit www.dryadpress.co.za to read more about all our books and to buy them. You will also find features, links to author interviews and news of author events. Follow our social media platforms on Instagram and Facebook to be the first to hear about our new releases.

Dryad Press is supported in the publication of this book by the Department of Sports, Arts and Culture, via the National Arts Council of South Africa, and the Presidential Employment Stimulus Programme. We extend our grateful thanks to these organisations, without whose assistance this publication would not have been possible.

Contents

Foreword

    – *Gabeba Baderoon*   1

Essays

    Inside the Outside: How a Poem Can Still Grow in the Glare of a Writing Workshop
    – *Kobus Moolman*   11

    Written by Others
    – *Phillippa Yaa de Villiers*   27

    Writing for Podcasts as Creative Practice in the Arts
    – *Annel Pieterse*   41

    Technologies of Conquest: On Writing the Dystopian through South Africa's Past, Present and Possible Future(s)
    – *Masande Ntshanga*   61

    the hamster forgets: a zuihitsu on remembering writing queerness and community in this body
    – *vangile gantsho*   77

    The Strongest Effect by the Lightest Means Possible: A Note on the Life and Art of Ernest Mancoba (1904–2002)
    – *Ashraf Jamal*   93

    Probing 'Place' as a Catalyst for Poetry
    – *Vonani Bila*   111

    Dance Curator as Archivist: JOMBA! Memory and Mourning
    – *Lliane Loots*   131

Writing Body as Land & Land as Body in
   Mine, Mine, Mine
   – *Uhuru Portia Phalafala*   149

'What's Up?': Using WhatsApp Group Chat to
Teach Undergraduate Creative Writing
Workshops during Covid 19
   – *Meg Vandermerwe*   169

Making *Nagmusiek*
   – *Stephanus Muller*   183

Concert Note – Remember Who You Are
   – *Liesl Jobson*   197

Reviewing as Attentive Praxis
   – *Wamuwi Mbao*   217

The Writer as Reader: Reflections on Poetry
and the Avant-Garde
   – *Simon van Schalkwyk*   233

Academic Writing: Starting, Stopping and
Coming to Grief
   – *Sally Ann Murray*   253

About the Editors, Artist and Authors   279

Foreword
Gabeba Baderoon

Can the creative arts be at home in the university? It is true that the university has offered degrees in music, drama, filmmaking, dance and visual arts for decades – but are the practices and ethos of creative praxes *at home* there? What possibilities exist for the university as a place of belonging for the arts, for creative making? This book risks bold responses to these questions: perhaps the creative arts can teach the university again what it could be. I see such belonging as always provisional and in conversation with meanings that escape the academic.

In the essays gathered here is a plenitude of ideas, experience and reflection on the *making* of art and the *doing* of teaching creativity by artists who also teach other artists. The variety, different scales and gratifying piquancy of the essays are deeply pleasurable and illuminating. There are accounts of how to teach in times of crisis, how to cultivate interiority yet address topics of larger amplitude, and the central challenge of how to write 'place'. But as I see it, one of the book's ambitions is to recharacterise 'the university' as a relational site where we can learn new, non-instrumental systems of value and therefore change the way we relate to the arts and the world. When we truly liberate our imaginations, we make visible what has no place in the value structure. In this, the book makes for a vital contribution to the pedagogy, theory and envisioning, not only of the creative arts, but of creativity itself. To practise such creativity is to approach the world with 'sharpened perception', in the words of the poet-publisher-teacher, Vonani Bila, who contributed to this collection the essay "Probing 'Place' as a Catalyst for Poetry".

The first time that poetry was rivetingly memorable for me was when I played Portia in *The Merchant of Venice* in Livingstone High School's annual Shakespeare comedy. I still remember my lines today: 'The quality of mercy is not strained. It droppeth like the gentle rain from heaven'. Next was when Jeremy Cronin gave a poetry reading at the same high school and I saw that despite the threats that loomed over dreams of freedom from a violent, authoritarian state, one could insist on dreaming. High school held more poetry than university, since for my first few years as a student at the University of Cape Town, I learned not how to be creative but how to become disciplined. By the time I enrolled for a PhD in English in 1997, all my interesting obliquities had been pared away in an agony of submission to authority. In my literature classes, I learned to despise what I felt closest to and value everything that lay outside of me. In contrast, when I took my first poetry writing class in 1999 (as an extramural 'hobby' class to the side of my studies, along with yoga, pottery and drawing), I found I could be honestly *not-knowing*. In his essay, Bila embraces this approach as a method: 'I see myself as a beginner whenever I sit down to write'. The thing I was learning assiduously to despise, the culture of popular reading, poetry and song that characterised my childhood – that is, what comes before and outside of the university – is the very stuff of learning and making poetry. As Bila recounts, he 'grew up listening to inventive poetry, myths and chants and performing cultural rituals by [his] clan' and in that corpus he learned 'poetry that challenges the sterility of accepted values, practices and norms; poetry that recreates'. Challenges. Recreates. This book conveys the pulse of a transformative moment for teaching the creative arts and making the case for the university as an enabling context, but also a boundary and provocation for reimagining teaching, critiquing and creating.

In late-capitalist culture, the university in South Africa has learned to mimic the language of production and measurement. Even so, the classroom, and particularly the arts classroom, refuses such instrumentalisation and resists the way the university has come to operate. Instead, the classroom is the site of resonance and transformation, which often becomes manifest over the long term. I see the arts as profoundly resistant to commodification, even as they rely on and are vulnerable to the demands of patrons who view them with a certain mesmerised fascination but a desire to remake them to their own measure of value. Thus, the university has made room for the creative arts in a way that often requires us to hide ourselves in metrics: annual reports, quality assessments, number of accredited outputs. However, as the essays gathered here reveal, the creative arts hold the potential to teach the university how to value itself differently. For one thing, an understanding of the power of creativity could prompt 'the university' to step more willingly outside its long-held boundaries. For what one knows can make one unresponsive to some of the very energies that could open up the field. If we don't recognise this, then we are limited to a lonely and colonial view of the world. As the essays in this collection affirm, being alert to the boundaries of the university's authority is crucial – in other words, attending to the dynamics of creativity near the institution, around the institution. In the university. Outside the university. How can these be creatively connected? High-status institutions tend to be less brave and interesting places for the creative arts than unruly, overlooked spaces where innovation can thrive. The essays in this volume illustrate this reminder.

When I first entered the creative writing classroom in 1999, I found it so strangely wonderful that I read many guides to learning and teaching writing to understand what was happening to me. I was trying to solve the mystery of the *at-homeness* that I had thought was impossible in a university. None of what I read was satisfying to me. None approached the mysterious loveliness of being a student who could once again trust the unknowability of the experience of learning. This book of essays would have satisfied me. To the audience who will discover it, I offer a guide to the many delights that are to follow. In form and theme, the chapters themselves practise a deeply gratifying range of voice and expression. The capacious form of the personal essay makes possible an intricate entwining of the autobiographical, the historical, the philosophical and the poetic into the vital meaning of creative writing. The erudition of the authors' allusions, such as is evidenced, for example, in Simon van Schalkwyk's essay, "The Writer as Reader: Reflections on Poetry and the Avant-Garde", is striking.

Given that many of the contributors to the book are also teachers in university contexts, it's apt to think a little about teaching, and its importance. The university has to learn again to treasure teaching. Teaching is always a charged relation, infinitely and mutually influencing – and the challenge of excellent teaching is to cultivate practices of growth as well as creativity. Included in this are questions of authority and fragility, practices of tenderness and care, and the capacity to feel a way hesitantly towards newness. If we think of writing (or choreography, podcasting or criticism) as a practice, so too is teaching. Such a practice, considered *creatively* rather than instrumentally, would ensure a softness, a *give* to the space of teaching. It would inspire different forms of hospitality, of relations to authority, of receptivity to newness. It would also introduce healthier relations to approval and critique – teaching creative people how to deal with praise is to teach them to protect the originality, stubbornness and unknowability of their ideas. The less recognisable we are, the more we are open to new possibilities. A long time ago, I learned that writing that engaged with politics, economics, history and collectivity was corrupted by ideology. Only the psyche was a legitimate terrain. In conversation with the artists gathered in this collection, I learn more about the profound promise of a new relation to teaching through the creative arts.

For the writer, tuition in 'creative writing' teaches creativity and not just fluency in genres of writing. Creativity does what other approaches struggle to do – it breaches boundaries of class, status and configurations of race through the unpredictable and resonant possibilities of invention. The role of the teacher in transforming a life – particularly that of someone who feels overlooked, misunderstood or disregarded – through even small acts such as lending a student a book, or writing a line in an essay's margin, is a central human narrative impossible to dismiss as a cliché due to the evocative detail and force of every such story. Teaching creativity doubles that transfiguring power. In this deliberate fluidity, the university can become a place for reshaping the possibilities of creative writing and creative making more broadly, bringing the power of imagination and idea and practice into generative encounter. Yet, for it to do so, those of us who are in the university must be careful not to claim too much authority over the creative arts. Because higher education traffics in authority; after all, a tertiary degree confers a fluency in the language of power – the university has also been a place against which artists have had to struggle. Colonial models of authority have often made the university a place of toxicity and domination. Teachers trained in the Global North, or hewing to the standards of the Global North, have drawn lines of non-recognition around certain kinds of dance or poetry or music, excluding the necessarily complex-otherness-making-remaking-re-birthing of what is emerging from the South. So, the university is also a boundary that drives creativity outside of itself by failing to recognise certain forms of practice. To become a worthy home for the creative arts, the university must become a more open place, a more creative place; open to fragility, inconclusiveness, multiplicity and incompleteness. In the face of institutional preferences for certainty and mastery, the essays in this volume embody just such a hospitality to practices of creativity from both inside and outside the boundaries of the university.

What you will encounter in the essays in this collection is creative multiplicity: Uhuru Phalafala's writing on 'wake'-fulness, enchantment and body-earth; Kobus Moolman's delicacy of beginnings and of coming 'crabwise' to the craft of writing; vangile gantsho's defining of the self with soft boundaries through a generous practice of recognition, listening and healing; Sally Ann Murray's movement across, within and between modes to find purchase in a latent, hybrid writing marked by a friction and distinctiveness that is perpetually in motion; Bila's writing of the poetry of the failed and the outcast, through the 'raw music' of the 'everyday'; the dynamic potential of teaching and writing explored by Meg Vandermerwe, who found that her students' fluency in WhatsApp offered a powerful resource for teaching prose despite the challenges of no access to electricity or quiet. Like Vandermerwe, Annel Pieterse is always stretching her medium, beyond radio into podcasts, imagining new relations of intimacy and resonance with audiences.

For all these contributors, the lesson is how to go beyond formula, how to write 'being' and 'place' and 'people' anew, especially the lonely, ugly, devastating landscapes that live in our bodies, as Phalafala tells us in her breathtaking account of her grandfather's broken breathing after absent decades on the mines. And in a country built on removing people from their homes, erasing their homes, creative makers must be willing to craft such *not belonging* – of being from no place. Ashraf Jamal traces his always-receding subject, the indefinable Ernest Mancoba, a masterly figure almost irretrievable to history and art – the essayist writing in language equal to his luminous and elusive subject. We also share the vivid private archive of Masande Ntshanga, who reads in the public library, watches Captain Tsubasa on TV at home, and plays 'Golden China TV Game' (the name for the early incarnation of Nintendo) on the console his mother buys him to keep him safe inside; from this archive comes the autobiography of the words 'native' and 'zone', tracking the crafting in his science fiction novels of an accurate and visionary history. Also vivid is Van Schalkwyk's parsing of the irretrievable subjects of avant-garde signs that refuse transparent meaning, leading him to imagine 'poetry as that form of language in which the boundaries between sound and sense are particularly porous'; and Stephanus Muller's account of creating his opus *Nagmusiek* emerges through a long process of learning, research, scholarship, and 'strategies of fragmentation, insertion, and creative re-imagining', which itself prompts further inventions of film, music and writing, an infinite responsiveness.

In my own dream of how creative writing might flourish in the university (and near and around it), I see artists of different fields learning near and around one another. For instance, writers would learn from musicians, and visual artists would learn with dancers, all newly and multiply aware of the breath and the body as technologies of creativity. Lliane Loots's archive is the body in motion, movement that is always evanescent and deliberately temporary. Impermanence has always implied 'unrecorded' – except when writing curates an archive of impermanent motion, and when ideas become cemented into givens. In her reflection on her dual musical and writing practices, Liesl Jobson finds that these twinned arts reach otherwise inaccessible parts of the self – that she is 'writing against self-erasure and self-destruction; music making for the silenced and wordless parts of [her]self'. As this suggests, a university hospitable to the arts needs to accommodate the drama that comes with artists and the awkward wildness of their imaginaries. It needs to teach artists a continuing mode of becoming and exceeding boundaries, without schooling them in self-regarding, self-destructive, often abusive personae (often learned from male artists from the North).

The profound hospitality that writers can bring one another in such exchanges is evident in Wamuwi Mbao's essay on reviewing, in which he views writing not as a finite object but as a space of relation and mutuality. His deep attention to the dimensions of a work elicits subtle understanding in readers, but also invites us to linger, inviting a futurity to our relation with writing that always promises further engagement and reciprocity. Such openness to relation is also present in Phillippa Yaa de Villiers's stunning deliberation on generativity and boundaries, both in the form of the porosity of motherhood, and in the way she as writer draws from other poets, specifically Phalafala, whose themes of breath and excavation in her epic poem *Mine Mine Mine* translate in De Villiers's essay into 'a strange radiance' that crosses the borders of writing and self. At its best, the teaching of creative writing can draw on these energies of mutuality, inventiveness and inspiration, and also cultivate in writers an appreciation for the practices of care and skill in the discipline.

This is a book for practices and pedagogies to which South Africa has come late; creative writing, for example, was only admitted to the university in the 1990s. Our belatedness sometimes makes us emulate too closely models from the Global North, and in other ways has made possible a bracing inventiveness, something not seen elsewhere – something that is equal to the realities we face and which forges new, urgently needed visions of the future. The essays tender a bold vision: how to make a hospitable space for artists, writers and critical creatives in the university and beyond. While we need medical aid, forms of recognition and support, we also need short-term residencies, flexible positions and ongoing relations. We need the university to see the teaching of the creative arts as teaching 'the how' of creativity and cultivating a whole ecosystem of readers, writers, performers, thinkers, makers and audiences. It needs to see itself with humility as *part* of this ecosystem – even if a particularly central part, laden with apparatus through which to grow and disseminate culture. To fulfil its deep promise, the university must evade the guardians of its disciplines and its own habits of authority. It must recover its playfulness and a lack of earnestness. While it might be said that the university has for decades welcomed theatre, music, dance, photography, architecture, visual art and film, each time stretching itself to accommodate them, it has also clamped down on these energies, tightening the air around them as a condition of entry. Instead, the university needs to build a home for agile, capacious, continuously evolving imaginations that practise habits of liberation, not strategies of containment.

We need not follow the model of the Global North. We need to find our own ways to measure creative success, to teach, to research, to write, to perform, to publish, to think and to review. So let us, in the South, cultivate a certain faith and stubbornness in defence of the difference of the models we are crafting both inside our universities and outside them, and not be derivative of the more glamorous and well-resourced Global North. Let us respect all the dimensions of the university – the classroom, but also the extramural, the extracurricular, the adult classes, the outreach, the 'afterschool', the voluntary, the student clubs, the families of those who got in, and those who didn't get in … for they are also the university – as places where knowledge can be creatively made. And since the university is, at its best, an eternally alive place, how about the arts connecting with one another? The dancers with the writers, the sculptors with the musicians, with with with … in practices that reach far beyond token 'interdisciplinarity'? How about we recognise that artists are bruisable; that our emotional structures have wide latitude that encompasses the bliss of creating and of pleasure, but also avoidance, loss, grief and trauma? How about the university understands slow maturation, indirectness, vulnerability and the unpredictable trajectory of creativity? How about we make translation central to our vision of creative making, whether literally, in the writing across many tongues (in a multi-lingual country, we must love, embrace and train ourselves in such linguistic translation), or in a more figurative enmeshed web of modes and styles and disciplines and cultures?

How about …? How about …?

I find it a source of joy that students, teachers and exponents of the arts are crafting a place of belonging, freedom and inventiveness for poetry, choreography, essaying, scholarship, teaching and performing in the university, making it a home hospitable to delicacy of perception, intuition and an openness to form and expansive themes. Let us continue to cultivate that.

Inside the Outside: How a Poem Can Still Grow in the Glare of a Writing Workshop

Kobus Moolman

Beginning

Where to begin? Begin on the outside. And then work your way in. Gradually.
How to begin? With one eye on the surface. And the other turned in.
And the third eye?
Looking up at the mountain. Or off into the distance of the desert.

The word 'poetry' derives from the Greek word *poiesis*. And intriguingly, *poiesis* does not refer only to the writing of verse. It simply means 'making': to make, in general. To make a boat, for crossing from one side to the other. To make a house, for sheltering from the wind and the rain. To make a bed. A cup for drinking. A stringed instrument. A pair of boots for walking into the distance. A poem too, for that matter.

How to proceed? Crab-wise.
With one unsteady step forward and two steps stumbling back.
With one word placed down uncertainly after the other. Over and over and over again.

> You can write on a wall with a fish heart, it's because of the phosphorous. They eat it. There are shacks like that down along the river. I am writing this to be as wrong as possible to you. Replace the door when you leave, it says. Now you tell me how wrong that is, how long it glows. Tell me.

Anne Carson said that (*Short Talks* 56).

Leaving an afterglow on the heart long after the words have left the lambent surface of the page.

'People go looking for one thing, and find another [...] Perhaps for something to be found, the only thing that matters is that there be searching – certainly that is the way in the writing of poems.' Jane Hirshfield said that (15).

Small yellow Cape canaries, finches actually (*Serinus canicollis*), search outside my window for the tiny pollen cones that have fallen onto the ground from the row of Monterey pines (*Pinus radiata*) in my neighbour's property.

'It is impossible to write meaningless sequences. In a sense the next thing always belongs. In the world of the imagination, all things belong. If you take that on faith, you may be foolish, but foolish like a trout.' Richard Hugo said that (5).

'But he had only ever owned one pair of boots his whole life. And they were black. And they followed him wherever he went.' I said that ("A Short Walk").

The Problem

I have to say it. I am a fraud. And I am a liar. For there is a fundamental contradiction at the heart of my creative life and practice.

As a writer – as a poet, a playwright, a writer of short stories – I believe that my works reach their completion best, their true fulfilment, after being left alone in the dark: private, uninterrupted and unwatched, germinating silently beneath the heavy earth. Polish poet Zbigniew Herbert, in his poem "The Longobards", wrote: 'In darkness and in silence my body was ripening' (138). And here instead of 'body', I think 'words', 'body' of words. And this is more to me than a belief. Much more. In daily, nightly, painfully slow practice, this approach, this methodology, as it were, has been confirmed over and over to me. It is I suppose, in some senses, an unashamedly anti-rationalist approach. And it has everything to do with surrender, with acquiescence, with trust. Trust that beneath and deep within that dark soil, something indeed is happening. That the dark is, in fact, in D. H. Lawrence's words, 'a living dark' (iv). That it is – to continue my admittedly clichéd metaphor of vegetation – rich, fertile, fecund. Productive.

Of course, I cannot claim any originality for this idea. In a letter of 1817, John Keats described poetry's relationship to the unknown, to mystery, to his brothers George and Tom. In this letter, he famously ascribed poetic inspiration to a kind of anti-talent. 'Negative Capability', he called it, and explained it as a writer's ability to accept 'uncertainties, mysteries, doubts, without any irritable reaching after fact and reason' (53).

And Athol Fugard in his *Notebooks* wrote:

> How thin and insecure is that little beach of white sand we call the conscious. I've always known that in my writing it is the dark troubled sea of which I know nothing, save its presence, that carried me. I've always felt that creating was a fearless and a timid, a despairing and a hopeful, launching out into that unknown. With me it has never been so much a question of something to say as of something, or nothing, to find – the "searchingness" someone called it. (73)

And yet, at the same time, I am also a teacher of creative writing, a teacher with almost twenty years' experience in supervising a wide range of undergraduate and postgraduate student projects. I believe that writing is a manifestation of new understanding or configurations of knowledge, and that these forms of knowledge, while hermeneutical, open-ended and actively evolving, are not ultimately either abstract or arbitrary. There is a definitive making involved. A thing is made. Brought into the world and then left there. *Poiesis*: a bringing forth. And this thing can be looked at and turned upside down and inside out, and understood. And if it can be understood, then it can be taught. And the understanding of it can be taught. But most importantly, the making of it can be taught too. For writing is a cognitive process. It is not, ultimately, like breathing, which happens without will or reflection or the necessity for understanding even. And part of my method of teaching this making – of guiding other writers through the making of their own pieces – is the workshop format.

In her article "The Rhetoric of the Prose Fiction Workshop", Jean McNeil describes the workshop model of a creative writing class as

> a peer-evaluation seminar where students, presided over by a lecturer/teacher, read and evaluate student work in progress. The ethos of the workshop is that each member offers a response to the work in progress of their peer, a response which can be analytical, subjective, thematic, technical or an amalgam of the above. (133)

Granted, in any creative writing workshop, the text is still largely emergent, in-process. It is, as McNeil goes on to argue, largely

> a series of suppositions, experiments, gestures and explorations, no matter to what degree its author might believe it is finished work. In reality, in the [...] workshop we are tasked with assessing the potentialities and intent of the text: what is this piece of fiction *trying* to be? What is its optimal expression of itself? (133)

My employment of the workshop model does not, of course, equate to an unproblematic adoption of this teaching/learning methodology for discovery and invention. Finuala Dowling confessed to the following: 'I am slightly allergic to the word "workshop" with its undertone of good works and hidden agendas, and its slight odour of damp garage' (1). And so there will always remain the question of how to breathe life into this potentially exhausted method.

Nevertheless, largely because of its flexibility and its receptivity to a multiplicity of individual approaches, the workshop format in creative production has formed the basis of my group facilitation as well as my one-on-one teaching and supervision. And in its most fundamental logic, the workshop model is premised on the idea that knowledge can be reviewed, shared, dissected and put together again, all in the full glare of other people. Public, probed and prodded, scrutinised.

Without prejudicing the ultimate outcome.

Is there thus a tension in me between the writer and the teacher? Between the champion of the dark, the ungraspable and the unconscious, and the pedagogue of explication, illumination and argument?

Am I saying one thing to myself, and another to my students? Or is this possible tension between these two facets within me based on a false understanding of so-called inspiration and the processes of artistic creation, of *poiesis*?

Are there in fact, ways in which the mysterious space of individual creative production can be preserved and even deepened during and through a collaborative workshop?

The Challenge

> To speak with blind alleys
> about what's facing,
> about its
> expatriate
> sense –:
> to chew this
> bread, with
> writing teeth.

Remember this poem by Paul Celan (*Snow Part* 51). I will return to it later.

Another admission first.

I am not a gardener. I cannot grow anything. I do not have green fingers. Unlike my grandmother, who could push the proverbial dry stick in the ground and it would grow. If anything, you could say that I have green eyes. I like to look at the things that grow – the wild banana and the fever trees outside my window, the yellow pincushion proteas, the spekboom and the spinach. And I like the way that these things taste – wild grass, eggplant, broccoli, peas in their pods (if the baboons don't get to them). And I like the way they smell – orange blossom, jasmine, dhanya, yesterday-today-and-tomorrow – drenched in memory and evocation. And I can stand for hours (not literally) watering them. But, I have never been good at growing them. I suppose I don't understand how growing works. I think I understand the inside life of a stone more than the life of a vegetable or a flower.

But one thing I do know. You cannot grow anything by digging it up all the time to see how it's growing. To see what's happening down there, inside the invisible dark. That much I know.

So how then can I suppose that it should be any different when it comes to teaching the making of a poem in the context of a writing workshop? Is there a difference between the maker who makes and the maker who teaches the making?

My approach has always been to bring these two aspects together in the learning space. And thus I learn, as we learn. And thus I have learned (slowly, painfully slowly) to understand and follow the inward way that a poem has of coming to be itself, being itself, the ways a poem acts out its constituent parts inside itself, the ways it presents itself to itself, its internal operations. And in the same way, I can bring this experience and this understanding to the classroom, and I can fast-track the process for the students. As Hugo explains:

> A good creative-writing teacher can save a good writer a lot of time. Writing is tough, and many wrong paths can be taken. If we are doing our job, creative-writing teachers are performing a necessary negative function. And if we are good teachers, we should be teaching the writer ways of doing that for himself all his writing life. We teach how not to write and we teach writers to teach themselves how not to write. When we teach how to write, the student had best be on guard. (64)

Now to return to Celan.

There is a 'blind alley' that faces itself. It leads nowhere but back into itself.

The poem's central gesture ('to speak') – its speech act – is an address to and with this sense (what he calls an 'expatriate sense', Celan himself being a kind of expatriate in Paris) of being in the world, while also of being a writer ('with writing teeth'). A difficult phrasing to follow, I realise. But this circular pattern in the poem is worth bearing in mind. It is crucially teased out, self-prospected, in his 1960 "Meridian" speech on being awarded the Georg Büchner Prize for Literature, where he discusses searching for and finding 'something – like language – immaterial, yet earthly, terrestrial, something in the shape of a circle' (*Collected Prose* 50).

So I go back to the beginning, and I begin again.
Begin on the outside. And work your way in.

> We had been talking life, fruit and vegetables. Now it was time to keep quiet. Shhhhh. Ladies and gentlemen, it is time to throw down your bones. Someone has to fill the hole of this grave.

Mangaliso Buzani said that in the long prose poem "A Naked Bone" (73).

The Method

In his seminal essay, "Tradition and the Individual Talent", T. S. Eliot describes a poet's mind as a kind of scientific laboratory or chemistry testing kit: 'a receptacle for seizing and storing up numberless feelings, phrases, images, which remain there until all the particles which can unite to form a new compound are present together' (*On Poetry and Poets* 72). What matters, for Eliot, is not the 'intensity of the emotions, the components, but the intensity of the artistic process, the pressure, so to speak, under which the fusion takes place' (*On Poetry and Poets* 72). So, what matters is not the individual qualities of all these disparate components (elements, to continue with the language of chemistry), but rather what happens when they are combined or fused under pressure, a process that would seem to unlock some hiddenness, some myriad potentialities, previously absent. A kind of whole as more than the sum of its parts. Hirshfield explains:

> Creative discoveries are made by generative re-combination: disparate elements brought together in a way not previously seen, then recognised as making a useful whole. Cognition begins with the construction and distinction of patterns. (36)

Pattern is an important word and concept. It is tempting to dive straight into its deliciously cool significations and resonances. But I don't want to get ahead of myself.

So back for a moment. In order to go forward. 'You say I am repeating / Something I have said before. I shall say it again. / Shall I say it again?' (Eliot, *Collected Poems* 201). The 'searchingness', Fugard termed it (73).

What is there about poetry – about what poetry is and how it uniquely functions – that can be activated by the writing teacher in order to counter the glare of the workshop format?

The departure point for me is in Terry Eagleton's conception of a poem as a 'phenomenology of language' (21). In his incisive and accessible book *How to Read a Poem*, Eagleton presents, among other things, a defence of the language of poetry as primarily a thing in itself:

> Poetry is a kind of phenomenology of language – one in which the relation between word and meaning (or signifier and signified) is tighter than it is in everyday speech. There are several different ways of saying 'Take a seat', but only one way of saying 'The hare limped trembling through the frozen grass'. Poetry is language in which the signified or meaning is *the whole process of signification itself*. It is thus always at some level language which is about itself. There is something circular or self-referential about even the most publicly engaged of poems. The meaning of a poem is far less abstractable from its total process of signification than is the meaning of a road sign. This is not to say that you cannot give a summary of a poem's content, just as you can of a police cadet's manual. But the former résumé is always likely to be less informational than the latter. Poetry is something which is done to us, not just said to us. The meaning of its words is closely bound up with the experience of them. (21)

Think about Celan's 'blind alleys' that face back upon themselves.

Or this by Hirshfield: 'Poems, if they are any good at all, hold a knowledge elusive and multiple, unsayable in any other way' (36). Unsayable in any other way because the saying is not a window through to something else; the words of a poem are our experience of them. I will let Eagleton back in again, because he expresses it so well: 'A poem constitutes the very things it is about. In this sense, every poem curves back on itself' (69). In this sense, too, arguably there is no *about* in a poem. At the risk of inviting accusations of aestheticism, the How is as important as the What. Or a more accurate way of saying this is that the subject of a poem (the about/what) should always serve the language of the poem, and not the other way round.

This is an important first step in understanding for students who sit together in the white humming light of the seminar room around the very large table – so large there is barely space for them to pull their chairs out before they hit the wall. While in the tree outside (why have I not noticed what type of tree it is?) a pair of grey hadeda ibises (*Bostrychia hagedash*) have raised their three chicks in a scrappy, precarious nest.

Names are important, you see. All things have names. Nouns are important. They can be shared around a table. I'll give you mine, if you give me yours. They can swell in the mind to three times their size. And they're so much more important than adjectives. Except the very simple kind. Keep it simple. Always. Especially if the subject is large.

> follow me
> close your eyes
> think of the moon
> contemplate my river
> and let us cross

The Congolese poet Tchicaya U Tam'si wrote that (3).

Listening to the Inside of the Outside

So let us cross over and continue on the dark side of words, where the shadow of language casts its weird light on Celan's 'blind alley' that faces itself. Under terrible pressure, the white-hot intensity of a poem's language – a pressure not unlike the electromagnetic force within an atom – the poem crystallises. I have borrowed this word from Carson, who argues: 'To understand and to keep, in however diminished a form, some picture of the inside crystal of things […] is a poet's obligation' (*Economy of the Unlost* 70). Of course, I admit that the spatial metaphor of inside versus outside is misleading. We cannot slowly peel the exterior of a poem away from its interior, and be left holding its appearance in our hand, like a long coil of orange peel. I resist the dichotomy or dualism that this spatial analogy implies – although we love to speak about Form and Content, Language and Meaning, as if they were distinct and independent. A better analogy would be the Möbius strip, which possesses only one side (and only a single boundary), although it looks as if it actually has two sides. Or a sheet of paper, where the verso cannot ever (at least not in this world) be separated from the recto.

Rather, my use of the term 'inside' refers usefully to the experiential moment of writing, the act of poetic creation when the student writer is looking down and listening from within to what is going on all around them and within them and within the poem itself, in a state of what Celan in his "Meridian" speech calls 'attention' (*Collected Prose* 50). Whenever I talk to students about this idea of inner attentiveness – sitting around the big table in the seminar room or around the desk in my small office with my back to the window – the lines from W. B. Yeats's poem "Long-Legged Fly" come to mind:

> His eyes fixed upon nothing
> A hand upon his head.
> *Like a long-legged fly upon the stream*
> *His mind moves upon silence.* (381; emphasis in original)

So, the workshop space, far from being a space of self-consciousness and comparison, even judgement, has the potential to become a place of encounter with the 'inside crystal of things' that Carson describes (*Economy of the Unlost* 70). And this encounter can be facilitated through a conscious but gradual nurturing of trust, openness and introspection that amounts ultimately to a process of listening. Listening *to* and also listening out *for*.

This double method of listening is significant. And with students I always use the analogy of a singer in a choir who might close one ear with their hand so that they can hear themselves, attend to themselves.

So. Listen out *to*, and listen out *for*, what?

Finally I can come back to Hirshfield who argued that 'cognition begins with the construction and distinction of patterns'(36). And what is pattern? Pattern is shape. Pattern comprises the characteristic features and identifiable traits of something that give it its distinctiveness, its identity.

And pattern, as in music, as in architecture or design, is repetition.

And in the writing workshop, through attentive listening, students can be guided on how to recognise, how to hear and see (poetry is always a coordination of ear and eye) the internal self-referential logic and coherence that underpins the voice and the energy and form of each of their poems. However transgressive, twisted or weird this logic might be. I cannot stress this latter point enough.

I am always reminded here of Samuel Taylor Coleridge's argument in the *Biographia Literaria* that each poem always 'contains within itself the reasons why it is so and not otherwise' (117).

And so one of the ways that I conceptualise the writing workshop is as a space where students can discover inside their poem the 'reasons why it is so and not otherwise'. So that as they consciously enter into dialogue with the evolving nature of their poem in the writing and re-writing phase, they can make informed choices about its formal characteristics: punctuation, register, mood, length of line, stanzaic structure. Whether wide open and expansive as a field, as in the work of Charles Olson or Mark Rothko, tight and formal like Emily Dickinson or Gwen John, or cruel and crude like Hiromi Itō or Egon Schiele. (I frequently use visual prompts or inspiration in the workshop.)

So that, ultimately, these complex formal and expressive choices will cohere and fit together, and belong and support each other, slotting in and helping the poem move along, instead of hindering it, slowing it down, and ultimately undermining it. As C. D. Wright argues: 'The need for form arises not so much for containment but for support. Form naturally determines the poem's movement, whether it be gradual, teleological, furious or travelling in reverse' (8).

And because of the internal patterning of a poem, I always argue that nothing is insignificant, that every full stop, comma, capital letter or line break is important and functional and contributes to the overall effect.

Yet, how does a student do what I am asking of them in the workshop? How do they achieve this?

I always encourage the student to address the materiality of what they are working with (the individual words, the lines, the sounds, the language itself, yes, ultimately, the language itself), and to ask of this concrete material the same question as above: why are you so and not otherwise?

Another way of putting this would be to say: always ask of these elements what do they want to be, where do they want to go, how do they want to get there? By way of the clear, direct path through the dark forest like Raymond Carver or Makhosazana Xaba? Or circuitously, continually doubling back upon themselves like Fred Wah or Joan Metelerkamp, for example?

Of course, pattern, repetition, is nothing without its counter, which is silence. Or space. The not said. The withholding. What Wallace Stevens (in his poem "The Snowman") intriguingly, even frustratingly, called the 'Nothing that is not there and the nothing that is' (178). Music helps in this case. In the workshops, I often use minimalist composers, such as Arvo Pärt and Philip Glass, to help students attend to the deep well, the dark unseen that must be left behind and between their words. The weight of absence that speaks. The weight of non-presence that gives form to presence. (I refer students to the idea of positive and negative space in drawing.) The weight of time that is the backdrop for everything we say and do. And I immediately recall the words of Mxolisi Nyezwa from his article "Trauma and Image": 'Poetry is the antithesis of death, enlivening our actions and our experience of existence to achieve a sense of new meaning. It is the duty of poetry to keep everybody alive' (20).

But listening, as I discussed earlier, is also a listening *to*. Listening to everything that I have just elaborated on above. Certainly. But more than that. Listening to the poem in its unfolding in the present. Listening to the moment of the present in its material distinctiveness, while at the same time open – wide, wide, wide open – to all possibilities and different solutions. Listening with one ear closed and the other open. Celan described this process in his "Meridian" speech as a poem 'travel[ling] a certain space in a certain direction, on a certain road'. The idea of movement, becoming, is central to both the method and the nature of poetry for Celan. He continues:

> The poem is lonely. It is lonely and *en route*. Its author stays with it. Does this very fact not place the poem already here, at its inception, in the encounter, *in the mystery of encounter*? The poem intends another, needs this other, needs an opposite. It goes toward it, bespeaks it. For the poem, everything and everybody is a figure of this other toward which it is heading. (*Collected Prose* 49)

And in the same way that in the workshop the poem can be '*en route* [...] in the mystery of encounter' into a deeper sense of its potential and what it is, so too of course is the student writer.

En route to a deeper sense of their humanness. And the elusiveness and precariousness of being human.

It is no small thing at all.
It is always a risk. There is no other way. Whether for a student or someone who has been writing for twenty years. It is always a wager. A step toward and into the dark.

With only the small light of the hand to guide.

'With the hand running. Following the writing hand like the painter draws: in flashes. The hand leads to the flowers. From the heart where passions rise to the fingertips that hear the body thinking', as Hélène Cixous describes it (156).

The workshop can contain and it can activate this mystery of making. The workshop can be the place where a form of thinking and speech different from the solitary experience can be energised, where the glare of the outside does not preclude the intensity of the inside, where instead another pressure can fuse language and emotion into a new compound.
And so, as Eliot writes in "Four Quartets", 'In my end is my beginning [...] What we call the beginning is often the end / And to make an end is to make a beginning [...] And the end of all our exploring / Will be to arrive

where we started / And know the place for the first time' (*Collected Poems* 204, 221-222).

So I return. Re-turn to face the 'blind alley' of the page.

So we, sitting around the seminar table or my office desk, shuffle our papers, shuffle our feet, look up, then down. We smile, and make the leap.

Bibliography

Boruch, Marianne. *In the Blue Pharmacy*. Trinity University Press, 2005.

---. *The Little Death of Self: Nine Essays toward Poetry*. University of Michigan Press, 2017.

Buzani, Mangaliso. *A Naked Bone*. Deep South, 2019.

Carson, Anne. *Economy of the Unlost*. Princeton University Press, 1999.

---. *Short Talks*. Brick Books, 1992.

Celan, Paul. *Collected Prose*. Translated by Rosmarie Waldrop, Carcanet, 1986.

---. *Snow Part*. Translated by Ian Fairley, Sheep Meadow Press, 2007.

Cixous, Hélène. *Three Steps on the Ladder of Writing*. Columbia University Press, 1993.

Coleridge, Samuel Taylor. *Biographia Literaria*, edited by Adam Roberts, Cambridge University Press, 2014.

Dowling, Finuala, editor. *Difficult to Explain*. Hands-on Books, 2010.

Eagleton, Terry. *How to Read a Poem*. Blackwell Publishing, 2007.

Eliot, T. S. *Collected Poems: 1909-1962*. Faber and Faber, 1963.

---. *On Poetry and Poets*. Faber and Faber, 1969.

Fraser, Kathleen. *Translating the Unspeakable*. University of Alabama Press, 2000.

Fugard, Athol. *Notebooks: 1960-1977*. Ad Donker, 1983.

Glück, Louise. *Proofs & Theories: Essays on Poetry*. Ecco Press, 1994.

Herbert, Zbigniew. "The Longobards." *The Poetry of Survival: Post-War Poets of Central and Eastern Europe*, edited by Daniel Weissbort, Penguin, 1991.

Hirshfield, Jane. *Hiddenness, Uncertainty, Surprise: Three Generative Energies of Poetry*. Bloodaxe Books, 2007.

Hugo, Richard. *The Triggering Town: Lectures and Essays on Poetry and Writing*. W. W. Norton, 1979.

Keats, John. *Letters of John Keats*. Oxford University Press, 1954.

Kroll, Jeri and Graeme Harper, editors. *Research Methods in Creative Writing*. Palgrave Macmillan, 2013.

Lawrence, D. H. *Selected Poems*. Penguin, 1979.

McNeil, Jean. "The Rhetoric of the Prose Fiction Workshop – an Analysis of Teaching Methods at the University of East Anglia." *Current Writing*, vol. 27, no. 2, 2015, pp. 132-138.

Moolman, Kobus. "A Short Walk." Unpublished poem, 2012.

---. "Teaching the Practice of Writing Poetry in an Academic Environment." *Current Writing*, vol. 27, no. 2, 2015, pp. 124-131.

Nyezwa, Mxolisi. *New Country*. UKZN Press, 2008.

---. *Song Trials*. Gecko Poetry, 2000.

---. "Trauma and Image." *The Fertile Ground of Misfortune*, edited by Stacy Hardy and Robert Berold, Institute for the Study of English in Africa, 2017. pp. 19-21.

Stevens, Wallace. "The Snowman." *Collected Poems*. Faber and Faber, 2006.

U Tam'si, Tchicaya. "Agony." *Selected Poems*. Translated by Gerald Moore, Heinemann, 1970.

Wright, C. D. *Cooling Time: An American Poetry Vigil*. Copper Canyon Press, 2005.

Yeats, William Butler. *Collected Poems*. Macmillan, 1973.

Written by Others

Phillippa Yaa de Villiers

Mother,
my phantom limb-o.
My ghost of a ghost of a ghost of a hand
stroking the infant face in wonder.
Where did you pour your awe
at the miracle produced
by your own body? I with my own son
awakened to such a strange radiance that
unexpected itself out of my whole vocabulary,
turned me inside out, there with the pulsing placenta
dismissing the rules and upending the grammar.
And all I could think was
it's all me, it's all me, it's all
mine, mine, mine …
(De Villiers, *Unpublished fragment*)

While drafting this essay in October 2023, I went to a launch of Uhuru Phalafala's epic poem and family memoir *Mine Mine Mine* at The Commune in Braamfontein. In this, her debut publication, literary scholar and poet Phalafala evokes the life of her late grandfather, who contracted silicosis while working as a migrant worker in the asbestos mines at various localities in the country. Phalafala's reading/performance vividly depicted South Africa's racist, extractivist mining history and its wide-ranging effects on the family networks of miners, particularly the women and children. Phalafala delves into her family's experience, revealing the human cost of the search for precious minerals. The musicality of her performance set something off in me, and the next morning I woke up singing a version of the poem at the beginning of this chapter, a poem that refused to be silent until I had written it down. It seemed that Phalafala's excavations had turned some of my own dirt; the poem returned me to the common themes of motherhood, loss and redemption.

Like all writers, the sounds, images and ideas of others accompany me as I carve my own path out of the labyrinth of contradictions, impositions, judgements and denials that plague my writing process. Let me be frank: while I am trying to write, that very same brain, with an equal energy and determination, is laying traps, attacking and undermining me when I presume to opine or even imagine. Perhaps the greatest obstacle to an artist is their ego; inflated with pride and arrogance, or filled with the bitter soup of rejection. Either way, it distorts the 'truth' that emerges in bursts, scribbles and tears. By the time that you, the reader, are reading this book, however, I will have smoothed out the utterance. The poem has already changed, as the words bump against new resonances that the world around it exposes each day. For example, a week later, I was pleasantly surprised, and then immediately unconvinced, by my use of 'unexpected' as a verb. Perhaps it won't even become a poem, but will simply exist as a figment, an illustration of a process. If there is a line that still feels hot in three months' time, I will gently wiggle it into shape. If I am lucky, you, the reader have developed a relationship with the poem. The poem, like Phalafala's, may have triggered a sound somewhere in your being. The words have reshaped themselves to fit the meaning you require; tickled in this way, your poetic apparatus might shoot out a poem in response.

This essay deals with life stories, and draws from memoir, theatre, biography and poetry in an attempt to explore the ethics and techniques by which one writes one's life. Poetry has played a significant role in the excavation of my story. Rather than stating any precise technical practices, I want rather to trace how the relationship between writer and reader begins with the writer's contract with language – their poetics. Writers draw from the unique expression of our formative models, building on the language family storytellers have shared with us, layered with the cultural register of idioms and imperatives. Added to this, the reservoir of our creativity is enriched by the collective lode of the artists whose work inspired us, a shifting tide of expression that we wield to our particular purpose, which is mostly to say, as Keorapetse Kgositsile argued, 'this is who I am' (19). Finally, this essay considers the consequences of wresting from the spectres of shame, fear and illegitimacy, the right to define oneself – to describe one's life in the language of one's personal preference and capacity.

A discussion about ethics and writing will inevitably involve the use of 'truth' or integrity, but a writer's 'truth' may be based in complete duplicity. What lies between fact and numinous fantasy is the province of artists, and has special significance for the maker of worlds in words. As a child, I generally believed that what the adults who acted, decreed and decided on my behalf – what they told me – was true. (I say that, but it is not the full truth. Since I can remember, a sense of uncertainty about these 'facts' hovered at the edge of conversations.) When I was twenty, my father revealed that he was not my father, my mother was not my mother, and none of the people I thought were mine, were mine. My father's news was devastating, but I only knew how devastating years later, in therapy. I was angry with my parents for lying to me and disappointed by their refusal to take responsibility for the consequences of those lies. In any case, my mother had already disinherited me for my involvement in student politics and we were not on speaking terms. I simply got on with my life as I had always done, dissembling. Apartheid with its sinister network of laws, including closed adoption, was still strangling South Africa. Strongly identifying with what I now understood were the oppressed, I began to explore the stranger in the mirror. I had grown up reading books and watching plays and movies, and enjoyed expressive exploration. Although I took photographs, sang, danced and acted, my most enduring and enriching mode of expression was writing.

The end of Apartheid signalled an end to segregation legislation, and gradually many South Africans were able to live openly as African, Coloured and gay. Adoptees had new access to genealogical information and consensual contact with birth families was permitted. Everyone, it seemed, wanted to add their name to the roll call of the new nation. Magazine articles, as well as biographies and autobiographies, memoirs and notebooks proliferated – from Winnie Mandela and Zelda la Grange (Nelson Mandela's personal assistant) to Hugh Masekela, sports figures and countless struggle veterans and a few villains. Nancy Jacobs and Andrew Bank note that biographies and autobiographies dominated the domestic non-fiction market, with over 800 works published in the (then) 28 years of democracy (Jacobs and Bank 166). For many, these texts seemed to appear compulsively, directed by forces beyond ordinary consciousness. Commissioned by ancestors, or with a juridical mission – impelled by the buried victims in personal narratives – South Africans took up the pen or faced the screen to make sense of it all. Gabeba Baderoon, in the introduction to *Our Words, Our Worlds: Writing on Black South African Women Poets 2000–2018*, observes, 'poetry written by Black women in South Africa came to remake public space' (qtd. in Xaba 1). This 'public space' was made accessible to me through the practice and power of poetry; it was through my association with Makhosazana Xaba and Myesha Jenkins that poems and sentences began to appear, confirming my membership of this important cohort of South African writers.

After studying during the states of emergency in the eighties, I had begun my career as a journalist. But I wanted to work with imaginary stories, so I went to Jacques Lecoq's international theatre school in Paris from 1989 to 1991, returning to South Africa just as it was coming into itself as a democracy. I started as an actor, and over the next twenty years complemented physical theatre and dance with television writing: in about 2001, poems began to appear alongside the scripts. I found it easier to access a feeling of presence and being fully alive through poems and physical movement than through narrative and plot, and everything I said seemed more real in the presence of others. Collectives like Cape Town's WEAVE, Johannesburg's Word N Sound, and Current State of Poetry, and the numerous poetry sessions that took place all over the country, invited people to share their lives in poems, birthing many of us as poets. I developed confidence from the critical engagement with the work and camaraderie and solidarity in these spaces, particularly at Jozi House of Poetry,[1] which I attended from 2002 until 2018.

My father's revelation did not produce an immediate desire to write my story, because I had no information, and couldn't conceive of a speaker or narrator. Fantasy was more accessible than reality. In 1997, while working as an actor, I wrote a short story about a circus crossing Africa; it centred on a dwarf called Piece-of-Shit, whose parents abandon him in the forest because the villagers in that area saw dwarfism as a deformity and a curse. The circus, run by ringmaster Callahan, adopts Piece-of-Shit. The tightrope lady and the dwarf fall in love, and months later she falls to her death while carrying his child. I never published the story in manuscript form, but it became the play *fall, i catch you,* directed by Warrick Grier and starring Tshepo Maseko, Sue Pam-Grant, Toni Morkel, Hannah Kantazi and me, which ran at the Market Theatre and at the National Arts Festival in then-Grahamstown, now Makhanda.² At the time, I had the bare facts about my own adoption into a White family, and *fall, i catch you* conveyed some truth about that experience. The feelings of abandonment and self-loathing, and the compulsion to perform to earn a place among people, were aspects of my inner life for which I had no words – but under the skilled direction of Grier, the characters expressed that story.

Ignorant of the Apartheid policy, my biological mother relinquished me for adoption in 1966, without the knowledge of my Ghanaian father. Due to my race, two academics, Professor Phillip Tobias and his colleague, Dr Hertha de Villiers, were appointed to decide whether I was a fit candidate for adoption. It was determined that I was not, but in September, De Villiers adopted me in strict secrecy. Although the mystery of my origins was hardwired into me, after my father told me the truth in 1986, I began to access flashes of what Jackie Kay calls a 'blazing burning curiosity, the all-consuming insatiable appetite for self-knowledge' (*Red Dust* 47). Kay was adopted by a communist couple and she and her brother of African descent grew up in a small, exclusively White community in rural Scotland. The Kays' political consciousness imbued Jackie with a sense of pride and courage, and she became a prolific writer of plays, poetry, novels and short stories. I, on the other hand, was somewhat muted until I found my biological parents, and began to write myself out of the silence. While I was professionally researching and writing other people's stories for television – for *Soul Buddyz*, *Soul City*, *Thetha Msawawa*, *Cha Cha* and other television series – I began writing poems and it became easier to find the words.

The writer is me; I am making up this story, which is 'true'. Some parts of the story are factually verifiable, like the fact that I moved into my adoptive home on the day that Hendrik Verwoerd was assassinated. Others are not verifiable – in particular, the circumstances that drove my mother to give birth to a baby fathered by an African, in Apartheid South Africa. Documented or not, proven or not, both are forms of historical fact, and they provide more than a background; they build a *stage* on which the drama will unfold. My story is nothing like those of the South African writers who defied Apartheid censorship laws, speaking out at great cost to their lives and careers. Their contribution represents a valuable resource, providing individual observations of collective trauma. Creative writing complicates grand narratives, providing the small song of the individual. Despite grand intentions to make Apartheid-era novels, poems and other art forms part of school and university curricula, many of these stories have disappeared. A 2023 creative writing class stares blankly when asked if they know the work of, say, Sandile Dikeni or Sipho Sepamla – not to mention the writing of Dennis Brutus or Jeremy Cronin. Our current sense of history and, consequently, literary value is not uniform, and is complicated by global publishing, the ubiquity of the Internet, and competition from other forms of storytelling. Within the maelstrom of technology, however, writers continue to *write*.

South Africans do not have a unanimous origin myth; our history is foundationally contested. The literature of the Caribbean, in comparison, is predicated on a universal acknowledgement of the facts of colonialism and slavery and the heinousness of the system that brutally displaced Africans to the other side of the world. This allows Caribbean writers to write whatever they write without having to rewrite history. On the other hand, South Africans are at various stages of unlearning the toxic habits that racialised their moral code. Jacobs and Bank posit that the interest in biography, autobiography and memoir was informed by curiosity 'as well as the need to engage in some process of inner reckoning, of coming to terms with the pain and suffering of Apartheid as narrated in accounts of the life paths of others' (166). They further suggest that a later cohort of readers, after Jacob Zuma's presidency, is 'groping towards re-imagining political possibilities in the light of a depressing spiral of revelations about corruption, failing social services and ultimately state capture' (Jacobs and Bank 166). The compulsion, in my case, was to share in words the strangeness of my personal circumstances, and to work out which of my experiences were beneficial, and which I could jettison. As a student in the eighties, I saw the apathy and casual racism of the majority of White people I encountered as a collective moral failure. My father's revelation allowed me to free myself, to some extent, from Apartheid White socialisation – and to pick the friends whose ideals aligned with mine.

I only discover what I think when I have written it down. This backwards way of orienting myself in the world has been the bedrock of my writing practice. Honestly, Kay's 'blazing burning curiosity' (47) only set in when

I had actual people in reach. It took years of writing and sharing poetry to allow for the substantially larger project of my autobiographical play, *Original Skin*, to take shape. I could never write a tome, solid and well-referenced. Like everything I write, it is fragmentary and alternates registers and modes between poetry, monologue and narration. Reading Kay's first poetry collection, *The Adoption Papers*, which she performed as a radio play, was inspiring and suggested new possibilities for telling my story. However, due to the violently acrimonious breakdown with my adoptive family, I chose to semi-fictionalise the story and change the names. As with *fall, i catch you*, I substituted how certain events *felt* to me for the 'truth' of the facts. It is close to dissembling, but without malicious intention. Like someone who has to claim that strangers are their family, I bend the 'truth' to make it work for me, almost without realising it. For example, I was not left in a box on the doorstep of the Princess Alice Home, but my mother's relinquishing me, a Black child, in Apartheid South Africa, made me feel as if I had been discarded. The warmth with which Kay writes of her parents is markedly different from my relationship with my parents, which is filled with conflict and betrayal.

Two years before the play was finished, the facilitator at a workshop for emerging writers at the Market Theatre Laboratory asked us what we were trying to write. When I shyly admitted that I was writing about my life, he said: 'Why should anyone care to read your memoir? You haven't yet *done* anything to deserve their attention'. He had a point. All I had done was live my life. I wasn't a famous activist, a pioneering scientist or a dedicated teacher. I was a somewhat spoilt, biracial adoptee from the far north of Johannesburg – the area now known as Midrand. I was, myself, a nobody of note. Barbara Boswell titles her rich study of Black South African women's writing, 'I wrote my story anyway', and that is exactly what I did, with the example and encouragement of texts like James Baldwin's *Autobiographical Notes* and Audre Lorde's *Sister Outsider*. I can't claim exclusive authorship of the play; perhaps that is written into the mechanics of making theatre. Robert Colman, the veteran theatre-maker, actor and director, co-wrote and directed *Original Skin*, and the title was his idea. Finding a doll's park bench in a second-hand shop gave me the idea for the plot: a woman is clearing out her childhood bedroom after her parents have left the house. Some lines from the opening monologue:

> A child's room is a boat, a ship of dreams,
> our first transport.
> Under starry skies we navigate
> our frail personalities into the ocean of life,
> our parents, two gods holding our course
> in their hands, our sun and moon, our stars,
> the earth beneath our feet,
> our certainty.
> My parents made this room for me:
> this shelter from the brutal kick of racism.
> (De Villiers, *Original Skin* 5).

Colman wrote the biological mother's monologue, and helped me develop the different voices and physicality to present the various characters. A cabaret actor, he also brought humour and music to the play. Our shared background in improvisation meant that we were used to finishing each other's sentences, building on the seeds of good ideas, coming in with a flourish at the end. This collaboration was like musicians listening deeply to each other in a band, as they play together. Unlike writing, which remains, the creative process is transitory: experienced, shared and forgotten.

The performances revealed what none of us could have anticipated – neither the dismissive facilitator, nor Robert and I. The story resonated with unexpected people, like the Market Theatre Laboratory's Zulu administrator, who, after watching the play, came to tell me that he had never met his father. An American actor who was volunteering at Cotlands, a home for abandoned babies, musingly reflected on how easily altruism can become narcissistic, because parenting is an exercise of power. I myself was amazed at how invested people were in the narrative, which drew mixed reactions. A teenager at the Grahamstown Schools' Festival complained that the play made 'White people look bad', and a Wits law student could not understand why I had written the play at all.

The question of 'truth' was the major sticking point, and some of the confusion lay in the use of a particular, sensitive metaphor. The setting is the child's bedroom, and the speaker, describing her mother, says,

If this room were a boat, I would lay her washed body in it
and cover it with lilies; light incense and candles and place them
around her head, and then I would pour petrol over it
and set it on fire, and I would gently push it out to meet
the setting sun. And as the night advanced, I would watch
my room of pink and white blazing in the dark water.
And I would look up at the stars
and I would plot a new direction.
(De Villiers, *Original Skin* 5)

Audience members were outraged that I would burn my adoptive mother; after all, she had rescued me. But in 2010, I did a reading of *Original Skin* for my biological father Sam and my brother Damian, and Sam said, 'As a poet, your work is not the same as a documentary producer. Your job is to make us feel'. My biological father is not a poet or an artist, but he articulated what 'truth' means, how it feels and how it shows up in the work.

It had taken me a fair amount of effort to build the courage to write, perform and tour *Original Skin*, and it has yielded a number of beneficial results. Telling my story, developing an interested cohort of fellow writers and readers, has reshaped my relationship with the collective. Opportunities to study, to travel, to perform and to teach arrived, none of which would have happened had I not written the story. The poem "Going Down There" explores the consequence of numerous rapes, and while launching the anthology *No Serenity Here,* an academic in Shanghai asked me repeatedly whether it was true that I had been raped 'at 6, 11, at 13, at 17 and 19' (*The Everyday Wife* 52).

I am not exaggerating when I say that this question is eviscerating. To have been violated, then to have written about it, and to have to defend what has been written – the prospect of not being believed – strikes me to the core. Yet I keep going back. As much as one can be a victim of circumstance and actual violation, writing carries its own power dynamics, elegantly explored by Sindiswa Busuku-Mathese in the critical reflection part of her Master of Arts in Creative Writing. Her presentation at the 2017 Writing for Liberty Conference (convened by the University of the Western Cape and Lancaster University) spoke to the ethics of writing about people who don't have equal access to language or register, and resonated with the demands contained in the #FeesMustFall and #RhodesMustFall campaigns. Busuku-Mathese (whose first collection, *Loud and Yellow Laughter*, won the Ingrid Jonker prize in 2018) is a young Black South African adopted by a White man in 1990. Her careful portrayal of her father renders him in his own voice and is a feat of creative writing. Interestingly, Busuku-Mathese conceives the collection as a play, opening with lists of major and minor characters, and with poems staged as scenes with actual stage directions and lighting cues. In "I Asked My Father Who He Was", the scene plays out:

> Between him and me there is a table, on the table, a bottle of whiskey and two glasses.
> No one sleeps. Tell the moon, no one.
> [dim the house lights]   [pour a drink]
> There is no more to tell/ who is she/ my mother?/ the other she/ I only know my mother
> and with her (he)/ my father/ and the other he/ he turns his face away from me.
> (Busuku-Mathese 50)

The scene is completed by two short monologues in blue and green spotlights respectively, borrowing from her father's voice to offer a glimpse of each of his parents. The intimacy of the image brings Busuku-Mathese's memory into the reader's private realm.

Staging one's life puts it at a remove, by lifting scenes from the everyday and infusing them with sensory detail that does not require verification; a scene is believed through the shared experience of sentience, being entirely plausible, and somehow *real*. It is a fabrication so skilfully rendered that we do not question whether the poet discussed family with her father over whiskey. Unlike biography or even memoir, Busuku-Mathese's poetry allows the banal to effect a secular transcendence, dissolving the boundary between writer and reader. And whether or not Busuku-Mathese's scenes actually happened, they are emotionally true.

While biographies of important figures like Dikgang Moseneke (head of the Constitutional Court) may entail many elements of lived fact, they may not present information that makes people laugh aloud or cry. We might not be able to relate to or identify with someone of Moseneke's stature, except in an aspirational sense, but we might relate to this:

> My Masters has fallen by the wayside; and the army begins baying at my heels; ordering me to come and do camps. Desperate, I ask around and locate an offbeat human rights lawyer. I visit his office; he has egg on his tie; he promises to get me off the hook. (Davey 123)

Derek Davey (musician and journalist) is one of thousands of South Africans who has self-published a memoir recounting the bands with whom he played and the festivals and venues – many now defunct – at which they appeared. A journalist by day, he also reflects on the climate for journalists during the Mbeki and Zuma presidencies. While there are no rules about the aesthetics of memoir, the unspoken contract the writer has with the language in which they express themselves (their poetics) is revealed and can productively complicate the aesthetics of a genre marked by the universal merit of everyone who writes their life story.

The book *Essays on Life Writing: From Genre to Critical Practice*, edited by Martine Kadar, focuses on various literary and non-literary texts, particularly by women, and attempts to define and describe life writing as a scholarly genre. The editor distinguishes between biography, autobiography and life-writing in the introduction by providing an etymological history of the terms: 'life writing [...] is a less exclusive genre of personal kinds of writing that includes *both* biography and autobiography, but also the less "objective," or more "personal," genres such as letters and diaries' (Kadar 4). While there is much in the collection that is valuable, my view is that the use of the term 'genre' is misleading. I understand genre to refer to a particular *way* of writing or making, and one that seeks to categorise products rather than speak to process. To put some writing into a 'genre' pre-emptively assigns aesthetic definition and terms to material that is still finding its balance and voice. Furthermore, it suggests a writerly consciousness that may not yet be present. A person chronicling a process or a memory is not necessarily making art, yet when we read Mary Wollstonecraft's travel diaries with knowledge of her literary stature, we mark these letters as a contribution to the genre of travel writing. When Noni Jabavu set about telling the story of her family in *Drawn in Colour*, she was already a writer, a journalist and editor, so we count her work as a contribution to the genre. On the other hand, the letters I sent to my friends during my travels in the eighties were not a contribution to a genre; I was just offering glimpses of my life.

Every writer finds their readers in their own way – I found mine by telling stories, initially trying to make sense of my personal contradictions, in poems, stories, plays and film and television scripts. The transition from performing one's words to publishing a book seemed momentous for me, and riddled with anxiety. The accountability that print demands from me manifests in a new tension, between one's 'truth' and how others who are connected to the experience may express the truth. This seems distant from the network of editors, publishers, designers, booksellers, distributors, festivals and writing competitions that either enables or disables a writer's access to readers, but it all starts with someone relating to what you write.

For some writers, the point of writing is not commercial or academic, but *vital*. Tracing that moment, Binyavanga Wainaina writes:

> I am starting to scribble my thoughts, to write these moments. It is when this is all done that I do what I do best. I look up, confused and fearful, all accordion with *kimay*; then soak in the safe patterns of other people, and live my life borrowing from them; then retreat – for reasons I don't know – to look down, inside the safety of novels; and then I lift my eyes again to people, and make them my own sort of confused pattern. (152)

Precision, truth and authenticity are entirely subject to the contract Wainaina has forged with creative, idiomatic language. Beyond Kadar's argument that 'life writing is a way of looking at more or less autobiographical literature as long as we understand that "autobiographical" is a loaded word, the "real" accuracy of which cannot be proved and does not equate with either "objective" or "subjective truth"' (10), lies the fertile discipline of writing. Reading can be generative, as writers respond to a passage that leads them to the unexplored lacunae of their existences, to write and discover what they thought, and whether it was what they meant.

Kadar goes on to describe how the 'involved reader takes great pleasure in inventing a persona for himself or herself as he or she reads' (11). This dialogic sense of the relationship between reader and writer, with the text in between, approximates theatre without the immediacy of reaction. The writer is staging glimpses of a life, the authenticity of which is technically unquestionable. Wainaina was trying to 'make sense of things on the written page. At least there, they can be shaped. I doubt myself the moment I think this' (152). Although he passed away in 2019, his words remain with me in an eternal present.

The 'truth' of a story is complex; it contains verifiable and unverifiable facts. The details of particular events contain unspoken, perhaps unexamined, aspects of what the protagonist felt and observed at the time. The only claim to the authority of emotions, fantasies, stories or notions lies in how well the writer makes them available to readers. Reading triggers memories, memories trigger words; the process is ongoing, for one can never tell, beforehand, what a story will do. The unpublished fragment of the poem that begins this essay possibly never will exist outside of this place. Like the reams of film on an editor's floor, it may become something, but who knows?

Endnotes

1. Many of these platforms are explored in *Our Words, Our Worlds: Writing on Black South African Women Poets, 2000–2018,* a comprehensive account of Black South African women's contributions to poetry in the first two decades of this century that incorporates work by writers such as Myesha Jenkins, Qhakaza Mthembu-Mohare, Natalia Molebatsi and Malika Ndlovu.
2. The play is quite well documented and a number of reviews appear online.
3. For further details regarding the adoption process at the time, see Christa Kuljian's *Darwin's Hunch: Science, Race and the Search for Human Origins*, specifically the chapter titled "There is Reason to Be Suspicious" (150), where the process and procedures relating to my adoption are dissected in detail.

Bibliography

Baldwin, James. *Collected Essays*. Library of America, 1998.
Boswell, Barbara. *And Wrote My Story Anyway: Black South African Women's Novels as Feminism*. Wits University Press, 2020.

Busuku-Mathese, Sindiswa. *Loud and Yellow Laughter*. Botsotso Press, 2016.
Davey, Derek. *Three Foot Tiger: A Musical Memoir*. 2nd ed., Self-published, 2020.
De Villiers, Phillippa Yaa. *The Everyday Wife*. Modjaji Books, 2010.
---. *Original Skin*. 2nd ed., Home Truth Productions, 2012.
---. Unpublished Fragment. Unpublished Poem. 2023.
La Grange, Zelda. *Good Morning, Mr Mandela*. Penguin UK, 2014.
Lorde, Audre. *Sister Outsider: Essays and Speeches*. Revised ed., Crossing Press, 2007.
Jacobs, Nancy J., and Andrew Bank. "Biography in Post-Apartheid South Africa: A Call for Awkwardness." *African Studies*, vol. 78, no. 2, 2019. Accessed 1 May 2020.
Kadar, Marlene, editor. *Essays on Life Writing: From Genre to Critical Practice*. University of Toronto Press, 1992.
Kay, Jackie. *The Adoption Papers*. Bloodaxe Books, 1991.
---. *Red Dust Road*. Picador, 2010.
Kgositsile, Keorapetse. *Approaches to Poetry Writing*. Third World Press, 1994.
---. "'This is who I am.' A Conversation with Poet Keorapetse Kgositsile." Interview by K. Mensah Wali. Sampsonia Way, 25 June 2012, http://www.sampsoniaway.org/literary-voices/2012/06/25/%E2%80%9Cthis-is-whoi-am-%E2%80%9D-a-conversation-with-poet-keorapetse-kgositsile/
Kuljian, Christa. *Darwin's Hunch: Science, Race and the Search for Human Origins*. Jacana, 2016.
Madikizela-Mandela, Winnie. *491 Days: Prisoner Number 1323/69*. Pan Macmillan, 2013
Masekela, Hugh, and D. Michael Cheers. *Still Grazing: The Musical Journey of Hugh Masekela*. Jacana, 2016.
Moseneke, Dikgang. *My Own Liberator: A Memoir*. Pan MacMillan, 2016.
Phalafala, Uhuru. *Mine Mine Mine*. University of Nebraska Press, 2023.
Wainaina, Binyavanga. *One Day I Will Write About This Place*. Granta, 2011.
Xaba, Makhosazana, editor. *Our Words, Our Worlds: Writing on Black South African Women Poets 2000–2018*. UKZN Press, 2020.

Writing for Podcasts as Creative Practice in the Arts
Annel Pieterse

Prologue

In 2019, a close friend approached me with an idea. He had a story to tell. He was going to make a podcast. And he wanted to do it in the style of the seminal American podcast *Serial*, a true-crime narrative podcast that began in 2014 as a spinoff of the public radio show *This American Life*.

When season one of *Serial* dropped, listeners had followed it as avidly as viewers now follow their favourite series on streaming platforms.[1] It was a live investigation, and every week a new episode was released, detailing updates relating to the criminal case. The podcast's popularity brought renewed attention to the plight of Adnan Syed, a young man convicted of the 1999 murder of his girlfriend, Hae Min Lee.

My friend Deon is a gifted writer, a born investigative journalist and ruthlessly determined. He had been the victim of sexual abuse in his teens, and he had been digging for information on the perpetrator. He had found evidence, spanning decades, of a string of similar young victims across South Africa. Deon planned to seek out survivors and gather enough witnesses to enable the police to prosecute the serial predator, while documenting the investigation in the style of a narrative podcast – a live investigation, just like *Serial*.

Inspired by a line from Donna Tartt's 1992 novel *The Secret History*, the title of the podcast would be *My Only Story*. Deon had already plotted the first episode, which would provide the backstory to his own encounter with the predator, but he needed to 'get tape'[2] around Stellenbosch and Cape Town, where these events had occurred, and he wanted me to go along. He needed support, and had been playing with the idea of an investigative partner – a Watson to his Sherlock, as it were – an interlocutor. I said I would think about it, and he left me with a copy of Jessica Abel's *Out on the Wire: The Storytelling Secrets of the New Masters of Radio*. It didn't take long for me to agree. How could I not? It would be the birth of a new story, in a new medium. I was about to learn a lot.

Introduction

In this essay, I reflect on my journey with the narrative podcast as creative medium. The essay is reflexive, in that I loosely adopt a structure that is common to many narrative podcasts: a 'sexy anecdote' (Glass qtd. in Abel 113) at the beginning functions as a 'hook' to draw in the audience, and is followed by a short introduction to the topic, providing a frame for the listener that helps them focus their attention on a central idea or theme. This central theme is then explored through several dramatic acts, each act consisting of a sequence of scenes. Through a process of framing, signposting and reflecting, the narrative moves toward a conclusion or, if unresolved, a question.

My essay is thus divided into two 'acts'. In Act 1, I describe my observations on writing for podcasts as a praxis at work in my classrooms, where I teach 'Writing for Podcasts' as a semester-long elective seminar option to small groups of second-year undergraduate students in an English Studies department.

Act 2 returns to *My Only Story* as an example of a successful South African narrative podcast, in order to examine more broadly how this success is achieved.

I performatively[3] evoke the structure of the narrative podcast in order to signal a conscious and calculated shift away from the conventions of the academic essay with its basis in print and traditional publishing. I adopt this strategy for two reasons. Firstly, it allows for a subjective and personal reflection on my academic and teaching practice. On this point, Rebecca Ora, writing about the podcast as a performative documentary mode, notes:

> The podcast, so often a second-hand narrative embedded firmly in personal voice, can be a probing and interrogative medium that happens to be frank about its imbrication within the personal experience, rather than to be summarised as narcissistic portraiture. (118)

In other words, it is a medium that, at its best, reflects the rigorous critical engagement of academic research, while simultaneously foregrounding the subjective, personal voice of the narrator.

My second reason for adopting the style and structure of a narrative podcast episode in writing this essay is because I am struck by the correlations between the process of researching and writing a narrative podcast, and the process of academic research and writing. Dario Llinares has identified the podcast as a hybrid medium, 'an amalgamation of creative audio experimentation with the fundamental spirit of intellectual curiosity and the idealised aspects of the internet's communicative potential' (124). He conceives of this experience

> as a kind of positive destabilisation; an exciting and potentially revelatory disruption of the boundaries that tie disciplines and fields of inquiry to specific forms of expression and institutional practice. In this sense, I have come to think of podcasting as a 'liminal praxis': a mediatory practice that emerges out of an idiosyncratic yet fluid set of technological, economic, creative, social and disciplinary conditions, and which, concomitantly, imbues a questioning of the logics and effect of the mediation itself. (124)

I turn now to Act 1, to explore how I have observed this 'liminal praxis' at work in my classrooms.

Act I: In the Classroom

In my course, we focus on narrative podcasting – rather than interview or conversational podcasts – as the narrative podcast is the format that intersects most productively with the 'work' traditionally associated with a literature department. We analyse examples of existing podcasts to understand how the material – which usually includes conversations and interviews – is combined into a narrative structure.[4] The broader category of narrative podcasts can be divided into either fiction or non-fiction narratives. In fictional narrative podcasts, such as *Welcome to Night*

Vale and *The Magnus Archives*, a recurring character narrates the events in a series of stand-alone episodes that develop into an overarching plot. Non-fiction narrative podcasts have varying formats. In *This American Life*, for example, various stories, told by different narrators, are organised around a central theme, which is introduced by the host of the show, Ira Glass. *Serial*, on the other hand, is one story told, week by week, by a single narrator. Either way, the style of narration is usually personal and intimate.

Narrative podcasts are notoriously labour intensive as they are heavily edited: music, ambient sound and sound effects are woven together with interview tape, scripted narration (which is sometimes re-enacted), and archival sources in order to structure scenes, evoke unspoken levels of the story, and punctuate action (Abel 148). While the importance of sound is central to the production of narrative podcasts, it is not always practical in a classroom environment, and I shall return to this point.

As a creative practice, writing for podcasts lends itself very well to a student-centred approach. It allows students to refine skills that aid them in their more traditional academic work, such as concept formulation and development, independent desktop or archival research, personal interviews, and logical structure. The idea of writing for a listener demands that students think carefully about how information must be framed and signposted. Related to this last point, the need for reflection as a strategy to keep listeners orientated and engaged develops the students' critical and reflective faculties. The ability of podcasts to foreground the subjective, personal voice of the narrator also encourages students to develop and articulate their own opinions and interpretations of the topic.

In my experience of teaching a course on podcasting, many students who find traditional academic writing challenging, are nonetheless able to conceptualise, write and record powerful and insightful podcast narratives. They often draw on their broader theoretical and practical training for inspiration. In my classroom, recently, for example: a student drew on insights gained from a colleague's seminar on patriography to explore her relationship with her deceased father; a mature student combined his love of composing and sound engineering with his interest in artificial intelligence (AI); and students studying Law and Sports Science explored aspects of their course work or experiences through their narratives.

Aside from these direct links to their training and course work, popular topics include: family genealogy, relationships with family members, or the life stories of family members; advocacy narratives related to mental health, identity politics, neurodivergent or differently abled experiences in education and on campus; biographical and historical writing; narratives of community, and true crime stories. Students who choose to work in fiction mostly work in the realm of speculative fiction. Recently, there has been an increase in students who enjoy desktop role-playing games (RPGs) – usually Dungeons and Dragons – and who have conceptualised their podcasts as companion pieces to the game. A student from a rural village in KwaZulu-Natal submitted a script that harnessed the potential of the sound medium for oral storytelling to share a story inspired by a local tale she had grown up with. Unfortunately, she was not able to record it, but the concept points to a way in which the podcast medium might facilitate non-Western forms of storytelling.

Although writing for podcasts naturally presupposes writing for an audio medium, I have not made it mandatory for students to record the final draft. While there are several free applications and websites available, recording, mixing and editing calls for some technical skill and practice, and is time consuming. The outcomes of my course require that students are able to master the structure and conventions of a narrative podcast – an exercise that can also be assessed through a process of scripting. Students therefore have the option of submitting either a 2 250-word script, which includes a proposed soundscape, or a 20-minute recording. The students develop their concepts towards a draft script throughout the semester. Every week, they follow a prompt and submit work to the online forum, and this 'process work' forms part of their assessment. Students who do ultimately generate a recording, are therefore working off a drafted script.

However, to ensure some level of audio interaction for all students, I include a short exercise where students are required to record only their voice in a reading or re-telling of a 500-word scene they have drafted. This exercise opens up new aspects of narration, live performance and delivery. There is a substantial difference between the style and effect of literary language intended for reading, and that of language intended for an oral delivery and aural reception. Initially, students tend to struggle with this distinction, and hearing their work read aloud helps them to understand the specific function of voice in a sonic medium like the podcast. They are encouraged to think of the final delivery and effect in terms of their natural speaking rhythms, and then their writing tends to improve significantly. Some students who are not necessarily good writers, are good storytellers and performers, and so this exercise also provides insight into classroom diversity insofar as learning and presentation styles are concerned.

In this particular practice, peer-to-peer engagement and feedback are crucial, and encourage students to think of knowledge as a collaborative process of co-construction. This process also mirrors the industry practice of the 'edit', which is central to developing a narrative podcast for publication. In the edit, the reporter works through various iterations of the narrative with a colleague, or a group of colleagues that includes other reporters, editors and producers. The edit is a collaborative practice, which, in the words of Glass, gets you 'instant feedback that *lets you know what you think*' (qtd. in Abel 114; emphasis my own). This is an important point. Studies on students' approaches to learning show that students will often adopt either a 'surface approach' that involves memorisation and rote learning, or a 'strategic approach' that involves working out what a lecturer 'wants' and producing work with that in mind (Entwistle 596; Entwistle and Entwistle 208). The mode of the 'edit', however, facilitates an environment where students are expected to test their ideas on peers as well as the lecturer, and work out for themselves what they think.

In the classroom setting, this dialogic creative process is modelled in our weekly meetings. Students divide into smaller groups to share their work and receive feedback from their peers, before electing their 'favourite' for that week from their respective groups to pitch to the class as a whole. This election process is guided by the question: if you were going to invest time in listening to one of these podcasts, which one would you choose, and why? The class as a whole then discusses the strengths (and shortcomings) of these selected pitches, and makes suggestions for improvement. During these sessions, I also give pointed guidance on problems that I know from experience are common to the group as a whole. In this way, students gain insight into how their story is being received, and where an audience may need more framing or structure. Fellow students grappling with similar challenges are then able to transfer these insights from peer feedback to their own work. These sessions also aid in developing presentation skills in a relaxed, informal setting. Many students have discussed the value of these sessions in promoting a more engaging classroom experience and a self-reflexive, self-driven learning environment.

So, what are the limitations in 'writing for podcasts' in a classroom environment? The fact that most of the students do not, in fact, record the script that they spend all semester developing for an audio narrative is certainly a limitation, but one that can be quite easily addressed through the incorporation of a lower-stakes assignment. As with more traditional forms of academic writing, source and reference management are often problematic. Ideally, a podcast has a website where each episode can be accessed along with its show notes and a transcript. The show notes should have a comprehensive reference list of secondary material referred to in the episode. Along with the show notes, the podcaster is also expected to acknowledge sources verbally during the episode – but this needs to be done without disrupting the flow of the narrative. So, for example, in episode one of her podcast *Out on the Wire*, based on the book of the same title, Abel includes an excerpt from a short YouTube video where Glass discusses why people get into creative work. She introduces it seamlessly:

> When I type 'Ira Glass' into Google, the second suggested phrase is 'Ira Glass the gap'. Which means this lo-fi video on YouTube of Ira talking to Current TV about storytelling gets more searches on Google than his actual show. Not more listens, mind you. Let's be clear. But this idea has definitely hit a nerve. ("Eureka")

This introduction is followed by the full video clip of Glass talking to Current TV, which is almost two minutes long.

In the classroom context, this practice of verbal acknowledgement can lead to potential issues around source management. Students are alerted to these alternative referencing conventions, and – instead of show notes – they are expected to submit a reference list in MLA format that includes the sources consulted during the research process. The majority manage this well. However, students who struggle with this practice in conventional writing also struggle in this hybrid mode. As to recent concerns about students' potential use of artificial intelligence (AI), I have not yet detected signs of writing produced by AI. Given the highly personalised topics, the process-oriented nature of the work, and the centrality of subjective 'voice' involved in writing for podcasts, I consider the potential for AI abuse quite low.

A further limitation is that the podcasts cannot be published or used for research. Many students choose to write about someone else's life experience, and these narratives are not always available in the public domain. Students therefore have to interview their subjects in order to obtain a record of their story. According to the Stellenbosch University regulatory policy on ethical teaching and research, students are not required to obtain written informed consent from interview subjects if the interview is used in the context of a class assignment, as opposed to research. However, without ethical clearance, the episodes cannot be publicly released, which means that students are unable to discover how the episode functions in the distribution channels for which it is hypothetically intended. The writing-for-podcasts exercise thus remains predominantly speculative, or putative.

A related question of ethics arises from the fact that many of the students want to write about their own experiences, or those of close friends or family members. These experiences are often traumatising or otherwise emotionally charged and psychologically difficult. Students who choose to write about their own mental health struggles or history of abuse have usually already processed these experiences to some degree in therapy, and they view the writing as congruent with this processing. However, some students shy away from sharing their writing with the class because it is so personal. Students who choose to interview family members about a particular story have also reported the need to back off from certain lines of inquiry because it was upsetting for the interviewee, or because it brought interpersonal tensions to the surface. Since these experiences are an inevitable part of the interviewing process, a seminar such as 'Writing for Podcasts' does need to offer quite substantial engagement with ethical interviewing practices, as an additional research skill.

The seminar 'Writing for Podcasts' was originally conceptualised as a practice-based course to introduce students of literature to the narrative potential of a new, aural medium.[5] As I have outlined above, the process of producing a narrative podcast offers many opportunities to develop research, interviewing, writing and editing skills. Students also have the option to develop practical skills related to sound production, and to familiarise themselves with a non-traditional form of research and medium for publication. Owing to certain limitations, it has not been possible to test the success of these exercises as actual podcasts in the world, which raises the question: What makes for a successful narrative podcast?

Act 2: Out in the World

To answer this question, we return again to where our journey started. The first episode of season one of the podcast *My Only Story* (a Fairly Famous production with publishing partner News24) was released early in November 2019, with follow-up episodes released every Thursday, for three weeks. When perpetrator Willem Breytenbach was finally arrested, the news made national headlines.[6] It became the most successful podcast in South Africa at the time, with more than 130 000 listens by late 2021, and it was awarded bronze in the Serialised Podcast category at the 2020 New York Festivals Radio Awards. To date, it remains a benchmark of narrative podcasting in South Africa.

Season two, *My Only Story: Back to School* – a co-production of the My Only Story Non-Profit Company and News24 – exposed a 'ring of predators' operating across some of South Africa's most prestigious private schools. It soared to the top of the South African blog charts on Apple Podcasts a day after episode one was released ("*My Only Story* Tops the Charts"); it won gold in the Serialised Podcast category, and bronze in the Narrative/Documentary category of the 2022 New York Festivals Radio Awards. It was also awarded gold in the Podcast and Radio category at the 2022 One World Media Awards in the United Kingdom.

The breakout success of *Serial*, on which Deon modelled *My Only Story* and *My Only Story: Back to School*, can be attributed to multiple factors. According to media scholar Richard Berry, while the premise of *Serial* was original for audio podcast, it mirrored successful narrative forms in other media, such as the classic serials of radio's past, as well as audiobooks and television series (170-171). As a serialised crime story and live investigation, *Serial* engaged audiences in multiple contexts, including: 'social settings, on traditional media, and perhaps most significantly, in a slew of podcasts about the podcast' (171). The podcast thus had mass appeal, but it also engaged audiences both intellectually and emotionally (171). However, it was not only the innovative concept and narrative that led to this engagement. As the executive producer, Glass, acknowledged, it was a lucky congruence between really good new podcasts, and changing technology that made podcasts more freely available to more people (qtd. in Berry 171). *Serial*'s success can thus be attributed to a combination of factors 'in which technologies, brands, social sharing, and engaging content all play a part' (Berry 171).

The local and international success of *My Only Story* can be attributed to similar factors: the structure and format were still relatively novel in the South African context in 2019, and the ease of social sharing facilitated by digital technology ensured a wide reach for Deon's story. This prompted listeners to respond with additional information, which in turn led to the investigations in *My Only Story: Back to School*. Furthermore, in partnering with News24, Deon was able to draw on the resources of an established and respected media brand. Although podcasting offers creators an 'uncontrolled space' where amateurs can 'compete equally with traditional media' (Berry 172), the top-performing podcasts remain those created by services, brands and individuals with public profiles. This point is borne out by the fact that in January 2023, the majority of the top fifteen narrative podcasts, according to online magazine *Time Out*, were those affiliated with major public broadcasters and other traditional media outlets.

I started this essay with Deon's story, since that is also where my own journey with 'Writing for Podcasts' began. It is therefore fitting to include some of his insights about the reasons for the success of *My Only Story*. Consequently, in a personal interview conducted with Deon over two days in September 2023 at his home in Johannesburg, we discussed all things podcast. What follows is an edited, shortened and restructured version of our conversation.

> DEON:
> When I decided to do something about Willem Breytenbach, initially I wanted to write a book, and a series, and a film, and … [laughter].

And then in the end, because I loved *Serial*, like everyone else really, that opened my eyes to what could be done, and I've always wanted to do *Serial* for South Africa.

So I wanted two things to happen in season one: I wanted lots of people to know – I wanted it to be a big scandal and I wanted to do it in a way that I could afford.

Which then turned out to be audio because you know, podcasts were not that big in SA back then.
I thought well, if I'm going to write something like *Serial*, I have to understand the structure because in my view, great writing is 50 per cent invisible. It's about the deep structure behind it that the reader doesn't notice but feels.

So I went on this autodidactic journey.

ANNEL:
So you immersed yourself in narrative structure for television series and creative non-fiction and documentary, and then, through a process of deconstructing, and reconstructing and synthesising what the successful ones did, you figured out how to do it yourself?

DEON:
Yes. And I knew that I did it, when I could see how *Serial* does all of it. A key thing I realised was that in *Serial*, Sarah Koenig is a protagonist on a quest. And then *Serial: Season 2* was a flop – or it was quite good actually, but people didn't relate to it the same way. In *Serial: Season 2* and *Serial: Season 3*, Sarah Koenig was no longer the protagonist, she was just the narrator – like a voice-over artist, almost. It wasn't about *her* wanting to know. In my view, what makes it compelling, is 'why are *you* doing this story?' It's more compelling when the narrator has skin in the game. So, when I was thinking about how I was going to do *My Only Story: Season 2*, I took this into account.

Because even though I was not the primary protagonist on a quest, there was a reason for me to be telling this story. Which is set up in the first act. I have skin in the game, I am this character who has been through something and now my new arc becomes growth beyond what I managed to figure out in the previous season. I didn't want to make the second season about me because it wasn't about me. But I'm still a character, I still need to do things. I mean people often talk about my 'bravery', and I unfailingly point out that I wrote myself quite sympathetically. But also, there are things you do to make a protagonist more sympathetic – I mean, this is deep structure, it's well catalogued.

ANNEL:
Okay, so can we talk a bit about structure? Because I think, in terms of non-Western storytelling forms and writing from South Africa, a three-act structure doesn't always accommodate traditional modes of storytelling. But at the same time, the three-act structure is the [dominant narrative structure] in cinema, television and now podcasting. So, what is your view on the three-act structure as the organising principle?

DEON:
Well, as somebody who has been deeply familiar with the three-act structure for about five years now, I am not married to it, beyond the fact that it demonstrably works. And I've put together these narrations myself, and I make sure to have act climaxes in the right places, because it makes it exciting […] Storytelling requires telling people one fact at a time, and only when that fact is most impactful. I heard a sentence in a documentary, where the narration went something like: when we got to the house, he was dead in the bathroom still wearing all of his clothes. The more dramatic and interesting way of telling exactly the same thing, is to go: When they got home, he was in the bath. He was fully dressed. And he was dead. I mean there's the thing: something changed, there's a reversal.

It is no longer what I thought it was, and that's what makes it exciting.

ANNEL:
So the three-act structure tends to be imposed by mainstream narrative convention, because that makes money, right …?

DEON:
I'd love to meet that kind of narrative in my own life. It doesn't guarantee money – all it does in the right hands is guarantee suspense. Western storytelling is popular all over the world because [it guarantees suspense] – you want to keep listening. And as a writer, as a podcaster, as an author, all you're there to do is to stop people not listening.

And here is the thing: the three-act structure is not what governs the narrative podcast. It has a different act structure. It follows the lead of television drama, which came about with [network] television when you have to break for ads. Traditionally, something that fills an hour of airtime would be 48 minutes long. That gives you twelve minutes in four acts and here it becomes crucial to get the act climax right, because you are going to have ads, and you want to make sure that people are not going to use that time to change the channel. The great insight of podcasts like *This American Life* and *Serial* was that for audiences to get used to a new form of expression, we needed to remind them of TV dramas.

Serial took that to mean that you have to give people an act climax every fifteen minutes. Everything – except the absence of visuals – is semiotically put together to make you think of television drama. You have a bit more flexibility with podcasting because it doesn't have to be exactly on fifteen minutes or exactly on twelve minutes, but I keep all my acts between thirteen and seventeen minutes, and then add a short one at the end. The last one is always short. So, scene, scene,

scene, scene, act climax every fifteen minutes. Because that is the deep structure. And that is what keeps people listening. I think it was one of my key insights: *My Only Story* deals with child rape, which is the last thing any of us wants to listen to. It's a really difficult subject matter, so you have to get people interested despite themselves.

ANNEL:
Okay. So let's talk a little bit about podcasting in South Africa.

My sense is that we currently have three or four good narrative podcasts – of which two are by you – and they're either true crime or investigative. We don't really have something like *This American Life* where you have an episode that is a series of vignettes told by different narrators around a particular topic. What do you think is the reason for this?

DEON:
Because of resources. It is a form of journalism that takes extraordinarily long. If you want to make money through podcasting, you don't have to make a good podcast, but a frequent podcast. I mean, it takes me a year to do one season. And in terms of research, it takes longer. Season three should be out by [September 2024] and it's going to take a year to do it.

ANNEL:
How long does it take you once you've got the skeleton and you're satisfied and you've put everything together in Pro Tools – you've got your story and now it needs to be edited, or engineered – how long does this process take?

DEON:
It's probably the longest part of the process, but fortunately I can do it, because I can work Pro Tools, and I'm almost uniquely positioned to do this kind of work because I have a background in journalism as well as advertising – in production. In South

Africa, if you're a journalist, you work in a newsroom and you don't really get exposed to forms of communication that aren't in the voice of the outlet. And also, News24 can't employ me to do this full time because it would be difficult for them to justify [supporting] a journalist who spends a year on one story. To make it work – initially, nobody wants to sponsor a podcast on child rape – so it takes willpower and loads of resources because you have to stay alive. Which is why I'm now back in advertising.

ANNEL:
Okay. And many of the big successful North American and British podcasts are obviously affiliated with broadcasting, and they can make resources available for someone to spend a year researching one story.

DEON:
Right. And the BBC has always made documentaries and Radio 4 has always made documentaries, so it was the natural next evolution of what they're doing anyway.

ANNEL:
So South African journalism and South Africa's news media are actually not developed and well resourced enough. When it happens, it's necessarily independent – it's someone with a passion to tell a story.

DEON:
So, for documentaries, there is actually a model in South Africa that works. They have figured out how to monetise it. It gets commissioned by broadcasters. It's a whole different game.

ANNEL:
Yeah. And a documentary series will often get a companion podcast as well. So it seems like, if there [are] going to be resources made available to create a podcast, it's going to be as

part of an existing franchise around a story that's already been commissioned as a film or series.

Goodbyes and New Beginnings

Since these are concluding remarks in a reflective essay on writing for podcasts as creative practice in the arts, I offer the following as a series of small, juxtaposed scenes.

***

Typing up this conclusion, I am sitting in a university library in the Netherlands, where I have had the privilege of a four-week staff exchange. Here, many practical social functions, such as public transport, money management, sustainability and administration are managed through smartphone applications. Most businesses no longer accept cash, and Virtual Reality (VR) seems almost ubiquitous – there are headsets available for use free of charge in public spaces, and documentary filmmakers (and, perhaps more insidiously, corporations) are producing narratives designed for the immersive experience that VR offers. This is a society that, for better or worse, is turning increasingly to digital technologies as platforms for creative expression and to structure society and citizen participation.

***

I have attended a media conference, a documentary film festival, and a symposium titled 'Arts, Culture and Media: Beyond Distinction'. In all of these spaces of encounter, there has been active intellectual focus on the use of digital media, with questions about AI a key point, but also questions of multi- and cross-disciplinary practices, and cross-fertilisation between academia and industry, theory and practice. These conversations are in equal parts inspiring and exasperating: inspiring, since they point to the ways in which technology can facilitate reconnections with the 'world beyond the academy' in the words of bell hooks (xv); exasperating because they often assume equal access to cultural and technological resources.

***

As I was finalising this paper, I learned that, for the time being, the literature department where I have taught 'Writing for Podcasts' for the past three years, will no longer be offering elective seminars to students at second-year level. The undergraduate course is being restructured, and instead of electives, resources will now be redirected to support tutorials to facilitate the development of academic writing. As the name suggests, elective seminars allow students to elect a specialist focus for one semester. For many of these undergraduate students – such as my Sport Science or Law students – the English elective seminars incorporating creative practice are some of the only spaces where they are exposed to these practices. Whatever forms of creative practice are to be retained in this undergraduate course will therefore have to be conceptualised and integrated within the scope of main lectures.

***

Deon 'wants to put a full stop to *My Only Story*', and so season three will be the last. He no longer wants to be the 'child rape' guy. And as we've seen, narrative podcasting is labour intensive and there are insufficient resources for it in South Africa – unless you can monetise a podcast by catching the current wave of documentary popularity.

***

These four small concluding 'scenes' highlight a series of interconnected points for consideration. Increasingly, creatives are turning to digital platforms for the creation and dissemination of their images and narratives, and international trends in the arts suggest a growing shift towards dialogue and cross-pollination between academia and industry. In South Africa, however, we are faced with a specific set of local challenges that make these international models hard to follow.

The greater question of the future of podcasting in the South African context requires its own essay, but my experience suggests that, while the model of narrative podcasting established by the Euro-American trailblazers of the form is indeed resource and labour intensive, it is not impossible to produce a good amateur podcast. Every time I have taught this course, I have had at least four students out of every 22 who do record their episodes, and who do it very well. This success is determined by the outcomes of my course, rather than the demands of the existing industry. The trick is perhaps to look beyond the Western models that currently dominate the industry to local examples of popular storytelling formats – the telenovela comes to mind – to develop our own form.

I started this essay by signalling a conscious shift away from the conventions of academic writing. However, as I have argued and, I hope, illustrated, the process of writing for podcasts is not unlike that of writing an academic essay. If monetising the podcast is not the goal – if we think of it instead as a creative teaching and research tool, and as an alternative or adjunct platform for research distribution – then it lends itself very well to the development of research and writing skills.

Endnotes

1 *Serial* pre-dates the arrival of both MultiChoice's subscription video on-demand service Showmax, and streaming giant Netflix, which launched in South Africa on 19 August 2015 and 6 January 2016 respectively.
2 'Tape' is the term for recorded audio (see "Transcribing Tape").
3 I use the term 'performative' here in the sense defined by documentary film theorist Bill Nichols as a mode that 'emphasises the subjective or expressive aspects of the filmmaker's own engagement with the subject, and an audience's responsiveness to this engagement. [It] rejects notions of objectivity in favour of evocation and affect' (33-34).

4   In the traditional three-act structure – which consists of the set-up, the confrontation and the resolution: the audience is introduced to a sympathetic protagonist whose life is thrown out of balance by an inciting incident (set-up); the protagonist tries to restore balance through a series of rising actions, until a climatic point is reached where the protagonist definitively either fails or succeeds (confrontation); either way, a new balance is established (resolution).
5   While narrative radio is obviously not a new form, and although the narrative podcast shares with narrative radio the goal of audio storytelling, there are some key differences between narrative podcasts and traditional narrative broadcast radio. These differences include accessibility and distribution, format and structure, duration, monetisation and creative control.
6   Breytenbach was arrested in 2019 and charged with 14 counts of indecent assault or sexual assault, although some of these charges were later dropped. As of December 2023, the State and Breytenbach's counsel are deciding on plea and sentencing options to present to the court (Evans).

Bibliography

Abel, Jessica. *Out on the Wire: The Storytelling Secrets of the New Masters of Radio*. Broadway Books, 2015.

Berry, Richard (2015) "A Golden Age of Podcasting? Evaluating Serial in the Context of Podcast Histories" *Journal of Radio and Audio Media*, vol. 22, no.2, 2015, pp. 170-178.

Entwistle, Noel. "Styles of Learning and Approaches to Studying in Higher Education." *Kybernetes*, vol. 30, no. 5-6, 2001, pp. 593-603.

Entwistle, Noel and Abigail Entwistle. "Contrasting Forms of Understanding for Degree Examinations: The Student Experience and Its Implications." *Higher Education*, vol. 22, no. 3, 1991, pp. 205-227.

"Eureka." *Out on the Wire*, hosted by Jessica Abel, episode 1, 30 January 2023, jessicaabel.com/out-on-the-wire.

Evans, Jenni. "Breytenbach Still Thrashing out Possible Plea Agreement." *News24*, 13 December 2023, www.news24.com/news24/southafrica/news/breytenbach-still-thrashing-out-possible-plea-agreement-20231213.

Fink, Joseph and Jeffrey Cranor, co-creators. *Welcome to Night Vale*. Night Vale Presents, 2015-, www.welcometonightvale.com/.

Glass, Ira, host. *This American Life*, Chicago Public Media, 1995, www.thisamericanlife.org.

hooks, bell. *Teaching Community: A Pedagogy of Hope*. Routledge, 2003.

Koenig, Sarah, host. *Serial*. Serial Productions, 2014, serialpodcast.org.

Llinares, Dario. "Podcasting as Liminal Praxis: Aural Mediation, Sound Writing and Identity." *Podcasting: New Aural Cultures and Digital Media*, edited by Dario Llinares, Neil Fox and Richard Berry, Palgrave Macmillan, 2018, pp. 123-145.

Lukowski, Andrzej. "The 15 Best Storytelling Podcasts." *Time Out*, 10 January 2023, www.timeout.com/things-to-do/best-story-podcasts.

Manyathi, Nokuthula and Deon Wiggett. *Exodus*. News24 Podcasts, 2020, news24.com. www.specialprojects.news24.com/exodus-kwasizabantu/index.html.

"*My Only Story* Tops the Charts as News24 Reports on Tragedy at School." *My Only Story*, 17 September 2021, www.myonlystory.org/post/my-only-story-tops-the-charts-as-news24-reports-on-tragedy-at-school.

Nichols, Bill. *Introduction to Documentary*. Indiana University Press, 2010.

Ora, Rebecca. "Invisible Evidence: Serial and the New Unknowability of Documentary." *Podcasting: New Aural Cultures and Digital Media*, edited by Dario Llinares, Neil Fox and Richard Berry, Palgrave Macmillan, 2018, pp. 107-122.

Sims, Jonathan. *The Magnus Archives*. Rusty Quill 2016. Rustyquill.com. www.rustyquill.com/show/the-magnus-archives/. Accessed 14 February 2024.

"Transcribing Tape." *MML Podcasting Resource Guide*. Multimedia Labs at Brown, brown.edu/mml.

Wiggett, Deon. *My Only Story, Season 1*, News24 Podcasts, 2019, www.myonlystory.org.

---. *My Only Story: Back to School, Season 2*, News24 Podcasts, 2021, www.myonlystory.org.

---. Personal Interview. 9 and 10 September 2023.

---. "Teen's Suicide Reveals Shadowy Ring of Predators at Top SA Schools." *My Only Story*, episode 1, News24 Podcasts, 16 September 2021, www.news24.com/news24/video/southafrica/news/podcast-my-only-story-teens-suicide-reveals-shadowy-ring-of-predators-at-top-sa-schools-20210915.

Technologies of Conquest: On Writing the Dystopian through South Africa's Past, Present and Possible Future(s)

Masande Ntshanga

> We are the black violators
> of the machine rhythm
> in plastic cities …
> (Gwala 37)

The year is 1986, and my mother has just been driven home from the maternity ward where she gave birth to me. Frere Hospital is in East London, which is considered a part of White South Africa, and even though my place of birth makes me South African, my mother and I are denied citizenship, restricted instead to residing in its labour reserve, the Ciskei homeland. Here, we settle inside the Bantustan's biggest township, Mdantsane. My mother, a journalist, owns her first house in NU 1, or Native Unit 1, which I'll later learn is what we are: *Natives inside Unit 1*. This narrative is an arrangement of human beings that will never leave me. During the nineties, the division into Native Units will be sanitised into Zones, and even though I don't know it yet, I will repurpose the word Zone in my second novel, three decades later, to describe a future form of social engineering. In adulthood, I will also come to think of the homelands as technologies of conquest, and of our first house – which was founded on the National Party's experimentation with eugenics – as my first introduction to science fiction, and the first seeds of my second novel, *Triangulum* (2019).

***

The year is 1991, and my mother and I have moved from the township of Mdantsane to Bhisho, the capital of the Ciskei homeland. Nelson Mandela has been released from prison and I'm lying on our driveway, bleeding from my forehead. Later, when my mother asks me what happened, I'll tell her I jumped off our front gate, believing I could float. That I saw it on TV.

***

The year is 1992, and during the interregnum, before the ANC's negotiations can be concluded, the political agitation has seeped into us as children, and we are warned against approaching unattended packages on the street, explosives to obliterate our limbs. There is also a ban on singing liberation songs in public, where 'hippos', or armoured trucks, still patrol our neighbourhoods. In my room one morning, I use yellow, black and green crayons to scrawl the liberation party's colours on a wall. I look at this image and do not know what it means.

***

The year is 1993, and I miss the long walks I used to take around our neighbourhood. I miss the long walks I used to take around our town itself – from Tyu Tyu North to Parliament Hill. I miss the fragrances of friends' houses and being alone at the shops in the strip mall on Circular Drive. I miss absorbing the architecture of the CBD and watching the multitudes of men, women and children that course around its edges like a river. Eating bowls of *umvubo* in front of my mother's woodgrain Panasonic TV, I sit on our carpeted floor with my legs crossed, watching episodes of "Captain Tsubasa", a Japanese animation programme that is broadcast in the afternoons on CCV-TV. I make an attempt at drawing the characters from the show in my school exercise books, and often fall asleep on our lawn, watching complicated cloud formations, pregnant with sunshine and rain.

***

The year is 1994, and in her efforts to keep me indoors as much as possible, my mother returns from work one afternoon with an 8-bit gaming console.

The machine is packed inside a rectangular box with a label that reads 'Golden China TV Game', accented with golden flourishes to emphasise its name. Peeling the tape from the cardboard box in our living room, I do not know that what I own is, in fact, a 'famiclone', which is a replication of the original Japanese Family Computer, or Famicom, also known as the Nintendo Entertainment System (NES). I also do not know that the NES has become a behemoth, popular enough to warrant duplication such that in the former Eastern Bloc (the former Soviet Union), and now too in the Ciskei homeland, the Golden China TV Game is a common alternative to the original NES, cheaper and sold with cartridges crammed with hundreds of games instead of one. The cartridge my mother's brought home with her this afternoon contains "Rockman", a science fiction platform game in which, during the year 20XX, artificial intelligence robots, designed for industrial purposes, have turned against humankind. The hero is a humanoid called Mega Man, and by the time the game reaches me, it has sold over a million copies across the world. From this afternoon onward, I adore and treasure the device, waking up in the middle of the night to admire it, and turning it on with the TV muted, in order to delve into its 8-bit universe without waking my mother. I lose myself for hours inside its green and blue pixels, which are not only an insulation from the violence outside, but also an introduction to science fiction as a narrative form, the soil in which the seeds of my second novel, *Triangulum*, will germinate.

***

The year is 2000, and I'm fourteen and reading an issue of *TIME* magazine inside the public library in King William's Town (now Qonce), seated alone at a desk and learning about the capture of Onel de Guzman. De Guzman is a working-class computer science student, and an introvert like me; he's authored a global pandemic from the Philippines, infecting more than 45 million computers with the ILOVEYOU virus. Later, it will come out that De Guzman couldn't afford the Internet and had written the application to steal passwords in Manila so he could access it for free. His worm, which exploits a bug in Windows 95, will be discovered to have the same code as the application he'd described in his thesis at AMA Computer College, the school that had rejected the work the previous year. During his arrest, De Guzman is pictured with a pair of black oval shades. His skin is pocked from acne and his face is without expression. He is famous for his bashfulness, which I recognise. My understanding of the relationship between the poor and technology is cemented. I want to become a hacker.

***

The year is 2002, and I'm sixteen and enrolled in a boarding school in Pietermaritzburg. It's a fortnight before our summer break and our grade has been taken on a week-long camping trip to Greater St. Lucia, a protected wetland along the coast of KwaZulu-Natal. Here, all three classes that comprise my grade are packed into a wooded resort close to an estuary, where we're put up in bunk beds inside rooms we share between four of us. In the mornings, we wake at dawn to hike the dirt trails that spider jaggedly from the resort like a net of arteries, concealed under the dense lid of the nearby forest. During these hikes, we encounter barren earth, where the resort has felled trees for timber and mowed the forest floor into man-made meadows used for obstacle courses. Having been instructed to do a dozen laps, we hike back down the trails, limp from exhaustion, the sun beating down on the backs of our necks like a hammer. Inside our rooms, we take turns under a shower head, gasping at the pellets of icy water. In the evenings, the school enlists a team of local conservationists to educate us about the wetland, and so it is that one night, after dinner, I learn about the Dukuduku Forest. Earlier that afternoon, we'd ziplined from a cliff face and gone white water rafting through the Mfolozi's muscular torrents. Now exhausted, we sit around a campfire before being told about the troubles in the region. Two years before our trip, they tell us, the Dukuduku Forest was incorporated into the Greater Wetlands Park, into St. Lucia itself, and, owing to its rare ecosystem, it was named a world heritage site. Later, I'll learn that this means that its indigenous communities – a human population that had settled inside the forest for centuries and was reliant on it for shelter, medicine and sustenance – would have to be displaced. The local conservationists tell us that the forest's inhabitants are squatters with no legal claim to the land, that their presence poses a threat to the delicate landscape; for homework, we have to come up with ideas on how to assist them to see reason. The grade is silent. Then, a moment later, our boarding master, a man of German origin, gets up from his seat and turns to us, beaming with pride, confident of our compliance. Ensconced inside the ring of teenage bodies around the flame, I can tell this moment is instructive, but I cannot make sense of it. It will take me more than a decade and a half to make an attempt at doing so. I will decide to do this through a novel.

***

The year is 2005, and in my first year of university, I unenrol from computer science in order to major in English. In a tutorial one afternoon, I read a poem that likens living under Apartheid to living inside a B-movie. It is meant to describe the ersatz civilisation of White South Africa, but the poem's lines transport me to the pregnant silence of the Ciskei capital, where we'd filled up water bottles and called them petrol bombs for play, an eerie peacefulness gliding over a foundation of violence.

***

The year is 2013, and after several unsuccessful writing years, I finally complete a story titled "Space". It is set in Bhisho, where I spent some of my childhood, and it follows a group of pre-pubescent boys on an expedition to find an extraterrestrial that is rumoured to have landed in their neighbourhood. I choose this setting deliberately, finding the town's absence conspicuous in South African literature. The story wins a PEN International Award, and after that, I decide I want to write about Apartheid using science fiction, and with a focus on the Ciskei homeland, emphasising those elements that felt alien to me. Like the poem.

***

The year is 2016, and I'm on a tour in the United States for my first novel, *The Reactive*. I am coursing across the plains of Middle America when I conceive of *Triangulum* as a book. My tour began in New York City, during the Brooklyn Book Festival, and is set to end at Litquake[1] in San Francisco. Most of the tour has entailed a journey by car. My publisher, his production assistant and I spend hours talking and listening to music on the road, stopping over in small towns and cities for readings and book signings, eating vegan burgers and drinking cans of Miller Lite. As we travel, I realise that the landscape is beautiful. One afternoon, driving past an enormous cornfield, I imagine a character who is not quite human, but has spent her life on Earth, living and working as one of us, and now provides an appraisal of humankind, an account of her experience of the planet in the form of a manuscript. Later, I'll realise that the idea of her as an alien life form is not literal, but is instead the book asserting its genre to me. I will also learn that it is the writing process that helps me understand that the protagonist often feels alienated, as do I. I begin writing notes in the back of the car, *en route* to giving a talk and reading from *The Reactive* at the University of Wisconsin-Madison. Something is happening.

***

04/09/2016

The following is an account of the only known record of Patient #1, the first augmented human being in the latter half of the twenty-first century. Little is known about the patient's life from ages 0 to 30 – only that upon suffering from deteriorating eyesight at 31, she is said to have answered an advertisement on the deep web for the Triangulum Project. The record reveals a successful experimental surgical procedure, which involved incising the lens of Patient #1's right eye and infusing it with a prototype solution of untested nano-bodies, thus repairing the incision and diagnosed damage to the retina. In five years, Patient #1 is said to have suffered from bouts of blindness (a side effect of the procedure), made a recovery, and at 41, contacted the Triangulum Project again to request another infusion owing to its unrelated benefits.

***

The year is 2018, and an hour after submitting a draft of *Triangulum* to my US publisher, I retract it. I'm sitting alone at the counter of a bar in Melville when I email him. There must be more on native collaboration with the Apartheid government, I write, promising him that I'll deliver the final draft the following month. Two weeks later, I board an afternoon flight from Johannesburg to Cape Town and edit the tenth draft of the novel with a pen over a tray table. Two hours later, I arrive in Cape Town. Inside the airport toilets, the taps don't turn. I look up and see a sign announcing the water restrictions imposed on the province. I use hand sanitiser instead. In the forecourt in front of the terminals, I use an app to transfer R1 000 to an ABSA ATM. My wallet was stolen in Johannesburg and I haven't had a debit card since then, even after I took a bus back home to King William's Town, where I'd holed up in a cottage in my brother's yard to finish the first draft of my second novel. In the guest house in Stellenbosch, where the festival I'm reading at is taking place, a receptionist leads me to my room. I tell her 'global issues' when she asks me what I'll be talking about at the Wordfees Festival, which she admits she's never attended. I notice how beautiful she is. Her frame is small, her hair worn in bangs, and her smile pierces me. 'It sounds intellectual,' she grins, opening my door. Later that night, after my panel, I linger next to the stage, talking about *Portrait of the Artist as a Young Man* with an Afrikaans writer I once shared a panel with at the Goethe-Institut in Johannesburg. In my room, I make cups of instant coffee, and edit until one in the morning. Eight hours later, a shuttle arrives to take me back to the airport and I spend most of the flight back working on more edits, trimming down the manuscript from over 100 000 words.

***

The year is 2019, and *Triangulum* has been published. In an intimate, but full launch at an independent bookstore in Melville (where I live), I explain that as I was writing the novel I came to the realisation that South Africa's dystopian future could be imagined through its dystopian past; that Apartheid, during which I had been born, could be seen as the same tiered, technological and oppressive civilisation that is a common trope in science fiction narratives about the future; that the regime included human experiments and ecological disasters.

I confessed that I wanted to write about a character who felt alien, or alienated – about someone who'd lived most of her life with the sensation of being removed from people, but who, also, because of that, had been able to observe and document her life clinically enough to highlight the changes in our society over the course of five decades. The rest, in terms of the genres I decided to incorporate – mystery, coming-of-age, historical fiction, cyberpunk and espionage – had come after this idea, but soon became as essential.

In response to further probing, I say that the present is where the past and the future converge; South African history exists as a continuum, rather than as separate, conclusive chapters. In other words, I tell the audience – feeling as bashful as De Guzman during the press release after his arrest in 2000 – in order to imagine what could be, I had to steal from what had been. The reviews arrive a month later and are favourable – apart from one notable exception. In a prominent political magazine that mentions me on social media, one reviewer criticises the novel's characters for their flat emotional affect, before taking issue with the book itself for its implausibly bleak estimation of our future, citing George Orwell as a similar example. 'So we have 15 years to change our ways,' he writes, towards the end of his review. 'On the present showing, there's little chance of that. But even *1984* turned out to be an unduly pessimistic prediction. Or just a bit premature?' (Heyns). The reviewer concedes to experiencing a generation gap *vis-à-vis* the novel and to feeling strain from the proximity of his deadline, which I find understandable, having once written reviews too. The following year, the Covid 19 pandemic starts its devastating spread throughout the nation. On 7 January 2021, ten months later, George Orwell's dystopian sixth novel *1984* is reported as the best-selling title on Amazon, sparking discourse about its relevance in the age of Big Tech and modern fascism.

***

The year is 2021, and during the July riots, a warehouse belonging to UPL, an Indian-based chemical company, goes up in flames in Durban. News websites report that the warehouse contains millions of litres of insecticides and crop-solution products, way above legal limits. The toxins rain on land and river alike before seeping into the ground, into the water table. The warehouse is 400 metres from a school and upstream from a congested informal settlement. From the vantage point of a drone, the latter resembles a machine, a rusting circuit board, and for weeks, the Umhlanga lagoon and Uhlanga River bleed blue.

***

The year is 2022, and it is three years after the publication of my second novel. While teaching a Creative Writing Masters class for a professor on sabbatical at the University of Cape Town, one of my students (a documentary filmmaker and journalist from Nairobi) tells me that while industry leaders jet around the world to attend global warming conferences, the continent is seeing a rise in climate casualties; school girls are being withdrawn from schools in order to travel farther distances to draw water for their families, forcing them into adolescent marriages and damaging the social fabric of Kenya's pastoral communities for generations.

***

The year is 2023, and I'm preparing this paper inside my one-bedroom apartment in central Johannesburg. I assemble a series of vignettes that appear disparate at first, persisting in the hope that these fragments might reveal themselves to me. I do this in order to illustrate how science fiction, along with its dystopian elements, has always been a part of my life. This is how the genre arrived to me, not only by virtue of when and where I was born, but also through a contemplation of my past, present and future, which I've now found often merge into one. Even though the genre entered my childhood life as insulation from a revolution, I would return to it as an adult in *Triangulum* and realise that it could also operate as a weapon.

In his book, *Capitalist Realism: Is There No Alternative?*, Mark Fisher writes that it is easier to imagine the end of the world than it is to imagine the end of capitalism (8), a sentiment that, as I write, makes me think of our expat billionaires; feeling defeated by the excesses of the West, they misinterpret their despair for homesickness and an obligation to save our population, badgering our government to lower regulations enough for them to mine uranium and frack the basin beneath the Karoo. It also makes me think of an audience member, who earlier in the year at the

2023 Macondo Literary Festival in Nairobi, had asked me to sign her book before telling me that underpaid moderators in Kenya – all commissioned to review content on OpenAI's ChatGPT language model – had suffered from psychotic breakdowns, each paid less than two dollars an hour by a Californian company to read vast passages of text describing unspeakable acts of sexual violence. It makes me think of a dream I used to have as a child that never failed to make me feel leaden with dread as soon as I woke up. I was in the passage in our house in King William's Town, walking towards the kitchen, when I learnt that the house was abandoned. I ventured out to the cul-de-sac in front of our gate and discovered that it was the world itself that had been deserted. That I was alone. Looking up, I would see nothing but a vast steel machine, a complicated superstructure that hovered above me as silent as space, pocked with blinking red lights and breathing out funnels of black smoke as it encroached on Earth, closing in as if to crush the planet inside its indifferent and metallic clasp.

I had written *Triangulum* to seek refuge from the despair of our world, through an application of an imagination I'd found refuge in as a child. That much is true. But it had also been a means to chart a path that would liberate me from the hold of Fisher's sentiment. Although my second novel is a work of speculation on the future harm that late-stage capitalism could impose on South Africa – a conjecture of our trajectory up to the year 2043 and beyond – I had since its publication felt removed from the sentiment. Five months after the publication of *Triangulum* – while housebound during the first round of Covid 19 lockdowns – I established an experimental independent press, Model See Media, through which I released my third publication, *Native Life in the Third Millennium* – a chapbook of poetry, literary fiction and science fiction. Upon finishing *Triangulum* – which had been sprawling, necessitating a different editor in each press where it would be released in the United Kingdom, South Africa and North America – I'd wanted to downscale, feeling drawn to the idea of condensation. That was in terms of form, but the themes of the book came from two disparate events, similar to each other only in how they made me question the stability of my position in the world.

The previous year, I'd attended a lecture by American philosopher Lewis Gordon at a community centre in Braamfontein. It had been an introduction to, and an explication of, Black existentialism, a 'philosophical discourse that critiques domination and affirms the empowerment of Black people in the world' (Bassey 914). I'd pursued the scholarship of Africana existentialist philosophy ever since, encountering philosophers such as Mabogo Percy More and Magobe Ramose and decolonialists such as Catherine E. Walsh and Walter D. Mignolo, before returning to the poet Mafika Gwala, as well as the philosopher and activist Stephen Bantu Biko. I was still following this line of reading when, on 25 May 2020, George Floyd died at the hands of Minneapolis police officer Derek Chauvin, an act of brutality that spurred more than 10 000 protests in the United States alone, and culminated in a global quake of political anger and despair. Even as the coronavirus seeped into our population from unsuspecting cargo ships, railroads, coaches and aircraft, claiming close ones as well as strangers, South Africans would attempt to answer the call of Black Lives Matter from their own shores, questioning whether the nation's institutions had departed from their historical alignment with structural oppression – the sentiment being divided between 'no' and 'yes, but inadequately'.

During the protests, I also learnt that South African Internet infrastructure provider Openserve had released a media statement on 16 January 2020, revealing that two undersea cables that powered connectivity in sub-Saharan Africa had been damaged, affecting global capacity. It led me to the discovery of a project funded by Meta and other telecommunication companies called 2Africa, an international submarine telecommunications cable – 37 000 kilometres in length and stretching almost the circumference of Earth – that is to circumnavigate the coastline of the African continent, connecting it to Europe and the Middle East. Instead of being reassured, I felt cordoned off by the West, inside a ring of fibre, even as its hostility towards its most marginalised continues to mount. I thought of what this could mean for us, recalling Mignolo and Walsh's assertion in their book, *On Decoloniality*, that '[m]odernity […] is not a decolonial concept, but coloniality is. Coloniality is constitutive, not derivative, of modernity. [… T]here is no modernity without coloniality' (14).

Having no other recourse, I took the question to the manuscript of *Native Life in the Third Millennium*, deferring to the line of reading I'd begun the previous year, attempting to understand the intersection of race and technology, and eventually coming out of the other side, free of Fisher's hold. I no longer believed it was easier to imagine the end of the world than the end of capitalism. As a South African, I now understood that the two are one and the same, and that capitalism (the dominant order and logical conclusion of our hierarchical civilisation – how we imagine the world and construct reality) has to end. This means that the world itself, or at least how we know, understand and accept the world, has to end, which brings home the importance of speculative fiction, especially in the hands of the African writer, and how it could operate as a weapon. In writing my second novel, I had burdened myself with the question of how I thought humankind should proceed, but had had no clue as to where to begin locating the answer. I had created two opposing groups: The Returners and The Tank. The Returners were against all technological advances, believing that the Industrial Revolution had been a grave mistake in the course of humankind, one that had alienated it from both its nature and habitat. The Tank, on the other hand, were hackers, like De Guzman, who believed in the infiltration and subversion of our century's digital superstructure, which, more and more, had become a creaking edifice founded on the modern literature of code, a language that could be studied and then bent like all other languages before it. This, of course, is an argument that exists outside of the dramatisation of fiction, present, as it is, in various branches of philosophical discourse. For example, Mignolo and Walsh write that

> [i]f 'another world is possible', it cannot be built with the conceptual tools inherited from the Renaissance and the Enlightenment. It cannot be built with the master's tools, as Audre Lorde reminded us a number of years back, 'for the master's tools will never dismantle the master's house. They may allow us temporarily to beat him at his own game, but they will never enable us to bring about genuine change'. (18)

However, Lewis Gordon and Jane Anna Gordon offer a different stance on this same problem:

> Slaves have historically done something more provocative with such tools than attempt to dismantle the Big House. There are those who used those tools, developed additional ones, and built houses of their own on more or less generous soil.

> It is our view that the proper response is to follow their lead, transcending rather than dismantling Western ideas through building our own houses of thought. When enough houses are built, the hegemony of the master's house – in fact, mastery itself – will cease to maintain its imperial status. Shelter needn't be the rooms offered by such domination. (ix)

I'd wanted to write about technology and race, and from decolonialists such as Walsh, I had learnt that there were others like me. They might not have been born to the dystopian laboratories of the homelands, as I was – the Bantustans that had forged my imagination in the speculative – but they shared my desire in wanting to '[abandon] modernity's naturalised fictions and imperatives'. Like me; they identify:

> those in search of the relational and communal over competition, those endeavoring to move beyond the dictates and confines of government politics and uni- or mononational state forms, and those radically opposed to the financial hunting of consumers and corporations chasing for technoqualified workers to increase the armies of unemployed [...] and to disobey the universal signifier that is the rhetoric of modernity, the logic of coloniality, and the West's global model [...] connect[ing] and bring[ing] together in relation [...] local histories, subjectivities, knowledges, narratives, and struggles against the modern/colonial order and for an *otherwise*. (Walsh and Mignolo 13)

This deconstruction and pluralism, this imagining of an *otherwise*, I would later conclude, could serve as an iteration of how speculative fiction could function as an instrument of liberation in our global order. I thought of Biko, and his assertion that

> [i]n rejecting Western values [...] we are rejecting those things that are not only foreign to us but that seek to destroy the most cherished of our beliefs – that the corner-stone of society is man himself – not just his welfare, not his material wellbeing but just man himself with all his ramifications. We reject the

> power-based society of the Westerner that seems to be ever concerned with perfecting their technological know-how while losing out on their spiritual dimension. We believe that in the long run the special contribution to the world by Africa will be in this field of human relationship. The great powers of the world may have done wonders in giving the world an industrial and military look, but the great gift still has to come from Africa – giving the world a more human face. (51)

From *On Decoloniality*, once more, I recalled Mignolo and Walsh's assertion that 'complementarity and relationality in search of equilibrium and harmony are fundamental concepts in Indigenous philosophy from ancient times to today' (22). I thought of how, as a result of inhumane farming practices, the consumption of meat had become a political focal point in the West, and how the most salient part of the phrase 'human supremacy' was supremacy, meaning that once supremacy – or 'mastery', as Gordon and Gordon phrased it (ix) – was recognised as a legitimate way of ordering humankind, a hierarchical civilisation was inevitable. I stopped consuming meat after the publication of *Triangulum*, but I still believed that human beings were omnivores and that eating animals or not eating animals were two different approaches to the life cycle. The approach I'd chosen was for me to learn more about sentience but, like the philosophy of *Ubuntu*, slaughter still remained an ancient technology for Xhosa people, a ritual that augmented reality and unshackled it enough for us to commune with our ancestors.

Four years after writing and releasing my second novel, I was crossing the road on an afternoon walk in my neighbourhood, Montgomery Park, when, upon passing a small and vacant park populated by weeping willows and tall stalks of uncut grass still fragrant from recent rainfall, I began to imagine an alternative, a third route that could combine the efforts of the two opposing groups in *Triangulum* – The Tank and The Returners. Even though the idea was still concealed from me, I stopped in my tracks, filling with an excitement for all that I didn't know, that I was still to learn – an appreciation for the gift of creation and art, and a sudden and overwhelming confidence in the abundance of our planet. The moisture on the grass darkened my pants up to the knees as I waded towards the heart of the park, the sound of traffic dulling into a serene silence behind me. I thought how, despite the treatment of human life as disposable in our current order, a hall full of billionaires still couldn't create a single strand of hair; that it was nature itself (the engineer we'd lost our reverence for) that had programmed the code in our DNA and given us plants to sustain our hardware, sleep to replenish our software. For the first time in decades, I remembered the conservationists at the wooded resort in St. Lucia, and how the men and women entrusted with our education had failed to teach us that humankind wasn't separate from its environment, fêted for either its protection or destruction; instead, along with soil, water, sunlight, all living organisms as well as non-living elements, humankind was an invaluable feature of this world, locked inside a cosmic chain of interdependence with all that existed before us.

Endnotes

1   San Francisco's annual literary festival, established in Golden Gate Park in 1999.

Bibliography

Bassey, Magnus O. "What Is Africana Critical Theory or Black Existential Philosophy?" *Journal of Black Studies*, vol. 37, no. 6, 2007, pp. 914–35.

Biko, Steve. *I Write What I Like: A Selection of His Writings*. Picador Africa, 2017.

Fisher, Mark. *Capitalist Realism: Is There No Alternative?* Zero Books, 2009.

Gordon, Lewis R. and Jane Anna Gordon, editors *Not Only the Master's Tools: African-American Studies in Theory and Practice.* Paradigm, 2006.

Gwala, Mafika Pascal. "We Move On." *Collected Poems*, edited by Mandla Langa and Ari Sitas. South African History Online, 2016.

Heyns, Michiel. "Triangulum by Masande Ntshanga." *Noseweek*, 30 September 2019, www.noseweek.co.za/wp/article/triangulum-by-masande-ntshanga/.

Mignolo, Walter D. and Catherine E. Walsh. *On Decoloniality: Concepts, Analytics, Praxis.* Duke University Press, 2018.

Ntshanga, Masande. *Triangulum*. Penguin Random House South Africa, 2019.

---. "Space." *PEN South Africa*, 2013, pensouthafrica.co.za/space-by-masande-ntshanga.

---. *The Reactive*. Penguin Random House South Africa, 2014.

---. *Native Life in the Third Millennium*. Model See Media, 2020.

the hamster forgets: a zuihitsu on remembering writing queerness and community in this body

vangile gantsho

in thinking, i am walking alongside #AudreLorde #ToniMorrison #bellhooks #NtozakeShange #BettinaJudd #LewWelch #TylerPerry #LorettaDevine #KHo #TamikoBeyer #ClarissaPinkolaEstes #DaniilKharms #AnitaSethi #BernardineEvaristo #CherylMoskowitz #KimikoHahn #ChingInChen i am writing alongside AbazaliBam AmagqirhaAseKhaya OoGogoBasePhehlweni uMamuRolomana uBabuMuhambi i am thinking with ToniGiselleStuart VusumziNgxande LivulileGantsho SifisoGodsell SarahGodsell i am never alone under author nothing is ever new we are constantly writing in pursuit of an answer to a question that has been asked before the answer is written in the ether

***

I don't think there ever really was a war between the Hip and the Square, and if there is, I won't fight in it. I am a Poet. My job is writing poems, reading them out loud, getting them printed, studying, learning how to become the kind of [wo]man who has something of worth to say. It's a great job.

Naturally I'm starving to death. Naturally? No, man, it just does not make sense.
('Look, baby, you want to pay bills, go out and get a job.')

I've got a job. I'm a Poet. Why should I do somebody else's job too? You want me to be a carpenter? I'm a lousy carpenter. Does anybody ask a carpenter to write my poems? (Welch 3)

***

on pronouns
after Bettina Judd

i, she, we, us, me, our, mama, this body, gogo, dadobawo, makazi, makhulu is vangile gantsho, a poet-healer-publisher-daughter-mother-activist-friend-queer-blackwoman among the now living. also, collectively, the we no longer breathing.

sometimes vangile gantsho (i, she, we, us, me, our, mama, this body, gogo, dadobawo, makazi, makhulu) is a hamster, in a cage, on a wheel. and sometimes she is her grandmother's child.

***

Dear Saddi[1]

In three days, I will have been here for three months. And as much as I want to go home, I would be lying if I said I felt confident as a healer. I feel like andizazi ukuba ndenza ntoni. Abantu abadala bagqibele kudala ukuvuka and when they do, they speak a language no one understands. I can feel them when they enter the room but I cannot see them, and I cannot trust what I am thinking to be true. I cannot trust what I feel. I do not always know if I am feeling or thinking. There are so many pictures in my head. I am not always sure my eyes are open. They have always gotten me into trouble, now uBaba says I must let them all be free. I cannot trust that I will not get punished for them. That someone won't try to lock me up or give me a pill or fire me. Or that I won't feel like I'm drowning and drink myself to some shore.

Everything bleeds into everything. I worry I cannot teach because I cannot come to teaching without being igqirha. And I cannot be igqirha because I have too much English in my spine. And I cannot mother, because I cannot belong enough to my child (children, I worry my son will never receive me as his othermommy and building a family this way opens up so many wounds). I worry, Saddi. About everything. About this place that makes us sick and makes it near impossible for us to be well and live well, like we must always choose. To be honest or to be believed. To know or to work. And what if I never write anything worthwhile again?

***

in a village near my own, during a ceremony, someone's ceremony, kungena amagqirha amabini. they are well known. always together. two men. both unmarried. when they leave after intlombe, elinye igqirha says that this democracy is forcing us to love ezi moffie. sizakuthini? wonke umntu unamalungelo these days. this conversation is followed by utamkhulu asking what a man should do if his wife is disrespectful. my voice makes its way back up my throat. a bait i am willing to hook. i have been here long enough to know when to check my own pulse.

> but bein alive & bein a woman & bein colored is a metaphysical dilemma / i haven't conquered yet / do you see the point [...] my spirit is too ancient to understand the separation of soul & gender / my love is too delicate to have thrown back on my face (Shange 45-46)

i am the spectacle. the modern girl who found herself back here. so modern and so ancient she has forgotten how things are done anywhere. this is why i am not married.

***

my daughter asks her othermommy if she can have a penis her othermommy tells her that for now she has a vagina and her brother has a penis she is crying when she comes to me it's not fair mama i also want a penis i wish i could tell her how many times i have wished for the same thing for different reasons

***

in august, i dream we are at my grandmother's house but it isn't really her house. it is on a hill and from the top i can see both the kitchen door and the road. there is a parade making its way. lions and cheetahs and elephants. there is a giraffe and a crocodile. past the kitchen door, in our yard there are only hamsters. my grandmother is furious. we cannot join the parade as hamsters. she has never been a hamster. she says we have forgotten we are wild.

***

And always, we begin with Audre (Lorde). Do you ever feel like maybe someone's words live so deeply inside your marrow you cannot always tell whose blood is on the chair? Did Audre know when she wrote *Zami: A New Spelling of My Name* that by writing herself inside and always alongside her mother, she was mixing poetry and prose with country and family, and biographies and myth?

> When the strongest words for what I have to offer come out of me sounding like words I remember from my mother's mouth, then I either have to reassess the meaning of everything I have to say, or re-examine the worth of her old words. (Lorde 31)

> I remember how being young and Black and gay and lonely felt. A lot of it was fine, feeling I had the truth and the light and the key, but a lot of it was purely hell. (Lorde 176)
> I came from the valley
> laughing with blackness
> up between the mouth of the mountains I rose
> weeping and cold
> hampered by the clinging souls of dead men
> shaken
> with reverberations of wasted minutes
> unborn years.
> (Lorde 118)

At home, my mother said, 'Remember to be sisters in the presence of strangers.' She meant white people. (Lorde 81)

I [am] the story of a phantom people
I [am] the hope of lives never lived
I [am] a thought-product of the emptiness of space
And the space in the empty bread baskets
I [am] the hand reaching toward the sun
The burnt crisp that sought relief
(Lorde 118)

and in the brief moment that is today
wild hope this dreamer jars
for I have heard in whispers talk
of life on other stars.
(Lorde 100)

Did Zami know she was, through me, writing a zuihitsu? Or am I simply meeting her at an intersection? Touching her blood through language? Both of us coming to the page whole and in pieces.

Does it even matter that something is called a zuihitsu and something else is called innovative and fragments? In this world of invisibility … What is it that Shakespeare says?

What's in a name? That which we call a rose, by any other word would smell as sweet. (Shakespeare 2.2. 47-48)

***

Chin-In Chen in conversation with the words of Kimiko Hahn, says:

The zuihitsu, a kind of fungus poetics […] in which the writer follows the impulse of the brush in a seemingly random pattern, carefully constructed using poetic techniques of juxtaposition and fragmentation. A peculiar almost ghostly way of seeing.

Of shaping one's own sensibility, of leaving evidence on the page of one's own specificity. A pairing of ghostly fragment with a cascade of specific lists and queries. A question which could be asked – who slips between each printed line? Whose bodies are breathing there?

***

In her 1993 Nobel Prize lecture, umakhulu uToni (Morrison) uthi that some language is more barbed wire than salve. In her words: 'Oppressive language does more than represent violence; it is violence; does more than represent the limits of knowledge; it limits knowledge'.

***

queer

some definitions[2]

'differing in some way from what is usual or normal: ODD, STRANGE, WEIRD'

'How queer she is', the neighbours think 'to become igqirha after her family worked so hard to modernise.'

The unending myriad of ceremonies and required livestock gave them the queer feeling that perhaps she really had lost her mind.

*

'of, relating to, or characterised by sexual or romantic attraction that is not limited to people of a particular gender identity or sexual orientation'

When she fell pregnant, her mother, relieved, thought she had been cured of being queer.

*

'of, relating to, or being a person whose sexual orientation is not heterosexual and/or whose gender identity is not cisgender'

In Xhosa, the queer daughter who never marries and is always working outside during ceremonies is called unongayindoda.

*

'QUESTIONABLE, SUSPICIOUS'

She claims to be a serious writer but everything I have ever read of hers is queer.

*

'SICK, UNWELL'

Even though she had completed nearly five years of initiation, she was still queer and had to begin again elsewhere in pursuit of health.

***

> If there is any truth I can express (particularly as a queer woman of color), the only way I can come close to doing so is to pierce the veneer of transparency that we pull over language. To expose its materiality and enforced thinking. To begin to expose the ways language has been used for centuries as a tool to prop up systems of oppression, such as capitalism, racism, misogyny, and homophobia. And thereby attempt to communicate in a way that asks for a different kind of reading, of sense making, of connecting. (Beyer)

***

Dear Saddi

I am tired. I feel like I have not slept in months, and I haven't – if I'm honest. Everything is a lucid dream. Yesterday, a man came in with his wife. People have many problems. He is trying to get access to his father's inheritance but grew up using his mother's surname. He wants to change it but his mother – who has passed – refuses to give him permission. He resents her for not wanting him to be able to build a life for himself. His father left his mother to raise four children alone and started another family in Zimbabwe. I cannot imagine the money he wants is enough for such disruption. Amathambo athi he is cheating on his wife. She cannot give him children because the woman he is sleeping with has isimnyama and he keeps ejaculating it into her body. She has had four miscarriages and a stillborn. What brought them here is his arm. It has stopped working. Ubambisiwe. Baba asked me to help him, and I am filled with rage. I want to help his wife, but she has been assigned to someone else. I could feel that his stool is filled with blood. I could feel that his whole body is in pain. When I was steaming his body and rubbing out the thorns, he told me he wants children. It took everything in me to find a love to pour into him as medicine. To speak life into him – this coward man!

You said I am knives to you. I don't mean to be. But I am filled with rage, Saddi. Men take and break so much as if we have not been by their side. As if we have not taken their lashings onto our backs! And we must build lives with them? Surely there are other ways to preserve this black family! Surely, we cannot pin our future on such selfishness!
I told him that if he wants to have children he must grow into a father. He thought we had not seen his cheating in the consultation. He did not connect the dots. And my rage bleeds into my love, into my writing, into the classroom, onto the stage … onto you, Saddi. I am sorry.

And this rage is both blanket and road.

***

my daughter asks me what colour she is i tell her she is brown she asks me what colour her othermommy is i cannot unsay brown this intersection arrived sooner than i had planned i ask what colour does she think her othermommy is she says pink and then white and when I say yes she says aww mama i also want to be pink i love pink but mommy is like Elsa and Anna i also want to be like Elsa and Anna there is a towel on her head long hair i am ten in a danish friend's home playing with all her dolls she has real barbies with a full head of hair i am in a new school with my socks pulled up past my calves and pigtails on freshly relaxed hair i am amusing to the other girls who are also brown but you're the same colour as mama and makhulu and brother i'm the same colour as brother yes and mama yes baby you're the same colour as mama

***

> A woman's issues of soul cannot be treated by carving her into a more acceptable form as defined by an unconscious culture, nor can she be bent into a more intellectually acceptable shape by those who claim to be the sole bearers of unconsciousness. No, that is what has already caused millions of women who began as strong and natural powers to become outsiders in their own cultures. Instead, the goal must be the retrieval and succor of women's beauteous and natural psychic forms. (Estés 4)

***

Toni (Stuart) asks us to write our period story. Most recently, I was eMatatiela. Iqgirha lase mthata libetha abantu nge mvubu. The following day, ligxotha abantwana abancinci entlombeni. Aliyazi ukuba ishlwele salomntu bazokumsebenza liziveza ngabantwana. When I stand up, there is a red spot on my chair. I realise that I bleed everywhere. Onto everything. I leave my blood on chairs and children and lovers and readers and audiences and patients. My blood is spread wide across pages and continents.

***

AfroWomenPoetry (AWP):[3] *When and how did you discover poetry? Or was it poetry that found you?*

vg: Poetry found me young and searching and has stayed with me since. I've been writing since my father told me to put all the stories I kept making up into a book. We moved though, and I lost the stories along with my entire nine-year-old life's savings. Nonetheless … in high school, those stories became poems, and I began collecting them (terrible as they were). You could say the rest is history.

AWP: *What was it like for you growing up?*

vg: I am the third of four children by Kholeka, nee Mrwata, and Malixole Gantsho. The second child – my brother – did not make it and I am the only girl. (All the black women in my family have a story of at least one dead baby.) Mama is a nurse, who has been working since she was seventeen years old. She is 67 now, still working. uTata was a political activist-come government official-come aspiring farmer. He passed when I was 24 years old. Swallowed by a tractor while tilling his land.

We moved around a lot – because of utata. I began school at the age of four. Repeated grade one when I went from a Xhosa-medium school to an English-medium school, where a teacher told utata they couldn't teach me because I couldn't speak English, to which utata responded: 'then you cannot teach'. And so began the work of my linguistic dislocation.

Moving around taught me that books last longer than people, and telling stories was born out of necessity. My younger brother needed bedtime stories. And I was bored by the ones in the books we had, so we made them up together.

Home was home. Loving parents, the wide river between urban and rural, infidelity, the quiet violence of freedom, the sacrifice of wanting more for your children, the price of black bodying in a country like ours … a regular so-called black middle class upbringing. I hold my memories dear.

AWP: *Which elements informed your writing as you were growing up? Did the socio-political situation in South Africa shape your perspective on things?*

vg: I mean, I don't know any writer who isn't affected by their socio-political situation. Especially one who is an artist.

AWP: *How would you describe your poetics? What are the themes and stylistic features that characterise your poems?*

vg: I love a vast range of poetry. Lyrical, narrative, multiple forms … I really love poetry. Personally, I am interested in writing the political as personal. In confessional writing. But in all art, I am constantly searching for what shifts the ground I think I'm standing on. What touches Life's pulse and affects it.

I appreciate short sentences the way I appreciate long sentences and fragments and how beetroot leaves your whole plate purple. How this allows for me to exist in small particles that may not always fit into one sentence or thought or place, while being a part of something big and messy and uncontrollable. I am thankful for form that allows me to come to it complex and multiple. To be in community with other writers requires an unseen kind of discipline. Form that is intimate and promiscuous and feels like the wild woman archetype.

I'm currently enjoying prose poetry, am constantly preoccupied with line breaks, white spaces, caesuras. I write a lot in the first person (mostly because I love confessional writing, and I think this point of view gives the reader personal access to the emotion of the poetry … like being invited into a secret) but I am always feeling myself inside other people's shoes. I also try to write poetry that doesn't beg the reader to agree or disagree. That can present the beautiful and the grotesque with the same indifference. That allows observation to guide, without begging.

You could say I'm trying to become less needy through poetry.

***

> I have a term I came up with called fusion fiction – that's what it felt like, with the absence of full stops, the long sentences. The form is very free-flowing and it allowed me to be inside the characters' heads and go all over the place – the past, the present. For me, there's always a level of experimentation – I'm not happy writing what we might call traditional novels.

There's a part of me that is always oppositional to convention – not only counter-cultural and disruptive of people's expectations of me, but also of form. (Evaristo)

***

I

WRITER: I am a writer.

READER: I think you are s__t!

(The writer stands still for a few minutes, shocked by this new idea, and falls deathly unconscious.)

II

ARTIST: I am an artist.

WORKER: And I think you are s__t!

(Right then the artist turned pale as canvas, And shook like a blade of grass, And, unexpectedly, he passed away. He is carried out.)
(Kharms 64)

***

Did you know that a hamster is a rodent? And that some hamsters are so territorial that if they are put inside a cage with another hamster they may bite it? Kill it even? But a hamster is the first pet I was allowed to look after. In primary school, our standard one class had a pet hamster. Did you know there are wild hamsters? How would a hamster who has spent her whole life in a cage know what to do in a parade of wild animals? Not all wild things can be cats. But a wild cat cannot come back as a rodent in a cage, unless she has forgotten who she is or is being punished for something she has done.

***

We're allowed to be angry we need that knife. Here's what I think: I do not know if I am angry or a boy. I'd rather be a glimpse than a girl. Good. I'll rest here for now. Look: an animal in a meadow. A dark sky cutting a lake. A body of water in a body of water, slipping past a flat chest, a thin white cap, a loath wrist, trying to get someplace else. (Ho; emphasis in original)

***

bell hooks talks about space in literature. About what space is given to whom and what having space does. About the acceptability of linear narrative stories as opposed to more experimental works.

> When that feminist theory deemed most valuable is articulated in a form that does not allow effective communication of ideas, it reinforces the fear, especially on the part of the exploited and oppressed, that the intent of theorizing is not to liberate but to mystify. Anti-theoretical backlash tends to privilege concrete actions and experiential resistance to sexism, however narrowly focussed their impact. (hooks 36)

I think a lot about this. About the multiple ways in which we document and imagine, about whose language is valued and why that is the case. About whose ideas exist on the periphery of 'legitimate knowledge' and who becomes translated folktale or old wives' tales. About throwing the bones and reading an encyclopaedia. It is never assumed that the bone reader may also be terrified of not understanding the encyclopaedia, it is only expected that she must adapt and assimilate. In the continued words of bell hooks:

> As long as university settings are the central site for the production of theory and academics are simultaneously engaged in a competitive work arena that supports and perpetuates all forms of domination, feminist theorists will need to be conscientious about not supporting monolithic notions of theory. We will need to continually assert the need

for multiple theories emerging from diverse perspectives in a variety of styles. (50)

***

my body sprawls herself out onto my daughter's face says she is a temple says she is something sacred something the bible painted on a white a page something searching incoherent in pursuit of a virtuous woman searching inside a fingernail there is a whore and my hand is a spinster who left home to find a husband found an illness instead a dompas a man with a promise and fist and a hard penis found a trail of blue beads leading to a turquoise hut in her father's house brother's house this body is no house has no house has no husband is lying on a black floor with a chimney this body is over two centuries old is a fifteen year old girl inside an elbow what was she thinking listening to the wind what did the wind really say when she told them to kill all the cattle now her daughters are whoring in johannesburg without a language in their mouth some went across the ocean some drowned and the men they are whoring too her sons have no fathers have broken hearts and reddened knuckles have white teeth and soft lips her sons are liars and her broken heart this body is becoming stone rock imbokodo rolling up a hill starting a fire printing papers fighting a war this is a war not a metaphor a real war with guns and dead bodies and sometimes a funeral this is also a war a girl found chopped up in a plastic bag another taken at a post office this body is ugly maimed a dark fat body this body should be smaller more stealable desirable worth killing worth a hashtag at least this body should know that no one writes on landscape this body is tired tired of being tired tired of being tired tired of being tired tired of being a cliché this body will crack her own skull open in search of a temple in search of proverbs 31 in search of any scripture that did not arrive by water

this body is no longer mine is struggling to remember her way home her beads have been taken by the wind the same wind that stole the cattle and her child's father this body is a ravenous stomach with acid reflux this body is sick this is not a metaphor she is sick the doctors say it's fibroids says her lover gave her an std sexual spiritual sstd say she must be cut open this body has been cut open enough this body is the product of c-sections and systematic sterilisation and blood memory and unresolved trauma and silence is made by the lorde the lorde is faithful the lorde is livid the lorde is disappointed write nothing of the garden said the lorde use only the sources we provide read only the books we give you speak only the language we teach you you heathen body listen go back to the beginning you remember too much to be here start again the lorde is your shepherd you shall not want he leadeth you into white waters he delivers you into the arms of a man inside a house with a fence and a dog and two children and you must raise these children alone you are a nuclear now a full sentence a single line stanza reference author capitalism date 1652 can you not see this body is naked says bed instead of bird cannot speak english must be stupid has a stupid illiterate grandmother thank the lorde for the clever english teacher reference author georg schmidt date 1737 this body is written by the victor can no longer cross her legs will no longer be quiet when she cums carries drums in her feet carries drums in her chest grows a drum out of her whoring fingernail this body is fresh out of commas to give has no more brackets to hide her nakedness this body loves women loves men is narrative is lyrical is strange is odd is free is made in the image of the lorde

Endnotes

1 Saddi Khali is a US-born writer, producer, visual alchemist and dear confidant. He is also initiated as a spiritual healer. See www.saddikhali.com.
2 In conversation with the Merriam-Webster Dictionary.
3 These questions form part of a longer 2020 interview with AfroWomenPoetry ("Guest: vangile gantsho") but the answers have been re-written for the purposes of this essay.

Bibliography

Beyer, Tamiko. "To Fail and to Trust. Writing into Queer :: Eco :: Poetics." *Evening Will Come: A Monthly Journal of Poetics*, Issue 46, October 2014, thevolta.org/ewc46-tbeyer-p1.html.
Chen, Ching-In. "On Resistance: Backbreath." *Strange Horizons*, 29 January 2018, strangehorizons.com/non-fiction/columns/on-resistance-backbreath/.
Estés, Clarissa Pinkola. "Singing over Bones." *Women Who Run with the Wolves: Myths and Stories of the Wild Woman Archetype*. Random House, 1992, pp. 1-20.

Evaristo, Bernardine. "Bernardine Evaristo: 'I Want to Put Presence Into Absence.'" Interview by Anita Sethi. *The Guardian*, 27 April 2019, www.theguardian.com/books/2019/apr/27/bernardine-evaristo-girl-woman-other-interview.

"Guest: vangile gantsho." *AfroWomenPoetry*, 18 November 2020, afrowomenpoetry.net/en/2020/11/18/vangile-gantsho-2/.

Ho, K. "Readiness Assessment Form." *The Asian American Writers Workshop*, 31 October 2023, aaww.org/readiness-assessment-form/.

hooks, bell. "Towards a Revolutionary Feminist Pedagogy." *Talking Back*. Routledge, 2015, pp. 49-54.

Judd, Bettina. "A Note on Pronouns." *Feelin Creative Practice, Pleasure, and Black Feminist Thought*. Northwestern University Press, 2023.

Kharms, Daniil. "Four Illustrations of How a New Idea Dumbfounds a Person Who Is Not Prepared for It." *Today I Wrote Nothing: The Selected Writings of Daniil Kharms*. Translated by Matvei Yankelovich, Overlook Press, 2007, p. 64.

Lorde, Audre. *Zami: A New Spelling of My Name*. Persephone Press, 1982.

Morrison, Toni. "Toni Morrison Nobel Lecture." *Nobel Prize*, 1993, www.nobelprize.org/prizes/literature/1993/morrison/lecture/.

Moskowitz, Cheryl. "Follow the Brush: Making Zuihitsu Poetry." *Poetry School*, 2015, poetryschool.com/new-courses/follow-brush-making-zuihitsu-poetry/#:~:text='I%20like%20to%20think%20of,are%20difficult%20to%20pin%20down.

Perry, Tyler. *For Colored Girls*, directed by Tyler Perry, Tyler Perry Studios and Lionsgate Films, 2010.

"Queer." *Merriam-Webster Dictionary*, 2023, https://www.merriam-webster.com/dictionary/queer.

Shange, Ntozake. *For Colored Girls Who Have Considered Suicide / When The Rainbow is Enuf*. Collier Books, 1989.

Shakespeare, William. *Romeo and Juliet 1597 (Malone Society Reprints)*. Compiled by Jill Levenson and Barry Gaines, Oxford University Press, 2001.

Welch, Lew. "Manifesto: Bread vs. Mozart's Watch." *How I Work as a Poet & Other Essays / Plays / Stories*, edited by Donald Allen, Grey Fox Press, 1973, p. 3.

The Strongest Effect by the Lightest Means Possible 93

Courtesy Estate Ferlov Mancoba, Copenhagen

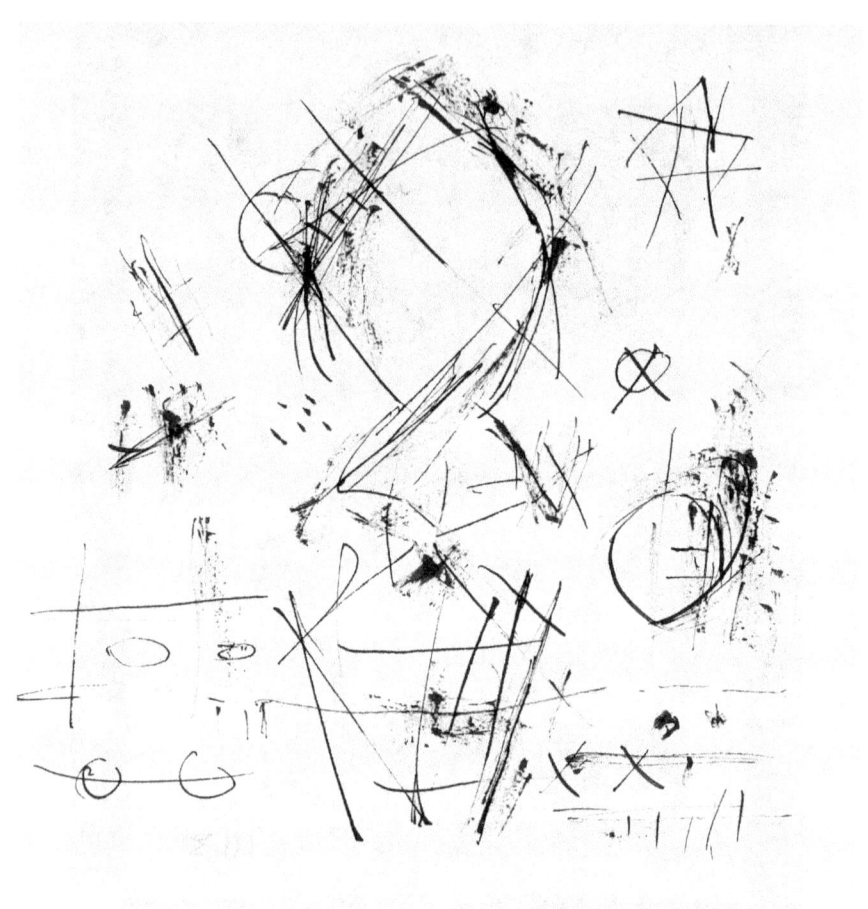

Ernest Mancoba, *untitled*, ca. 1965, Ink on paper, 50 x 32 cm
Courtesy Estate Ferlov Mancoba, Copenhagen

The Strongest Effect by the Lightest Means Possible: A Note on the Life and Art of Ernest Mancoba (1904–2002)

Ashraf Jamal

In an article in *The Guardian* in 2017, historical novelist Hilary Mantel reminds us that 'Evidence is always partial. Facts are not truth, though they are part of it – information is not knowledge'. For a poor historian such as myself, these are reassuring words. 'And History is not the past', Mantel resumes, 'it is the method we have evolved of organising our ignorance of the past […] It's what's left in the sieve when the centuries have run through it – a few stones, scraps of writing, scraps of cloth'. If Mantel's view is especially emboldening, it is because it eases the challenges presented by my own elusive subject – Ernest Mancoba, an artist about whom little is known and written. Little is available in the public domain, barring Elza Miles's biography, *Lifeline out of Africa*, published over twenty years ago, and a clutch of tenuous or provocative essays that Winnie Sze sceptically considers opinion pieces. As curator of a major retrospective of the works of Ernest Mancoba and his wife and fellow artist, Danish sculptor Sonja Ferlov, in Amsterdam in 2023, and organiser of a landmark symposium on the artist's life and work in Cape Town in 2020, Sze is well positioned to account for the lacuna, or vacuum, in critical and art-historical assessment. Barring Hans Ulrich Obrist's interview with Mancoba in Paris, a few months before his death in 2002, and Rasheed Araeen's jeremiad, Mancoba remains a spectral presence in the national and global imagination, and as such, deeply concerning; at best, the artist appears in the record of European Modernism as little more than a faint interlineary gloss. It is this absent presence that is especially intriguing, epistemically and psychically, a ghosting that has spurred my own engagement with the artist's life and work. What is it that informs his self-proclaimed 'invisibility'? How is that invisibility manifested in the artist's person and work?

While I would regard my own 'take' on Mancoba as an opinion piece of sorts, I believe avowed neutrality or objectivity in any interpretation of the artist would be disingenuous and illusory. I do, however, admit that to date the evidence at my disposal has been meagre. Still, I look forward to accessing the artist's private record, which includes ten years of video footage shot by his son, Wonga. For now, my approach has been speculative. I do not have anything to add by way of fact. But then, this was never my primary concern. Rather, it is the abiding mystique that envelops the artist that drew me in – a connection, a frisson, in the artist's person and creative expression that informs the precipitous relationship of Sartrean Being and Nothingness (states which, in large part, have informed my self-understanding and my understanding of art). Subsequently, this essay, or *assay*, is, as much, a personal examination. Through Mancoba, I also seek to understand my own snagged place in the world. However, in making this declaration I do not intend to place my subjectivity centre stage. Simply, I wish to confide my intimate *recognition* of Mancoba, and, by way of a disclaimer, to repeat that no neutrality, no objectivity, is truly possible in the assessment of the life of another.

Reading *A Life*, the Clement Greenberg biography by Florence Rubenfeld, I momentarily gasped. Greenberg spoke of Paul Klee, and yet it was Ernest Mancoba who came powerfully to mind. Klee's colours were akin to 'tints', Greenberg noted (qtd. in Rubenfeld 65). 'Light, tender, aqueous, thin', they resisted 'definite contours', were 'seldom thick or solid' (qtd. in Rubenfeld 65). Rather, it was colour that intensified and faded 'like light itself, translucent, vaporous, porous' (Greenberg qtd. in Rubenfeld 65). For Greenberg, such colouration achieved 'a kind of depth, but not one in which "real" events are probable. [...] Lines wander across areas of hue like melodies across their chords; surfaces palpitate, figures and signs appear and disappear. It is an atmosphere without dimensions' (qtd. in Rubenfeld 65). If Greenberg's words were uncanny, it was because they spoke of an artist who, far more than Klee, understood the precarity of creative expression, whose tenuous relationship with the self, with paint and canvas, defied record. What haunts me is the acute vulnerability of Mancoba's paintings – not only their formal ephemerality, but what their technical hesitance tells us about the man. Indeed, one could also consider

Mancoba's paintings as fragments gathered in a sieve – akin to Mantel's 'few stones, scraps of writing, scraps of cloth' – for such is the piecemeal and precarious nature of the artist's vision and being.

Mancoba left South Africa, then a British colony, in 1938, on a steamship bound for Southampton. His final destination was Paris, a city which, in his eyes, was by no means as bigoted or provincial as London. That he remained in Europe until his death in 2002 means that the greater portion of his life was spent in Europe, outside and beyond the world he knew for the first 35 years of his life. (I'm told his only two visits to South Africa were in 1993 and 1995 – for the opening of his first major retrospective at the Johannesburg Art Gallery, and the acceptance of an honorary PhD from Fort Hare University – dates, like bookends, that frame the country's first democratic election.) If this matter of his life in Europe is palpably important, it is because it makes his excision from European Modernism, in which he played a significant role, all the more concerning. Erasure, it would appear, not only informed the precarity of his being and artistic expression, but has proved seminal to his relative absence from European art history. That very little has been published on Mancoba – a gifted artist erased from European Modernism, but reclaimed by a democratic South Africa into which he was never born, and to which he never belonged – suggests a doubly exilic state. A group photograph taken in 1948 to commemorate the Høst exhibition in Copenhagen positions Mancoba on the peripheral back left of the frame. Unlike the figure on the far right, he does not lean into the picture, seems reluctant or perhaps embraces the futility of any comraderie. There he is, alone, peering from a distance, a widget, present-yet-not, functional yet inscrutable – *invisible* – or, after T. S. Eliot, 'glad to be of use, [...] but a bit obtuse' (7).

Reading Obrist's interview with Mancoba, recorded in Paris five months before Mancoba's death at 98, I was immediately struck by the artist's measured reflection; his ruminative calibration of North and South, Europe and Africa, the personal and intellectual; his striking suspicion of ideological affiliation and his deft weaving of theology and reason, faith and a heightened reflexivity. The conversation begins in South Africa, and, tellingly, with rebellion – that of Mancoba's 'clan', the Fingo people, who fought against King Shaka's oppressive rule and demagoguery in the name of 'democratic kingship'. Intriguingly, Mancoba connects rebellion with wanderlust ('fingo' means 'wanderer'), thereby triggering our curiosity about his own itinerancy and rebellion. As the only living son in a matriarchy, his is a quest for a brotherhood, which his mother foresees in Europe. This proves to be the case in his long-standing friendships with Danish artists Ejler Bille and Christian Poulsen. And what of his relationship with Constantin Brâncusi, the godfather of his son? Or with Alberto Giacometti? Or Mancoba's relationship with Aimé Césaire or Léopold Senghor? We know he failed to meet with C. L. R. James in London, and that this was a disappointment. He occupied the top floor of Giacometti's studio for nine years, interrupted by four years in a Nazi concentration camp. Arriving in Europe in 1938 was a significant year. The ensuing traumatic aftermath of a failed attempted fascist takeover by the Nazis certainly played a vital role in his re-evaluation of European values. Then again, Europe, by 1938, had barely recovered from the First World War.

My point? That European values were systemically destabilised in the early part of the twentieth century, that an abiding trauma infected every new ideal, every perceived change. It is in this profoundly damaged world that Mancoba arrived, dressed as a 'workman' in London, where, on the streets, he is verbally accosted by children who cry 'Nigger!' A perceived outsider and stranger from the start, Mancoba, doubtless, was forced to review his status as a Black man and artist in Europe. As to whether he forgave the children for the sins of their parents? The Obrist interview convinces me that he would have. Still, the full insult deserves our attention, precisely because it is imbued with the racist rot of empire, a rot that remains prevalent today – 'Nigger, Nigger go to hell. English, English ring the bell!' (Mancoba 10).

In his conversation with Obrist, Mancoba concludes his opening remarks by recognising the immense importance in his life of his mother, 'a fervent Christian', who treasured a book of African poetry – bound in cloth – a book of murmurings, a hiding place for the 'unspeakable' (7). There, in that book as a metaphor, we find Mancoba's personal understanding of art as a rune, a cipher or code for what cannot be spoken. Given the noisome New York–based Abstract Expressionism that would drown the world in its narcissistic din a decade later, Mancoba's marked quiet deserves our greater attention. Not only does his art anticipate

Abstract Expressionism, it also anticipates Tachisme in France. Deriving from the French 'tache' (meaning 'stain'), Tachisme conjures an art that seeps, spreads, dissolves the representational drive for perceptible forms and meanings. Indeed, it evokes a muteness, obscurity or enigma that speaks both to Mancoba's faith and his artistic practice. Barring his creative initiation in a Christian school in South Africa – his wood-carved Bantu Madonna being a sacrament to God – Mancoba forsook figuration as a declaration. Instead, in his paintings and drawings, the figure is obscured, becomes immersive, hallucinatory, barely present, and yet, immanent – a stain. This, doubtless, is symptomatic of his personal experience of invisibility in Europe and in South Africa. But to suppose the art produced is solely a psychological manifestation of his spectral relationship to being, is to personalise excessively a practice that, in my view, is as notable for distancing itself from penetrable conversation in its unspeakability, its self-alienation. It is Mancoba's gnomic nature that is most intriguing – his dissociative sensibility in the Eliotic sense, in which connection is deferred, and we find a separation of thought and emotion, a distinctively unromantic quality which, in my view, is in keeping with the fractured continent on which Mancoba struggles to find a home. Dissociation, in this regard, is not an error of being, but a symptom of non-being. One can choose to be noisome, hysterically so, or one can become a stealth machine; Mancoba chose the latter.

Unable 'to become either a citizen or an artist in the land of my fathers', Mancoba chose Europe (Mancoba 8). Or, it chose him, given the support he received from the Church and from artists to relocate. Seminal encounters in Cape Town in particular – especially with Lippy Lipshitz, who introduced him to Paul Guillaume's book, *Primitive Negro Sculpture,* an influential study said to have triggered Cubism and transformed Picasso into a superstar – would propel the move. After reading Guillaume's book, Mancoba 'began to think about how enriching it would be to have an exchange of ideas with such an open mind, who spoke with such deep respect about the expression of Africans, when I wasn't even considered as a full human being in my own country' (Mancoba 8). Inexistence precedes existence. It was to remain as a ghost, a haunting, in Mancoba's art. The commonplace description of him as a marginal and ephemeral figure in the CoBrA group (an influential art collective formed in Paris in the late 1940s, comprising artists based in Copenhagen, Brussels and Amsterdam) amplifies this acute sense of inexistence. That he failed to find himself mirrored in his adopted continent – other than in his relationship with his wife – reinforces my earlier remark about a doubled exilic state. What remains remarkable, and far more important, however, is the art that emerges from such existential dissociation, and the fervent optimism that nevertheless underpinned it. When Mancoba read Guillaume's book (which he sourced from the Cape Town Public Library, the staff member considering his loan request, coming from a Black man, strange, and his presence anathema), he 'soon understood' that he 'would never be able to feel free enough', in his 'mind', to 'express' himself as he 'fully [...] wished', that he 'would always knock' his 'head against the barriers which the colonial order had set up' in South Africa, wherever he went (Mancoba 9). That Europe would prove no different is another complex matter. For now, it is Mancoba's enthusiasm for change that counts, not the subtle slights that awaited him.

That Mancoba was sceptical of political gestures – during his time in Paris, he was keenly aware of the Black Francophone intelligentsia – further underscores the greater value he placed on art, which he saw 'also as a means to favour a greater consciousness in Man', as 'part of the struggle for any human liberation [...] without which any practical achievement would probably, sooner or later, deviate and miss its point' (Mancoba 9). The acuity of this remark must be fully embraced. It is the lack of refinement of the political sphere – its pragmatic emphasis on a fixed and non-empathic position, which invariably misses 'its point' – that ensured its ethical limit and failing. This distrust of political dogma – indeed, dogma of any kind – is Mancoba's abiding core. It is remarkable, however, that he refused to allow cynicism to contaminate this inherent distrust. Detachment proved a more honest stance. Regarding Senghor and Césaire's political position (although later he is careful to distinguish one from the other, challenging Negritude and celebrating Césaire's syncretism), Mancoba notes that

> the problem with their approach was that I never believed, for my part, that the racist ideology of the Occident is a problem of defective reason or insufficient comprehension. And I do not think, therefore, that it can be treated by forming new

> ideological concepts, like Negritude, anymore than I would imagine that the humanity of the white man might rely upon any virtual concept of 'blanchitude'. For you will never prove or disprove the truth of our common humanity, any more than a child needs material proof to instinctively know that his mother is his mother. No scientific or moral demonstration, no genetic test, nor any ethical imperative will ever add to this simple recognition, identification and love. (Mancoba 11)

Would that we, today, could heed Mancoba's wisdom, instead of wilfully balkanising the world, manufacturing difference, endorsing racism and systemic inequality, and producing dull counter-attacks that further ghettoise and entrench Blackness and Whiteness, say, at the drastic expense of a more empathic and incorporative vision of the world.

> I do not believe that we Africans, any more than other people, should need (as it would not diminish racism a jot) to show the white man how good we are at speaking or writing his language, performing in his sports, learning his customs, manners and intellectual actions, or to develop ourselves along the lines of his so-called 'universality', to be considered as human beings and his equals. Because the true universality is a common goal on the cultural, political and spiritual horizon that will be reached only when all ethnic groups achieve, through an authentic dialogue, the many-facetted diamond shape and the full blossom of the deepest and widest integrity. (Mancoba 11-12)

Mancoba holds a human-centric view, untainted by geopolitics, hemispheric and continental divides, or prejudice. From a historical materialist perspective, it may be considered naïve, but Mancoba never loses sight of existing inequality; he merely questions the mimicry of power and its reactive negation. He is disarmingly frank, in stating:

> I, for my part, have only relied throughout my life on two ideas – one, from the deepest heart of Africa which constitutes the

> basis of Ubuntu: 'Man is man by and because of other men', and the other, the precept of Christ: 'Do unto others as you would have done unto you'. I do not bother with anything else. (Mancoba 12)

The combination of Christian doctrine and African lore is not intended to signify a cross-cultural synergy but, in-and-through the barest bones of principle, to announce a simple austerity. The art is not to judge, hold predictively to inherited value, but to enshrine a raw human dignity. It is this austerity that defines Mancoba's human exchanges, and, significantly, the austerity of his art. In this regard, it is worth considering the decade-long relationship between Giacometti and Mancoba – given that they lived in the same complex, and Mancoba attests to their friendship, a declaration I imagine rare for the artist to make. What is friendship to a man on the outskirts of the norm? A man whose art emerges as a spectre, a ghost, barely substantive – as austere, one might say, as Giacometti's precipitous mortal punctuation marks (bodies without organs, skeletal, fibrous) – as sheer, as hallucinatory? Is this the bare forked animal that, for Mancoba, accounts for the fundamental yet rudimentary nature of his truth, or care for others? Is this his deepest African sensibility, reduced to its barest sinew, his Christian piety mutually reflective too?

When looking at Mancoba's ink drawings or his peripatetic brushwork, the febrile, loose, jagged markings suggest the search for some grip, some attachment – be it to a distant African aesthetic, or its potent re-emergence in European art – a Tachistic stain. In his conversation with Obrist, Mancoba notes that, in his painting,

> it is difficult to say whether the central form is figurative or abstract. But that does not bother me. What I am concerned with is whether the form can bring to life and transmit, with the strongest effect and by the lightest means possible, the being which has been in me and aspires to expression in the stuff, or any material that is at hand. (14)

That he renounces the either/or logic (of abstraction and the figure) further underscores the nonsensicality of the divide – for abstraction consumes the literal, and the body in turn is abstraction's excrescence, its suppuration, its brittle largesse, vanity and failure. As Mancoba smartly resumes, 'Our history has brought about, little by little, this dichotomy between abstraction and figuration which provokes, more and more, a terrible atomisation in the very essence of life' (Mancoba 14). It is precisely this fracture that accounts for the divisiveness of the current historical moment in which, absurdly, abstraction is pitted against figuration. 'In no domain more than in the arts has this systematic dichotomy caused such destruction of the very foundation to the human identity, as both belonging to nature and sharing in the essence of an ideal being' (Mancoba 14). Here we find a perfected distillation of Mancoba's world view. His is a frictionless world that overrides gratuitous and meaningless conflict, a world freed from the banality and hysteria of division, in which a foundational being and reality refuses historical burden or pragmatic political signification. The 'ideal being' exists under sufferance, with a great capacity for transcendence. That this being is destroyed in and through humanistic discourse – the humanities – accounts for its institutional bankruptcy today. For Mancoba, however, moral prurience, self-righteousness and ideological dogma remain the root ills of invention and truth – they negate the essence of an 'ideal being' (Mancoba 14).

What troubles Mancoba is 'the superficiality of academicism', or, more generally, prejudicial, exclusionary prescriptions to which his art and being have fallen victim (Mancoba 14). In a world as declarative as it is simulacral, 'we have lost the capacity to unite in our vision the outward aspect with the inner significance' (Mancoba 14). 'Our eye has been miseducated' and for Mancoba, the Greco-Roman ideal is the core of this miseducation (Mancoba 14). It is because of a peculiarly European culture of reason and beauty that African sculpture has failed to be recognised as an engine room of the radical transvaluation of human and aesthetic values, first triggered by Picasso. That Mancoba should also adopt the African figure as a spectral presence in his drawings and paintings reaffirms its critical place in European Modernism. This shift, however, is not merely a formal one, it is central to Mancoba's grasp of a great universal humanity, which European hubristic forms and beliefs have failed to embrace. If African sculpture matters to Mancoba, it is because of its evocation of 'inner being' through 'outward aspect' (Mancoba 14). This, in and of itself, is not a unique realisation; yet, such is the degree of attrition, that Mancoba is obliged to insist upon it. For even a dissociated sensibility requires a psychic congruence, some connection in the midst of an historical-epistemic-psychic collapse – the result of two great wars, a metastasised empire, the utter bankruptcy of core values and faith. And what of the art generated through this collapse? Here, the subject is Ernest Mancoba, and the solutions he struggled to find.

If African art matters for Mancoba, as it mattered to Picasso, it is because 'the object of African art is not to please the eye or the senses but to use art as a means, as a language to express feelings and ideas in relation to the present, the future, and the past, to discover new concepts by which to regard the world for the salvation of man' (Mancoba 15). Notwithstanding Picasso's white lie regarding the significance of African art, or his peculiarly European inflation of its noumenal and Dionysian power (a predilection shared by the members of CoBrA), or for that matter, its deeper, older root in Nietzsche's dichotomising of the Apollonian and Dionysian traits that inform and deform art, history and culture, one cannot dispute its force and impact on the European, if not (to date) the global imaginary. Seismic shifts are fickle. At this historical moment, we find ourselves returning to a simulacral understanding of truth, feeling, beauty; it is an age consciously cauterised, immune, dulled, in which African art, perhaps, no longer has a true place, its sovereignty under Modernism all too brief, its capacity to save the world null and void. Or so the neo-fascist naysayers would have it – the provincialists, nativists, puny brokers of a contracted little world, the very same one that Roger Fry in the 1920s abhorred. This world, this vision, is not Mancoba's. 'Man is One,' he declared, recognising that the racist and the bigot too have a place in a greater evolution – that is, if he or she is 'open to the Other, even to the ultimate Other […] with the knowledge, so well condensed by Arthur Rimbaud in his famous phrase, that: "Je est un autre" [I is somebody else]' (Mancoba 16). Only by allowing for such a radical transgression will one be able to see 'creations from the farthest elsewhere', and, in so doing, 'break free from our prejudices and our formalistic or ethnic enclosures' (Mancoba 16). Thus, Mancoba announces his own dissociation from that to which he remains so intimately connected, yet achingly removed. What, for him, remained catastrophically absent was 'a common acceptance and understanding' across cultures and ethnicities (Mancoba 17). This dialogue, for Mancoba, had tragically 'not started yet' (Mancoba 17). One can imagine the degree of pain suffered by the artist when faced with such a grossly inhumane failing.

In "The Erasure of Ernest Mancoba, Africa and Europe at the Crossroads", Laura M. Smalligan provides a compelling, if controversial, interpretation of the man and artist. Reasonably, Smalligan is concerned by the absence of Mancoba in the European Modernist canon, given his participation in CoBrA, creative life in Paris, and, primarily, his contribution to abstraction. While relieved, she is concerned by the re-appropriation of Mancoba by South African art historians. The return of a prodigal son is a noble story, but Mancoba was never prodigal. He recognised his extinction at home when he chose to leave; he did not anticipate his extinction in Europe. The timing of his arrival in Paris in 1939 could not have proved more fatal, given the start of the Second World War and his four-year incarceration in a Nazi concentration camp as a British subject and Black man. His was a freedom deferred, an identity repeatedly compromised, a talent delayed. When Mancoba speaks of a 'mis-educated' eye, one senses the cruel intimacy of this insight – his reduction to a skin colour, a subaltern status, a lesser continent. As for the art? This too was never satisfactorily understood as stemming from a forging at the 'crossroads' of a radical European aesthetic shift and a traditional African aesthetic economy. Largely, it is the latter that was presumed to inform his art – an African primitivism. I will not belabour the racism at the root of this assignation. And yet, to Mancoba's great credit, in his conversation with Obrist, he never berates the stunted and deformed perception of his person and art. 'The embarrassment that my presence caused – to the point of making me, in their eyes, some sort of "Invisible Man" or merely the consort of a European woman artist' – Mancoba is speaking of his wife, his partner and his soulmate – 'was understandable' (Mancoba 13). Prejudice cannot be blithely swept away. But it is what follows that deserves our greater focus, for Mancoba fully recognises his radical singularity: 'Before me, there had never been, to my knowledge, any black man taking part in the visual arts "avant-garde" of the Western World' (13).

While Mancoba understood the enormity of his place in the history of Modernism, few championed this deep self knowledge. That is, not until

Araeen, the Indian artist widely credited with being the linchpin in the revived interest in Mancoba's art. Which begs the question, can there be a revival when there was little interest in the first place? If Araeen's jeremiad is of importance now, it is because it is the first observation that starkly reconfigures Mancoba's place in Modernism, and Africa's place in that radical synapsis, for Modernism was no evolution, but the morbid result of a civilisational crack-up. According to Araeen, Mancoba not only single-handedly challenges the 'Eurocentricity' of Modernism, he also revises the vitality of Africanity therein. For, '[w]ith Mancoba, Africa's place is no longer peripheral to the mainstream history of modernism but central with it' (Araeen 7). As to where one wishes to position Mancoba in the 'crossroads', one thing is certain, his place, thanks to the efforts of Araeen, and others, especially in this revisionist historical moment, is now assured. Our challenge, then, is to reticulate this reconfiguration, see the many tangents and possibilities that have opened as a consequence of (what remains) nascent research. If Mancoba is indeed an anomaly, as Araeen understands him to be, what are the implications of the artist's outlier status in both Europe and Africa? Araeen is a celebrant of Mancoba's aversion to mimicry – 'colonial paternalism and patronage' in Africa and in Europe (7); it is interesting that Mancoba's rebellion does not emerge through a dissimulation and subversion of the language and economy of White power and mythology. There is nothing reactive in Mancoba's art and life. Even when triggered, he is careful to sublimate a given hurt or misunderstanding, precisely because racism, or any other prejudice, cannot be reformed rationally; it is a madness, willed, acculturated, insidious, ruthless. Which is why Mancoba's stance – an example Nelson Mandela would follow – is one that demolishes the myths of supremacy and inferiority from 'within'. This, Mancoba confides to Obrist, is achieved bodily, psychically, within the reservoir of his art, 'the strongest effect' of which stemmed from 'the lightest means possible' (15).

As I understand it, and my view is little other than conjecture, the driving force behind Mancoba's innovation stems from an acute inexistence in the art world – not being seen, other than through the optic of race as a Black man, a Black artist, an African. The rest, notes Smalligan, is erased. As she reasonably asks, 'What happened? Why has Mancoba been excluded from history?' Here, she is especially concerned about 'the complete absence of any discussion of Mancoba's involvement with CoBrA', perhaps because, after Araeen, he was someone 'who defied the colonial predetermination of their subjectivities' (Smalligan 265, 7). My point, however, is that this defiance is never deliberately conscious, never reactive. Mancoba's deepest yearning, the core of his art, was for the 'farthest elsewhere' (16). Entailing a renunciation of petty strictures, any bounded site of being, Mancoba's vision and world is not only one that others have failed to understand, it is also a vision and world that stems from his own radical un-accommodation. If how we position Mancoba matters – and this is Smalligan's key concern – it is because the artist cannot be nominally fixed. In this core regard, Mancoba is the embodiment of a displaced and errant being – translocal, migrant, symptomatic of a very different cosmopolitanism, devoid of any common ground, yet always *in situ* as some compellingly confounding widget, unnamable, unspeakable, mute yet sonorous – the embodiment of a restless and unfinished modernity, spliced along a frontier or a radically ambivalent zone of contact, the sum of regional, national and transnational intersections, the fleeting sketch of a struggle to maintain hope, some *uncertain* lucidity.

A Kafkaesque or Beckettian figure? A reverberation of a complex global trauma? After Jacques Derrida, we should remember that an erasure does not suppose a disappearance in its entirety. Mancoba, man and artist, is a striking instance of this nexus of the apparent and non-apparent. His paintings conjure this dance. Thus, it is insufficient to charge others for failing to recognise an art and being that is none other than *a disappearing act*. If Mancoba's art was not representative of the CoBrA movement, it is perhaps because he was unable to support their primitivist thrust, because, physically and psychically, he felt disinvested in this drive for which, incorrectly, as an 'African', he was perceived as an embodiment. Given that Mancoba (for me at least) is never a noun, but always adjectival – a thrusting, outwards, inwards, that refuses to coalesce – supposes a man, an artist, who was non-absorbent. A stain that could not be cleaned. An aberration, a nervous tick, a flaw or glitch – a-systemic, inconsolable, elsewhere. Hence, it is difficult to pin Mancoba down. A Black artist without a political agenda? What would that signify, given Blackness has always been objectified, understood nominally, the products of a Black artist is perforce some 'thing'? It is precisely because Mancoba refuses to be interpellated thus that we find ourselves productively searching for a more supple lexicon. However, what is indisputable is that he recognised himself as belonging to a vanguard, some 'farthest elsewhere' (Mancoba 16).

It is this non-absorbent quality, in the man and art, that places him outside of any explicable context and paradigm. Nevertheless, Smalligan is just in seeking answers, if only at a 'crossroads'. Concerned by Mancoba's restitution as a 'South African artist', she notes that thereby he has 'been ghettoized, celebrated as uniquely "African" but denied the possibility of being understood in a dialogue, not with other African art but with the work of European modernists' (265) – Giacometti, say, considered a great friend whose art like Mancoba's, suggested parsimony, some brute frugality, a precipitous void. Is Mancoba's art, then, morbidly intransitive and intransigent? Impossible to cohere? A radical experiment? In hindsight, given this moment in which Contemporary African Art has fast metastasised (the bulk of it Eurocentrically imitative), one can see why Smalligan is concerned with a cultural and epistemic misappropriation of Mancoba. While Mancoba might have sensed an 'African heartbeat' in his work (naming a seminal work 'Ancestors'), one cannot thereby consider his allegiances as being ever scrupulous (Smalligan 15). The wandering spirit, regarding his clan, the Fingo, is natal. Viewing Mancoba as a splinter adrift, tethered to Ubuntu and a Christian resistance to judgement, one cannot expect him to serve as an intermediary between worlds, for this supposes a rational and relational navigational capacity in which the artist assumes, in both, an emblematic role. On the contrary.

At each and every point, one cannot ignore Mancoba's liminality. How to maintain one's being when it is negated at every turn? How to sustain one's manifold self when, in truth, it is shattered? How does one find the wherewithal to bind oneself while one is unheeded, unseen, blind and blinded? Impossible. It is nigh impossible to maintain a core in the face of evisceration. This was Mancoba's reality. No righteous mirror was held up before him, no sanctimonious buffer against perpetual threat. Naught. Nothing. An echo? Sonar? A depth charge lost in a great vault of silence? How, in this fathomless silence does one speak? What must one announce? It is questions such as these that are the incentive and compulsion for this essay, for what Mancoba's life and art subtly yet excruciatingly reveal is the erasure of Black life and art within European Modernism. This decision is not merely prejudicial but epistemic, fundamental to the maintenance of a largely and peculiarly White male cultural mythology, Grecian in its core conceit. However, that being the case – commonplace in numerous critical positions currently undertaken – one cannot ignore Mancoba's more universal position – one that defies a raced and/or gendered cognitive and ideological stricture and avows a single and singular principle that 'Man is One' (Mancoba 15). That this transcendent view emerges in and through an acute sense of un-accommodation is all the more compelling. It is the existential complexity of his *non*-position that has proved the key intoxicant. In my view, it is insufficient simply to conceive of Mancoba's erasure from a historico-political point of view, which amounts merely to ideological commentary. A deeper explanation is needed – one that can conjure the artist's constitutive precarity, the root of his brilliance as a painter. If anything, Mancoba is an intriguing riddle. As a psychic excrescence, rather than a trope, he vividly embodied the Black artist in Europe in the 1940s. As a prisoner of war, or then again, simply a prisoner, he remained undivided in a divided world – austere, gentle, an artist who could barely touch a canvas, paper, and yet, in a fevered, tremulous, heartfelt, or calm instant, expressed precisely, minimally, the root of everything, be it the salvation of humankind, the sovereignty of care, the unbounded quality of grace, the solvent truth that overcame every hate, division, cruelty, or the heart and mind that it takes to be, to live and endure the madness all about. It is for reasons such as these (and far more than reason) that Mancoba has re-emerged as a soulful answer to the human and creative struggle. And it is because of this riddle, because of the gnawing evasiveness of Mancoba's art, that I have found myself – ensnared. For no artist to date has so utterly mirrored the void that informs my own life as a being and, especially, as a writer. Looking at a Mancoba painting or sketch – such as the untitled ink on paper drawing reproduced in this book at the beginning of this essay – the two mediums interpenetrate, and form a single fragility; it becomes immediately apparent that commentary will not do, for Mancoba begs alternative, acutely personal poetics. Hence my earlier dismissal of the fictions of neutrality and objectivity. Writers can never be mere commentators, or merely be writing commentary. The personal must find its way into the work that is thinking and feeling.

Reading Mancoba's conversation with Obrist, and, all the more uncannily, looking at and experiencing the acute fragility of his paintings, I grasp my own dissociated non-being, my own precarity as a putatively nominal creature – displaced from the age of nine, shiftless, adrift between schools and universities, countries and continents, hemispherically ill-aligned, neither Northern nor Southern, dislodged, disjointed, dispersed, a sketch or hallucination, the merest figuration in a febrile realm of marks.

Bibliography

Araeen, Rasheed. "Modernity, Modernism and Africa's Authentic Voice." *Ernest Mancoba: Drawings and Paintings from the Studio*. Stevenson Gallery and Mikael Anderson Gallery, 2014.

Eliot, T. S. *Collected Poems: 1909-1962*. Faber and Faber, 1963.

Mancoba, Ernest. Interview by Hans Ulrich Obrist. *Africa and Abstraction: Mancoba, Odita, Blom*. Stevenson, 2012.

Mantel, Hilary. "Why I Became a Historical Novelist." *The Guardian*, 3 June 2017, www.theguardian.com/books/2017/jun/03/hilary-mantel-why-i-became-a-historical-novelist.

Miles, Elza. *Lifeline Out of Africa: The Life of Ernst Mancoba*. Human & Rousseau, 1994.

Rubenfeld, Florence. *Clement Greenberg: A Life*. University of Minnesota Press, 1997.

Smalligan, Laura M. "The Erasure of Ernest Mancoba: Africa and Europe at the Crossroads." *Third Text*, vol. 24, no. 2, 2010, pp. 263-276.

Sze, Winnie. "'Je est un autre': Winnie Sze on Ernest Mancoba and Sonja Ferlov." *Artthrob*, 14 April 2023, artthrob.co.za/2023/04/14/je-est-un-autre-winnie-sze-on-ernest-mancoba-and-sonja-ferlov/.

Probing 'Place' as a Catalyst for Poetry
Vonani Bila

Creative writing is not always about getting published or receiving a grade, but is a practice to sharpen our awareness and appreciation of ourselves, familiar and unfamiliar landscapes and inscapes, and an opportunity to reflect key societal moments. Creative writing, and poetry in particular, allows us to connect with the written and spoken word, express complex ideas and reflect our experiences and imaginings with sincerity. It is about self and collective affirmation of the poetic craftsmanship without dwelling on collectivist and dogmatic thinking.

This essay explores community-orientated poetry approaches that reflect true and distinct images of society and the intimate physical textures of people's lives – our lives. It taps into meditations on place, familial relations and domestic life, and how this sociological alertness contributes to the demystification of poetry as an exclusive, elite artistic form for literary purists and followers of rigid procedures of composition. It highlights how community-oriented poetry workshops accommodate the literate and illiterate, and how poetry – be it lyrical, dramatic or narrative, oral or written – can offer a vigorous critique of society without sloganeering.

Poetry as I Understand It

In my community in Elim – Shirley village – both written and oral forms of poetry are highly regarded. However, the unpopularity of written poetry persists in terms of certain generalisations. They include associating written poetry with school – as a compressed and complex language, relying on obsolete words. Such poetry is considered difficult to relate to in terms of the common and everyday experience of the readers. I grew up with the notion that written poetry is demanding because of its many forms and technical requirements. It was only when I learnt that, in Greek, a poem is *creation* – meaning that well-composed poetry renews human existence – that I was comforted in the recognition that written poetry (like all forms of poetry) is not meant to be an elitist pastime or an intellectual exercise, but an engagement with all facets of the human experience.

When the educated fellows in my village want to brag, they throw a line from John Donne's "Death, Be not Proud", T. S. Eliot's "The Waste Land", John Milton's "Paradise Lost," any love sonnet by William Shakespeare or a psalm from the Bible. These great poems are quoted during funerals, weddings and graduation parties by men and women adorned with robes of academic excellence, and asterisks behind their names. Such speakers, orating from poems, don't see themselves as creators of new work; rather, they repeat the famous lines from the work of celebrated poets, often Anglo-Saxon. They hardly ever quote indigenous poets, no matter how skilful such poetry is. Some try to write, but the motive is usually the enticement of the money that publication may generate if the work ends up in the school system.

Speaking at the Timbila Poetry workshop held on 1 and 2 December 2001, poet Taban Lo Liyong argued that no poet should write for money:

> If you want to make money from poetry forget it, you will not make money from poetry anywhere. Maybe you can be rich if you write novels and maybe plays, but in South Africa not many people read. (314)

The currently more popular form of poetry (though historically ancient) is oral and performative, and is generally more accommodative than written poetry. I consider it to be less intimidating. Its language is rich. The oral poem records important events, moments and emotions without stringent academic formalism. It not only involves the poet in composition and presentation, but also engages the community or audience in the presentation. Duncan Brown observes:

> Oral literature and performance have been important features of South African society since the development of the earliest human communities on the subcontinent, from the songs and stories of the Bushmen and the Khoi to the praise poems (Zulu/Xhosa: *izibongo*; Sotho: *lithoko*) of African chiefdoms. In addition to prominent 'public' forms of panegyric to

> the leader, other forms of oral poetry have flourished – and continue to flourish – in African societies: songs to the clan; family songs (especially at weddings and funerals); love lyrics; children's verse; work songs; lullabies; personal praises; religious songs; songs to animals; and songs of divination. (2-3)

I grew up listening to inventive poetry, myths and chants, and performing cultural rituals by my clan. I found it to be interdisciplinary, providing glimpses into other facets of life such as history, sociology, anthropology, culture and religion. This understanding made it easy for me to connect with the poetry of Black Consciousness of the 70s, which was unsympathetic to Apartheid. Equally, I fell in love with the radical poetry of key Xitsonga poets James Magaisa, Max Marhanele and Benson Masebenza. I understood that the key public function of poetry –
written or oral – is, as literary scholar Casey Hayman (commenting on radical American poet Amiri Baraka) writes, 'its ability to speak, actively and directly, to the Black masses at large, to induce thought and action' (85). According to the Poetry Foundation, Baraka (like the projectivist poets) believed that a poem's form should follow the shape determined by the poet's own breath and intensity of feeling.

Kimberly Benston observes in *Performing Blackness: Enactments of African-American Modernism*:

> Baraka has always written within a sense of imminent crisis: his work derives much of its driving power from the assumption that the apocalypse is always about to be, that its arrival requires nothing other than the conjunction of changes, inevitable trajectories and his audience's decision finally to shed foolish delusions about the world and their own motivations. (194)

I am attracted to poetry that is rooted in the Black radical tradition, which is aimed at transforming society – the same way Steve Biko inspired the Black Consciousness poetry of the 70s and 80s in South Africa, and critiqued the barbaric system of Apartheid and racism without fear. According to Dominique Thomas, scholarship-to-practice curator at the National Center for Institutional Diversity, the Black radical tradition (popularised by Cedric James Robinson) is 'a collection of cultural, intellectual, action-oriented labour aimed at disrupting social, political, economic, and cultural norms originating in anti-colonial and antislavery efforts'. Mohammed Elnaiem observes that 'Cedric Robinson proposed that the Black radical tradition was necessitated into existence by "racial capitalism"'.

Unsurprisingly, I like poetry that is brave and fearless like a lion; poetry that strikes like lightning; poetry that challenges the sterility of accepted values, practices and norms; poetry that recreates. I prefer a poetry that calls a spade a spade, but woven and stitched in a crafty and nippy fashion. I like poetry that is rooted in people's lived experiences. A poetry that dramatises life anew. A poetry that breaks language open, demanding full acceptance of the vernacular – the patois, the local *Ringas*[1] – as noticeable in the work of Oku Onuora, Linton Kwesi Johnson, Mikey Smith, Kamau Brathwaite, Benjamin Zephaniah, Ike Muila and Jean 'Binta' Breeze. What I am advocating for is not new: German theatre practitioner, playwright and existentialist Bertolt Brecht, Brazilian theatre guru and political activist Augusto Boal, and Brazilian educator and leading advocate of critical pedagogy Paulo Freire have all called for people-centred art and education. As poet and playwright Angifi Dladla puts it: 'Students are not potatoes in a bag, but individuals with unique personalities, unique life experiences, and therefore unique needs that cry for individual attention, real growth and development' (11).

And, as Breyten Breytenbach writes, 'poetry is the breath of awareness and the breathing thereof […], for underlying the flow and the fall of verses are "natural units" of consciousness sculpted by rhythm, by recall, by movement reaching for the edges of meaning and of darkness' (15). For Breytenbach, 'the poem is a membrane, rippling, thrumming, reminding us that we are breathing organisms continually translating ourselves into spaces of the known and thus drawing circumferences around locations of the unknown' (15).

Making Everyday Poetry

I have always believed that poets should be encouraged to use place as a source of concrete images, and to write poems rooted in a concrete context.

In my 30-year journey of writing and teaching creative writing, and especially poetry – in often-neglected communities, rural and township schools, old-age homes, drop-in-centres, pre-schools and prisons – I have developed a set of instructional questions that poets must ask themselves in order to paint a picture of where they live and who they are. The emphasis of this approach is to encourage new poets to approach writing from the physical textures and details of their lives: what I've termed 'making everyday poetry'. The value of this methodology is an increased sense of place, recognition of their environment and heightened ability to witness stories around them, and eventually remake their world anew. Some of these questions relating to place are canvassed here.

Name the Place You Are Writing About

The ability to know the locale or situation of your subject matter enables a poet to be clear-sighted and to craft poems rooted in place and time – conscious of cultural, social and historical factors, mythic speculations and spiritual impulses. The context situates the poem, dressing it with the garments of the tradition of the place. The poem becomes an embodiment of rituals and evidences, practices and oddities, that define time and space. A poem grounded in place converts those depths of feeling and self-consciousness into an evocative organism. The place is a portraiture of memories – including childhood memories, songs, laughter, tears and loss. These memories return to the aged poet and guide them to see clearly, and to establish finer nuances such as speech patterns, dialects and cultural register. Memory helps a poet to look with detail and at length at the characters and objects that constitute place in relation to the envisaged story or poem, including the natural world of birds, stars, the moon, forests, rivers, mountains and spirits. Memory asks questions about representation and the description of objects and existences. It rescues poetry from mediocrity with the articulation of the particular. It makes writing concrete, coherent and a testament to everyday reality and existence as can be noticed in the concrete and resistance poems and woodcuts of the enigmatic South African poet Wopko Jensma.

In my attempt to understand and distil place, I've written several poems that are rooted in the actual place – the locale – and I have used the vernacular. My defiant narrative-cum-lyrical long poem "Dahl Street, Pietersburg" (*Handsome Jita* 58-66) is one example that satirically puts into perspective the lives of people treated as social discards located in a particular physical place. The characters are drunkards, vagrants, truck drivers, taxi drivers and sex workers. The prostitutes of Dahl Street dress in red lipstick, strut in broad daylight, often tipsy, trying to solicit the habitual truck drivers who sleep in their parked trucks along the road instead of wasting 'sleep-out allowance' at a motel. There are fat taxi drivers with thick neck pleats always munching something. The tough guys are gourmands. They eat *magwinya* and become round like the same *gwinya*.[2] They slurp cheap yoghurt and guzzle down *mageu* for stamina. They gobble boiled eggs, nibble fried corn, bananas, munching chips and crispy apple and pap, and gnaw *vleis* like stray dogs. They drink all types of herbal concoctions for virility. Here, you become a joke if you are a vegetarian, unless it's a prescription from the doctor. Dahl Street reeks of urine and grime, its inhabitants in thrall to liquor and sex. It is chaos and blaring *kwaito*. Yet what is common between sex workers and the reckless taxi men is the unspoken pain in their faces and a feeling of impotence. Equally, it's how they've both managed to straddle beauty and violence in a highly polarised society.

> Dahl street
> Pietersburg
> Reveling fatty boom-boom drunkard
> In tight jeans
> Sniff snuff
> Bloodshot eyes
> Dread-stoned woman
> Eats cigarette
> *Ke a o rata buti*
> *Vandag ke tsamaya le wena*[3]
> (Bila 59)

"Dahl Street, Pietersburg" describes the failures of post-Apartheid South Africa through the gritty images of denizens and outcasts. The persona is aware of the binaries – of us and them, rich and poor, modern and traditional, powerful and subservient. Inhospitable living conditions are characterised by sub-standard housing, mass unemployment, poor education and limited access to proper health facilities, to which the majority of these social discards are subjected. The poem's language is neither pure, nor sacred, but accessible, streetwise and sincere in relation to what people are experiencing in their everyday struggles. It's a language that carries with it the sound patterns, local cultural registers and pauses of the place, the staccato language of the ordinary person that must be preserved so that it doesn't die: 'She drinks *yonke nyakanyaka*' (Bila, *Handsome Jita* 60).[4]

The poem engages with the fragility of the human condition. There is no reason to censor the images of deepening societal decay. I write poems that combine emotional and political insights without sounding like a political hack or using poetry as a disguise for scholarly and rigid ideological argument. This approach is partly inspired by Boal's *Theatre of the Oppressed*, to which I was introduced to by Mike Abrams in the early 90s. Abrams was a cultural worker and political activist from Cape Town who ran a rural literacy programme at Akanani Rural Development Association, a political NGO in Shirley. He used drama to spark dialogue in the community so as to identify and solve their problems. Pat Bauer describes Boal as the 'Brazilian dramatist who created the Theatre of the Oppressed, a form of interactive theatre intended to transform lives, where spectators become inspired performers, seeking and creating solutions to social problems'. Of equal significance, Mike Abrams introduced me to the work of Freire, another Brazilian theorist and political activist. In our Thursday cultural meetings, Mike also introduced me to Brecht's writing. Brecht believed everyone should enjoy art and theatre, which should not be the preserve of the elite. "Dahl Street, Pietersburg" amplifies the philosophical groundings of Boal, Freire and Brecht.

When Timbila Poetry Project, a non-governmental organisation that I founded in 1999, hosted poetry readings at Waterland pub in Polokwane between 2001 and 2014, the audience included poets and non-poets, the literate and illiterate, students, workers and teachers. Patrons also included sex workers engaging in a transactional practice known as *mavuso*. *Mavuso* derives from *'vuka'* meaning 'wake-up'; it is money paid to a woman after spending the night with a man.

During the poetry performances, there was a sense of connection between the content being presented and the listening audience. Sex workers, who ostensibly came to the pub to drink, had an opportunity to encounter poetry that was not removed from their everyday social and political realities. To borrow Edward Hirsch's phrase, it was as if the poems had 'inhabited the reader's consciousness, the reader's body' (xi). Our shared experiences at the poetry performances led the Timbila office to campaign against the abuse of women and children, through poetry, drama and music. As Mark Waller observes in his foreword to *Handsome Jita*, 'the reason Bila's poetry resonates with a non-literary audience is because it speaks to their lives, their anger and frustration and desire for what should be – for the transformation of the outside landscape so that the inner one might flourish.' (vii)

Karen Press's poem "It Seems that if You Write" warns about writing about 'a place outside your heart':

> Your words get stuck in the furrows and ridges
> like shreds of meat
> Your mouth starts to sink like a hyena's lair.
> The place you were going to with your words
> has ended here.
> It will be found in the teeth of fossils
> dug out three thousand years
> and used to name the ones who ate you. (69)

Press's poem draws from the imagist and surrealist traditions, which emphasise brevity, precision and dramatised experience. Mick Imlah argues that imagism occasioned the introduction to the elite audience it sought for itself of several prominent features of modernist poetics – organic form, elimination of personality, rejection of public themes (689). In the context of my discussion, Press's poem illustrates what happens when you write with your feet hanging in the air, not firmly planted on the ground, in a place you can touch, smell and feel. There is nothing wrong with recreating the imaginings of the mind and heart, even when these are abstractions and influences from unknown places, but the danger is that the poem will lack coherence, internal logic and clarity of thought. It will only imagine the smell of the place, instead of whetting the reader's tastebuds with something real. Poems that are not rooted in place will be detached from the reality of the everyday. Press's poem warns about the dangers of not authentically including this sense of place when composing poetry.

What Is Interesting About This Place? What Do You Find Boring About It?

What you find interesting or boring about a place may serve as a trigger for a poem and its form and rhythms. I am fascinated by the liveliness of conversations in taxis, buses, trains, kitchen parties, weddings, funerals and all gatherings. They are like raw 'found poems' or 'raw music' before the stories and feelings appear in newspapers and magazines. I am fascinated by the folkloric tales, proverbs and idioms expressed effortlessly and casually by the elderly men and women in social gatherings; how they render their totems in such rich language, likening themselves to specific animals and reptiles. I am moved by certain particular objects that signify something in my life and the life of the community: a church hall, school, the umbrella thorn tree under which the community gathers for their important meetings; the binding cultural rituals that must not be questioned even when some, like male circumcision or the burial of a chief, hide cruelty; the gurgling or silent river where I used to swim and catch trout, and where Gideon Xidzinga drowned, and his decolourised stiff body was found floating after a week with eyes gorged out by aquatic creatures. I focus on the particular story within a wider context. I describe the particular. I breathe life into it.

A piece of excellent writing is an expanded view of the world that dwells in the subconscious mind of the poet. Black American poets like Yusef Komunyakaa and Amiri Baraka compose lyrical poems that chronicle the conflicts that besiege communities in America. They confront racism and historical suffering through their poetry, which is inspired by jazz and blues. They amplify the radical black poetic impulse. In Nigeria, the poet Tanure Ojaide meditates on place. James Booth describes Ojaide's poetic influences as love accounts, history, the beliefs and rituals of his Urhobo people and tribal antagonisms (454). What I find interesting about most villages in Limpopo are the mythical stories. In Shirley for instance, people relay tales of throbbing drum beats under water at the Dombani

Dam, where the sangoma's red and white skirts and vests hang on shrubs and trees. I grew up knowing that there was a *ndzhundzhu* – a snake-like goddess of the river that trains sangomas. Cattle herders and hunters claim to have seen the trainees dancing, clapping and floating in water before dawn. I'm just as fascinated by forests, rivers, mountains and their sacred tales – beyond the physical textures, there is the spiritual curiosity and familial relationships and experiences of place that must be expressed in poetry.

The particularity of this poetry doesn't prevent the poet from writing poems that explore art-making as a process, which incorporates abstractions and surreal images. A writer should establish their roots of influence because that will distinguish their poetry from the rest. The place, whether physical or imagined, is the identity, badge and shadow of the poet. If a poet is fascinated by folklore, oral poetry elements such as parallelisms, idiophones, riddles, proverbs, humour and lullabies will find expression in their poetry without necessarily limiting the scope and influence of their poetry. If a poet's primary influence is jazz, like Keorapetse Kgositsile, features of jazz poetry such as improvisation, rhythm, musical infusion and radical political messaging are likely to occupy the style and form of the poetry. Read Kgositsile's emblematic poem "If I Could Sing":

> I want to remain
> Wild
> Like a young song
> Unleashed
> Aspiring
> To the serenity
> Of a Japanese morning
> Hour
> (100)

I was introduced to the Turkish poet, Nâzim Hikmet, by Robert Berold during the Timbila workshop outside Tzaneen in 2004. Berold urged participants to use Hikmet's poem "Autobiography" as an inspirational template. Hikmet's poetry is regarded as poetry of witness since he meditates on exile, incarceration, death and escape in the face of forms of political extremities. I write my own precarities: misery and relentless poverty unleashed by capitalist governments on the poor; and racism and violence in all its many forms. It took me more than ten years to imitate Hikmet's poem, but once I did, I couldn't stop my writing hand from moving. I tried to maintain my communal, narrative and colloquial style, remaining faithful to confessional and experimental verse. Hikmet's poem is 59 lines, while mine is 1 238 and is included in the collection *Bilakhulu*:

> I grew up in a mud hut
> Drank water from the wells
> Slept on the itchy *majekejeke* mat on a cowdung-smeared floor
> At 10, I was still wetting myself in the night
> The millipede powder couldn't stop the habit either.
> (52)

Since being introduced to Hikmet's poem, I have used it often in writing workshops in Limpopo and across the country to stimulate an exploration of the self. During *My Story Your Story*, a community writing project in three schools in Limpopo, learners responded well to this exercise. Khanyisa Nkuna wrote the following: 'At 16 the world almost collapsed upon me / It flogged and dragged me away' (84).

While mentoring learners at Capricorn High School in Polokwane in 2004, I once again used Hikmet's "Autobiography" as a writing prompt. The learners matched Hikmet, pound for pound. Roshuma Phungo, a Grade 11 learner at the time, wrote: 'At 8 I was homeless / The extra child no one wants' (117). Manku Masemola, another Grade 11 learner, wrote a portrait poem, "Nokubonga":

> … she's only nine
> head of a household
> she's just a child
> the siblings she must fend for
> mama died
> last year
> of AIDS
> papa's a drunk

half-alive
*malome*⁵ pierced through her thighs
countless times
(113)

What is the Smell of the Place? Do You Breathe Polluted Air or Fresh, Healthy Air?

My cousin works as a coal miner in Emalahleni, Mpumalanga, the epicentre of coal mining. He describes the Emalahleni skyline as blanketed with a spiralling dark smog of coal. He says he doesn't like his job, but he doesn't have any other option. He coughs persistently, producing a thick brown phlegm. Sometimes he struggles to breathe, yells at no one in particular: 'All this shit is because I'm uneducated. I'm exposed to coal dust, yet I earn a pittance'. He says most of his co-workers with fragile lungs, as far afield as the Eastern Cape, have died of pulmonary diseases such as silicosis. Listening to my cousin's story, I am scared to visit Emalahleni. The water is polluted and the land is sterile owing to acidification of the soil. What I want to know is: who is responsible for fomenting this mess? The answer resides in the history of the place. And the place demands to be written, written into the place that is poetry.

One day, my friend Gomo gives me a lift from Louis Trichardt to Polokwane. He is driving a black hearse. I'm reluctant to get in until he shouts my name, and I join him in the front seat. When I look back, there's a rectangular wooden coffin with long rails along the sides. Gomo says he enjoys working with the dead: 'They are so peaceful. But hey, the rotting dead smell like dead elephants or rotten fish. It is musky and harsh.'

In January 2016, I spent over twenty days at Elim Hospital, nursing gun-shot wounds and broken bones. My stay resulted in the poem "New Surgery Ward, Elim Hospital":

Smells of fucked-up maleness trapped in a funnel of tears,
the stench of bodies pressed against each other,
sticky smells of patients smelling out of place –
of the forgotten citizens who can't smell themselves anymore.
(33)

An honest poem should reflect these smells – whether repulsive, putrid, stale, bitter, rancid, sour, airy, floral or sweet. Imagination should go beyond the plastic and beyond lip service; instead, it should conjure the precise intersections between the aural and olfactory; the physical and metaphysical; the conscious and unconscious. Smell provides a prompt to reframe memories of loss and desire; hope and despair. It is concrete and informed by the socio-political and cultural factors of lived experience. It makes the poem believable.

What is the Music of the Place? Is It Good or Bad Music?

The music of the place means different things to different people. For workers, daybreak is heralded by cockerels chanting their doodle-doo. Alternatively, silence over the depth of feeling of loss, despair and indignity can be so loud. Music of the place can mean release from the 'tyranny of conscious thought' and enjoyment in the songs of nature and the night. In my village, we dance when we are happy, when we are working, but also when we are grieving. Breytenbach says, 'when you hold a poem to your ear you hear the deep-sound, the movements we are part of, conveying not so much a literal meaning as an existential sense. It constitutes the spinal cord of remembering' (16).

Each and every place has its own kind of music, and poetry is central to sustaining the song, as it injects a new life into forgotten memories. Then there is the sad music we walk with: poverty, inequality, want, hopelessness, dehumanisation, powerlessness, traumatic childhood, denialism of sickness, mental breakdown, rampant violence, and power outages.

I recently used Eduardo Galeano's poetic prose piece "Jazz" as a writing prompt at a creative writing workshop in Mbombela. I asked participants to read the poem in silence. In the midst of the silence, I asked one participant to read the passage out loud. She read it as if she'd rehearsed it, with confidence, respecting the pauses, the ebbing and leaping movement of the writing. The older participants were reminded of their days as jazz fanatics and admired the fragmented sections and leaping movements in the piece. After our discussion, I read Galeano's piece again, admiring his ability to interrogate and meditate on the place:

1916: New Orleans: Jazz:

> From the slaves comes the freest of all music, jazz, which flies without asking permission. Its grandparents are the blacks who sang at their work on their owners' plantations in the southern United States, and its parents are the musicians of Black New Orleans brothels. The warehouse bands play all night without stopping, on balconies that keep them safe above the brawling in the street. From their improvisations is born the new music. (43)

When I was shot on 29 December 2015 in my yard, in the village that I had inhabited for 43 years, I realised that the music of my village was not sweet. I had always harboured an impression that the village was peaceful and violence-free – different from other townships where gates are locked as soon as the sun sets. I was wrong. The Ubuntu tree that had sheltered us during the boiling heat and torrential rains, had been mottled by ants and harsh weather. Its roots were dry.

The important thing to note is that the physical and emotional textures – sound, rhythm and colour – are primary factors in the making of a poem, but the poet's connection with the music of the place must be deeply embedded in the writing in order to avoid sentimentalism.

Have You Been to Town, Let's Say Polokwane or Joburg? What Were You Doing?

Travel is the best university. After visiting different places, I return a different poet. In Indonesia, I met a deified high Balinese Hindu priest (Gusti Putu Bawa Samar Gantang, master of Pencak silat), who introduced me to the Indonesian martial arts style, and who is king of mantra-chanting (or *Modre* in the Balinese language) poetry from Bali. Samar Gantang visited me at Shirley village a few years before I was shot. On hearing of my near-death calamity, he summoned his healing powers to try to remove the bullet lodged in my left thigh, and if that failed, at least to domesticate and neutralise its venom. The fully bearded seer and healer is revered for his ability to remove strange objects and organisms that malign people and their force (Rangda the witch) plant in our bodies – be it snakes, geckos, lizards, rings, scissors, stringed beads, birds, centipedes, necklaces, little horns, bullets, pieces of cloth, needles and nails. When I last saw him in Tabanan during the international poetry festival, I was so elated. It was like meeting a living deity. We stayed at the Gajah Mina Beach Resort in the mountains and palm tree forest near the Balian beach in Selemadeg village. Every morning, I walked alone to the beach, and planted my feet in the black sand that carried fragments of basalt – the dark fine-grained volcanic rock. I watched fishermen snorkelling and surf fanatics diving and catching easy waves. I didn't dare swim because of the dangerous currents, and the thought of meeting underwater reptiles or even Baruna, the god of the sea. Some tourists were kayaking while a few boats sailed. It was magic to be there. I could accept death from a volcanic eruption but not the gruesome deaths of South Africans. There was peace here instead of the barking guns that have become our music back home.

One night, we poets were seated at a long table, drinking unsweetened lemon grass tea decanted from a huge pot; gamelan music played softly in the background. We talked about the history of the archipelago, the burning mountains and volcanoes, hot springs, death and Balinese burial traditions. Samar Gantang emphasised that the Balinese Hindus worshipped several gods. It appeared everything had a god: the moon, the sun, the stars, death, everything had a god. Nature was revered. The Balinese were optimistic not only through their colourful attire and dance, but through their caring and warmth. During my stay there, I didn't hear a single gunshot.

In Bali, Indonesia, I witnessed the dead being cremated *en masse*, in public. Scores of people came out to witness the event. I learnt about the god of the wind and the god of fire. Watching things on TV or PlayStation, and listening to radio and digital platforms is good but not enough. Travel has taught me that borders are man-made and a futile exercise to exert imagined power. It has taught me that there is something special beyond the surface. The Tsonga people say, *'loko u nga fambi u ta teka makwenu'* – meaning, if you don't travel, you'll marry your own sister. Good poets travel. They are curious. They mingle with people from different backgrounds, cultures, races and personalities. They place themselves in the shoes of their subjects. They internalise the feelings of their characters. The experiences and memories of the roads travelled, seas navigated, geographies mapped, the people and objects encountered, and the sounds, sights and smells, enable the poet to visualise and write a wider and more meaningful and descriptive poem.

How I Write

I usually write what matters for me, and then go back and do line editing. I write what I feel, without a particular readership in mind, and trust that this creates music and structure for the poem. The Zen American Natalie Goldberg writes memoir using memory to weave her stories. She argues: 'We remember in flashes. You see a glint off a fork. Boom, you suddenly remember the hot dog you ate at Coney Island twenty years ago. It works in slices' (188).

Many of the poems I write have a strong narrative component, sprouting in accordance with my own rhythms, and out of necessity. Berold, a poet himself and a creative writing coach, says that when sitting down to write a poem, one should write with all the senses and with emotion, without explaining anything – leave the meaning to the reader.

I'm fascinated when my poems discover new vocabulary that is relevant to the ethos of the poem – making it a unique and independent construct capable of explaining itself without calling its author to the rescue. My poems are inspired by life, dreams, art, observations, struggle, stories that burst from people's lips and laughter and sadness in taxis, buses, trains, aeroplanes and boats; stories that keep me glued to the radio; newspaper stories that must be cut and placed safely in a file; interesting and unusual stories that my mother tells me; interpretation of photographs and art images; and some poems that come from the whistling grass and the howling wind, the rustling trees or even from silence. I can't ignore any of the things that comprise life. Life and all the objects must be carefully shaped and injected with breath. I read my poems aloud to synergise feeling and beat. I'm content when the poem works both on the page and the stage. I read my poems to other people, and I'm thrilled when younger poets memorise my poems and perform them in auditoriums and public spaces.

Like writer, critic, educationist and humanist theorist Es'kia Mphahlele, who considered himself a beginner whenever he stared at a blank page, I see myself as a beginner whenever I sit down to write. I treat the page as a field of vast possibilities. I break language open. I mix languages. I am playful, provocative, funny, subversive and sometimes free-wheeling.

Whatever I generate, I leave it to ferment like good wine, and I return to it after a few days or months to taste it anew, or to chisel it out, especially if it still has a spirit that talks to me. Then I explore what to cut or add in a poem, identify important lines and ways of sustaining my style, ways of shifting stanzas and sometimes lines without destroying the energy and cohesion of the poem.

I write lyrically descriptive poems that I carry with me in my heart; poems that are part of my skin and veins; poems that are part of my bones, muscles and bloodstream. I have little to hide in my poetry. I deliberately burn down the bush, patch by patch, and hope every word I plant will have a life of its own, cover the field with green shoots to form a coherent whole in the poem. I use plain language and I prefer poetry that is direct, but I hope it has intensity and richness, and carries several layers of meaning like the layers of a fresh onion. I think in associations, in images and in stories that take both the individual and society into perspective. My writing is a communal social construct that speaks to the condition of the marginalised – the denizen and excluded; a work that records stories and memories of the ordinary folk using everyday language so that even the illiterate can access the treasures of poetic magic without consulting a thesaurus or dictionary.

Berold argues that, when rewriting, the key is to become your own reader, so that the poem can speak to you – and it is easiest to do this after a lapse of time, when the emotions of the original impulse have dissipated and there is just the energy of the poem itself to show you what to do. He says:

> Cut anything vague, anything clichéd, any language that is not yours, any lines that do not belong to this particular poem no matter how attractive they seem, anything that is an explanation of something that the tones and images have communicated already. In editing a poem, give priority to the tones and music of the language.

In his letter to a beginner, Mphahlele observes:

Writing is that kind of creative art, just as you would imagine a wood carver making a figurine or making a bust of a human being. Chipping this side, chipping that way, chipping this side, chipping that side, chipping this side, filing here, filing there, shaping and reshaping and picking here with things, picking there with things, while it's still pliable, while the materials are still easy to use. It is that kind of creativity and creative experience. (329)

Conclusion

This essay seeks to impress on poets the importance of viewing their contexts with curiosity, to discover the arresting images and stories emanating from place and to harvest the melodies of place. The physical and emotional textures of a place, its sound, rhythm and colour, are primary factors in the making of a poem that is rich in sense-based images. A poet's connection with the music of the place must be deeply embedded in the writing in order to avoid sentimentalism. Such a poem reflects smells – whether repulsive, putrid, stale, bitter, rancid, sour, airy, floral or sweet. The imagery goes beyond the plastic and beyond lip service. It conjures the precise intersections between aural and olfactory; physical and metaphysical; conscious and unconscious. The experiences of travel, the people one meets, and the sounds, sights and smells, enable the poet to write a wider and more meaningful and descriptive poem, peeling off words and images that resonate with the place and its environs. Once this heightened sense of place is appreciated, poems generated with this awareness record not only the personal, but also a collective tale of the affected community.

Endnotes

1. *Ringas*, better known as *Tsotsitaal* or *Isicamtho*, is a South African vernacular urban dialect/creole derived from a variety of mixed languages. It is a *kasi taal* (township language) used 'through' another language – a type of basilect. While retaining its own defining features, it has no structure of its own, relying instead on the structures of the languages it uses. South African poets who have experimented with *Ringas* include Mboneni Ike Wangu Muila, Don Mattera, Sipho Sepamla and Kgafela oa Magogodi. Some catchy words and phrases include *heita* (hello), *ncaah/grend/*'double-dolly'/ *phashasha* (fine/ good), 'tah' (thank you), *danone* (dating a young girl), *danyani* (prison), 'tiger' (R10 note), *choko* (R20 note), 'clipper' (R100 note), *izinyoka* (thugs/thieves), *ngam'la* (white man/rich man) and 'Kosovo' (a dangerous place). 'Pulling a Kelly Khumalo' implies claiming to be a virgin when you are not, while 'Khanyi Mbau' refers to a gold digger.
2. *Gwinya* (plural: *magwinya*) is a South African fried dough ball, fluffy inside and crispy on the outside. In Afrikaans, it's called *vetkoek*. In the township, it's also known as *puff-puff*. It can be eaten by itself or with anything from sweet jam, atchar, polony to mince. It is a South African speciality that crosses the cultural divide. People who eat a lot of *magwinya*, especially taxi drivers, are fat and bulky.
3. *Ke a o rata buti / Vandag ke tsamaya le wena* means 'Dude, I love you / Today I take you home'.
4. 'She drinks *yonke nyakanyaka*' means 'She drinks everything that's cheap and bad'.
5. '*Malome*' is Sepedi (Sesotho sa Leboa) for uncle.

Bibliography

Bauer, Pat. "Augusto Boal: Brazilian Theatrical Director." *Britannica*, 5 August 2019, www.britannica.com/biography/Augusto-Boal/additional-info#history. Accessed 7 November 2023.

Benston, Kimberly. *Performing Blackness: Enactments of African American Modernism*. Routledge, 2000.

Berold, Robert. Personal interview with Vonani Bila. 13 July 2012.

Bila, Vonani. *Handsome Jita*. University of Kwazulu-Natal Press, 2007.

---. *Bilakhulu! Longer Poems*. Deep South, 2015.

---. "New Surgery Ward, Elim Hospital." *Voices Unbound*, edited by Heidi van Rooyen, African Sun Press, 2023, pp. 33-34.

Boal, Augusto. *Theatre of the Oppressed*. Pluto Press, 1988.

Booth, James. "Ojaide, Moses Tanure." *The Oxford Companion to Modern Poetry*, 2nd ed., edited by Ian Hamilton and Jeremy Noel-Tod, Oxford University Press, 2013.

Breytenbach, Breyten. *Intimate Stranger*. Archipelago Books, 2009.

Brown, Duncan. *Voicing the Text: South African Oral Poetry and Performance*. Oxford University Press, 1999.

Dladla, Angifi. "Growing Writers, Readers and Listeners." *The Fertile Ground of Misfortune: Teaching Practices in Creative Writing*, edited by Robert Berold and Stacy Hardy, Institute for the Study of English in Africa (ISEA), 2017, pp. 10-19.

Elnaiem, Mohammed. "Cedric Robinson and the Black Radical Tradition." *JStor Daily*, 11 November 2021, https://daily.jstor.org/?s=Cedric+Robinson+and+the+Black+Radical+Tradition.

Galeano, Eduardo. *Century of the Wind*. London, Minerva, 1990.

Goldberg, Natalie. *Writing Down the Bones: Freeing the Writer Within*. 2nd ed., Shambhala Publications, 2005.

Hayman, Casey. "People's Poetics: Amiri Baraka, Hip-hop, and the Dialectical Struggle for a Popular Revolutionary Poetics." *Massachusetts Review*, vol. 50, no.1/2, 2009, pp.82-97.

Hikmet, Nâzim. *Poems of Nazim Hikmet*. Translated by Randy Blasing and Mutlu Konuk Blasing. Persea, 2002.

Hirsch, Edward. *How to Read a Poem: And Fall in Love with Poetry*. Harcourt Incorporated, 1999.

Imlah, Mick. "Imagism." *The Oxford Companion to Modern Poetry*, edited by Ian Hamilton and Jeremy Noel-Tod, Oxford University Press, 2014, pp. 688-689.

Kgositsile, Keorapetse. *If I Could Sing: Selected Poems*. Kwela Books/Snail Press, 2002.

Lo Liyong, Taban. "Building Literary Communities." *Timbila 2002: A Journal of Onion Skin Poetry*, edited by Vonani Bila, Timbila Poetry Project, 2002, pp. 309-325.

Masemola, Manku. "Nokubonga." *Timbila 2005: A Journal of Onion Skin Poetry*, edited by Vonani Bila, Timbila Poetry Project, 2005, p.113.

Mphahlele, Es'kia. "A Letter to a Beginner." *Timbila 2002: A Journal of Onion Skin Poetry*, edited by Vonani Bila, Timbila Poetry Project, 2002, pp. 326-333.

Nkuna, Khanyisa. "Autobiography." *My Story Your Story*, edited by Vonani Bila, Timbila Poetry Project, 2018, pp. 84-85.

Phungo, Roshuma. "Autobiography." *Timbila 2005: A Journal of Onion Skin Poetry*, edited by Vonani Bila, Timbila Poetry Project, 2005, pp. 117-118.

Poetry Foundation. "Amiri Baraka." *Poetry Foundation*, www.poetryfoundation.org/poets/amiri-baraka.

Press, Karen. *The Canary's Songbook*. Carcanet Press Ltd, 2005.

Thomas, Dominique. "The Black Radical Tradition of Resistance: A Series on Black Social Movements." *Medium.com*, February 2019, www.medium.com/national-center-for-institutional-diversity/the-black-radical-tradition-of-resistance-7277f09ef396.

Waller, Mark. 'Foreword.' *Handsome Jita: Selected Poems by Vonani Bila*. University of KwaZulu-Natal Press, 2007.

Dance Curator as Archivist: JOMBA! Memory and Mourning

Lliane Loots

In this essay, I reflect on the politics of curation in the context of my 25 years of organising the JOMBA! Contemporary Dance Festival[1] in Durban, South Africa. I explore the potential link between being a dance festival curator and being an archivist interested in the forgotten, unrecorded, embodied histories of contemporary (especially African) dance. I set out, as a Southern-based feminist, artist-scholar and curator, to explore the intricate navigations of decolonial histories of curating and archiving dance in South Africa, interrogating *how* history is written (and *danced*); for *whom* it is presented and remembered; *what* has been left out and *why*; and *where* the personal and collective memories of alternative (and often invisible) dance histories are. Since so much of (dance) curation moves within the thorny arena of 'taste', I engage an autoethnographic frame as a way of situating all these discussions in a personal dance studies phenomenology. I engage curation and, cognately, archiving, as an act of memory, but also as an act of mourning.

Curation, perhaps best understood as the act of selecting and organising a defined set of artefacts or artistic works for presentation in an exhibition, show or festival, is a deeply political terrain. Curatorial practices have, according to Elizabeth Anne Bruchet, 'been subject to heightened levels of visibility and inquiry in recent decades' (2). This scrutiny is particularly necessary in contemporary Southern feminist spaces where knowledge pivots on contested ideas: who did the selecting, the organising and the defining of the ideas, artefacts and artistic works that count as viable and worthwhile? According to Michel Foucault, curating is a discursive construction that produces inclusions and exclusions, and parameters over what constitutes valuable art and artefacts. In this sense, curating becomes a way in which knowledge – and cognately 'truth' – is produced. To extrapolate, if knowledge (and truth) production is contingent on historical bias, curating can be (and has been) linked to paradigms that favour Western aesthetic-cultural traditions, and that comprise painful gendered and racial biases (among other numerous intersectional sites of struggle).

Jomba is the isiZulu word for jump. The dance festival was named in conversation with one of my colleagues in the Drama Department at the University of KwaZulu-Natal, Bheki Nkala. I jumped in, back then, but in my ongoing role as curator of the annual JOMBA! Festival, I need to reflect on my participation in cultural production, and in the production of knowledges that the curatorial act entails, variously including and excluding. I conceptualise curatorial practice in relation to the archival agencies of collecting and choosing, but also of preservation. I do so with an awareness not only that truth, memory and meaning are inevitably contested in the process of curating, but that, as Nayia Yiakoumaki's thinking around curating understands, every act of curating also *opens* (and activates) the archive (45). Curation as practice can move beyond the limits of what has been excluded (and why), towards re-readings and adjustments that appreciate that culture and meaning are produced continuously and often in a dialectical relationship with hegemonic truths and knowledge systems. Yiakoumaki is perhaps influenced by Jacques Derrida's idea of an acted-upon and active archive: 'As much as and more than a thing of the past, before such a thing, the archive should call into question the coming of the future' (34).

I have chosen to write this chapter as a type of personal remembrance, which is an archive too, of sorts. Here, I am claiming the value of autoethnography as a research method and a point of visceral theorising:

> [T]hose that complain that personal narratives emphasise a single, speaking subject fail to realise that no individual voice speaks apart from a societal framework of constructed meaning. There is a direct and inextricable link between the personal and the cultural. Thus, rich meaning, culturally relevant personal experience, and an intense motivation to know are what typify and strengthen autoethnography. (Wall 155)

Affirming a space to write and reflect on Southern feminist intersectional practices of curating/archiving feels significant, given histories where singularly loud voices and very visible bodies (usually male, abled, heterosexual, White, Northern) have generally decided, chosen, collected for, spoken for, curated and archived for 'others'. It is significant to affirm my own experiential narrative as I begin to unfold and question my place and space as dance archivist working on the African continent. Mine is not a definitive voice, but rather, one that I hope opens up, as Derrida suggests, a call to an approaching future of different and new knowledges via the archive (35). This exploration of curator as archivist necessarily engages with feminist, decolonial, and intersectional ideas and practices around the archive, emphasising Derrida's idea that the acted-upon archive is a hopeful 'promise of things to come' (34).

Jumping into JOMBA!

In 2023, the JOMBA! Contemporary Dance Festival turned 25 years old. As an annual contemporary dance festival based in Durban, it is currently the longest-running extant dance festival on the African continent. Despite the geopolitics of the Covid 19 lockdown, and the tenuous politics of retaining a space for critical contemporary dance in a South African arts environment that prefers to fund cultural practices expressly aimed at 'social cohesion and nation building' ("Funding Overview"), JOMBA! has survived, holding onto its self-defined mandate to support and nurture dissident and critical dance makers from Africa and further afield. This is also due, in part, to the unusual place of the festival, homed within the Centre for Creative Arts (CCA) at the University of KwaZulu-Natal. JOMBA! sits alongside four other international festivals hosted and curated by the CCA: the Durban International Film Festival, Poetry Africa, Time of the Writer, and ArtFluence (a festival that looks at arts and human rights). Emanating from a university space that promotes teaching, learning and research, perhaps an element of JOMBA!'s survival is its firm connection to an educational dynamic. Certainly, this unusual placing and university home base has also influenced my growth as an artist-researcher – as someone who fulfils roles as both an academic/teacher and artist working in dance. While curating a festival was not an idea I had for myself, circumstances opened this curatorial (and archival) path for me.

I consider myself an initially inadvertent curator: JOMBA! began on a dare. In 1996, the then-Dean of Arts Professor Michael Chapman set up the CCA, the mission of which was to promote, support and celebrate literature and poetry. Chapman, himself a South African literary scholar of international standing, imagined the CCA as serving and promoting the interface between academia and an ever-growing radical Southern African literary community. The appointed director of the CCA was Adriaan Donker, newly retired from his South African publishing company, AD Donker Publishers. Owing to a lack of office space on upper main Howard College Campus, Donker was sent to the bottom of campus and given an office in the hutments in the Drama and Performance Studies Programme. I was also new to academia, having taken up my position as dance lecturer half way through 1994, in what was then called Speech and Drama. Donker was allocated the office next to mine. Over the first year, we engaged in corridor banter and eventually began to meet for occasional tea in the office staff room. Donker was an inspiring man, who could talk about anything – from publishing to running the Comrades Marathon – and he expressed genuine interest in my dance work. Under his leadership, the newly- formed Centre for Creative Arts grew and originated, "Time of the Writer" and "Poetry Africa" – two literary festivals that continue to evolve, representing the many faces of literature in Africa, and globally.

One late Friday afternoon over tea in 1997, I shamelessly told Donker that he had a narrow arts focus with only literature and asked, 'What about a space for a dance festival?' Without even a pause, he replied, 'If you organise it, I will find some funds'. This was the moment of beginning. I walked away, humbled by his simple and profound confidence in me, and feeling a terrified delight in being offered this opportunity. I knew nothing of festival organisation, or of curation, nor of what it would mean to start on this curatorial journey. All I knew was that the contemporary dance hub of South Africa was firmly entrenched in Johannesburg at that time; the now disbanded Dance Umbrella SA was at its zenith and most of South Africa's notable companies (like Moving Into Dance and Soweto Dance Theatre) and big-name choreographers (such as Robyn Orlin, Jackie Simela, Sylvia Glaser and Vincent Mantsoe) were flourishing in Gauteng. It was my hope that this festival idea would enable Durban dance to engage, grow and develop.

I came to JOMBA! as an artist myself, and the beginnings were modest. I was at the start of my journey as a dance maker and had begun to be invited to perform my dance work at African and European festivals. Each time I toured, I encountered situations where I and the dancers I worked with were poorly treated. This ranged from not being fetched at the airport on arrival, to accommodation not being ready, being given weak technical support (which compromised performance), and late or forgotten fee payments. One thing I was clear about as I stepped into this thing called "JOMBA!", even before curating began, was that I wanted the artist placed at the core of the festival. I wanted to create a festival space that honoured dance makers by taking care with the people and the art being shared. I believed that if we could create an initiative that respected dance makers (in everything from publicity, to technical rehearsals and organisational administration), then audiences would follow. I envisioned JOMBA! as a space to which artists/dancers wanted to come because they were cared for. Given the treachery of South Africa's intersectional race, class, disability and gender histories, it felt – to me at that emergent moment – that we were embarking on an act of embodied radical politics akin to Ben Okri's understanding of artists as the conscience of a nation. We were intent on creating a kind landing for the critical, embodied and sometimes conceptually and physically dangerous art form of contemporary dance.

Opening Up the Art and Act of Curation

Looking back at the first two (even three) editions of JOMBA! (1998, 1999 and 2000), I remember my harsh learning curve as I began to understand curation. As a curatorial novice, I developed dance programmes featuring sometimes eight or nine works on one night, honestly trusting that because I could sit through three or four hours of contemporary dance, everybody could. But as I watched enthusiastic audiences dwindle over these marathon evenings, it became clear that something was not right. I also had the JOMBA! technical team approach me, in exhaustion, saying they could not continue to serve the needs of artists with this bulk of work. And so, slowly, my learning began. I started to see myself as a curator and not just an organiser, which was both a pragmatic and a deeply conceptual shift. Slowly, I navigated the idea that curation is a series of choices, and that far from being only personal, the decisions are also profoundly political. It was here that I set about rethinking the JOMBA! Festival, embarking on a more dedicated conceptualisation of curatorial practice, setting it in relation to the archival practices not only of collecting and choosing, but significantly, also of preservation. It became clear, in the scarcity of dedicated spaces for African contemporary dance, that any decision to programme a specific artist or dance company meant that JOMBA! was supporting and promoting that artist both economically (via small performance fees and grants) and through the visibility that was fostered and which allowed for the onward invitation and potential curation of work on other platforms and in other locales. The choosing (an element of curating) also came to be about decisions concerning what felt valuable (aesthetically and politically), and what dance forms and practices to support for onward preservation. These felt like heady burdens placed on what can be referred to as personal taste.

Sarah Pink in *Doing Sensory Ethnography* considers how ethnographic and autoethnographic research hinge upon posing questions about sensory knowledge. This is not something easy to articulate. Pink aims to comprehend how the researcher as artist (or in my case, curator) cultivates their practice through multi-layered lifetimes of sensory experiences that speak to the notion of 'taste' (xi). Choosing to make, or to do, or to curate are not actions that occur simply in a vacuum of socio- and geo-political knowledges. Pink harnesses an understanding of how 'thinking about and doing ethnography […] takes as its starting point the multisensoriality of experience, perception, knowing and practice' (xi). I am interested in this idea, wondering how 'knowing and practice' might be located at a visceral level of embodiment where the body as a whole makes decisions. As a dancer and choreographer, it is my daily habitus to move from one dance phrase to another in a series of seemingly instinctual movement choices in a choreographic process. Of course, this motility is not simply intuitive; it lies in 40 years of moving my body in various accumulations of cellular learning that are not only my own, as I also carry the palimpsest of absorbed influences from myriad physical dance trainings, dance teachers and dancers with whom I have worked and learnt. My dancing body is not only my body – it is an accretion of sensory knowledges that makes anything but 'simple' or 'instinctual' choices.

Opening up conventionalised notions of 'personal taste' is very productive for a curator and archivist. The curator – far from assuming that they instinctively curate what they like, and harnessing Pink's notion of 'multisensoriality' as an activated agency – makes choices based on a lifetime of learning and knowing that is not, and cannot be, separated from the political sphere. This is particularly pertinent for bodies that have been excluded – female, Black, queer, disabled, for example – for it prompts investigations into how a 'knowing' within intersectionally marginalised embodiments allows for a sensory practice that can offer curated and archived knowledge as a counter to hegemonic bodies. Moreover, a focus on the senses – Pink's 'knowing and practice' (xi) – becomes a way of understanding other people's danced experiences and identities. It becomes a means of exploring the invisible, the intangible and the unexpected, the unspoken, felt or sensed elements of a dancer's and choreographer's experiences.

The (Personal) Politics of Curation and Archiving

JOMBA!, being situated in Africa (and South Africa specifically), has an obligation also to explore the intricate decolonial navigations of how dance histories – in practice and in record – have been written, archived and presented; to interrogate *how* history is written and presented by a select few; to ask *what* has been left out and *why*; to query *where* the personal and collective memories of alternative and often invisible dance and embodied histories are. In short, how do the excluded bodies – among them female bodies, Black bodies, queer bodies, disabled bodies – find a way into curation and into the archive? This also speaks to questions of curation and decoloniality. Bear in mind that the JOMBA! dance festival is located within a South African university, which, like many other institutions of higher learning in Africa, tends to advocate decolonial educational practices, even while it is characterised by organisational systems that entrench versions of colonial ideology. This is a quandary. Nigerian born writer Harry Garuba unpacks two prevailing methods in which decolonial practices manifest in contemporary African universities. The first is to 'add new items to an existing curriculum' such that there is no real structural shift but an implied invitation is extended to those previously marginalised. The second, more demanding, approach is to 'rethink how the object of study itself is constituted and then to reconstruct it and bring about fundamental change' (Garuba). This is the version of decoloniality I favour for JOMBA!. As a dance curator, such decoloniality must entail the process of de-centering from epistemic adherences based on ways of being and knowing that are colonial, White, patriarchal, class bound, and able-bodied, dramatically reconfiguring what Savo Heleta calls 'violent normative ways of learning truth' (2). Decolonial influences impact the curation of JOMBA! and could be relevant to the historical, social and material realities of the dance (and academic) communities it hopes to serve. Acknowledging the type of archive I hope to evolve through JOMBA!, my curation has set out not only to offer a more accurate record of what has been included and excluded as valued dance history and dance making, but also to affirm (and every year to re-affirm) the importance and worth of what has previously been denied in Southern dance histories. In short, when curating JOMBA!, I have constantly engaged a consideration of the structural changes that need to be effected to habituated ways of curating and archiving dance. JOMBA! has become a holding space where alternative performance histories are curated, and repertoires emerge that negotiate intersectional, multi-layered forms of oppression (race, class, gender, disability, sexuality). JOMBA! as a process of dance curation is envisaged in a manner that allows a 'speaking back' to the dominant dance forms and assumptions that have been assumed to occupy the centre of danceography.

Historians like Steve Anderson and Genevieve Hart have argued that archives cannot be neutral; they are sites of contestation, control, and power: 'what is selected for archiving, how it is presented and who is allowed to see it, are all ways in which power relations are maintained' (25). In these (ongoing) examinations of the politics of archiving, I see (and have seen) my role as dance festival curator and not simply event organiser. I continue to curate and direct JOMBA! as a Southern dance arena that encourages contested South African/African dance spaces of and for memory. Dancers and dance companies who are curated are also archived and remembered. For JOMBA!, this act of remembering becomes the deliberative force in how dancers and dance companies are selected, and who partners with the festival in relation to issues of funding and collaboration.

I am further challenged in my curation by artist-writer Wanalisa Xaba, who tries to articulate how human bodies are receptacles of knowledge.

She reminds us that the body (and for Xaba, the Black body) is constantly in motion – moving, transferred and transferring. She conjures, for me, the idea that the movement of stories/histories – in short, dance – through highly politicised African bodies in motion, is an archive. I see my role as curator to set in motion the often forgotten or marginalised archive (and bodies), and to see what dances within it, counter to it, and alongside it.

My thinking about the archive, curation and the 'moving dancing' embodiment provoked by Xaba is also influenced by Diana Taylor, who offers a powerful further conceptualisation of the way in which externally formulated narratives of memory interact with embodied memories in the archive, and what she calls 'the repertoire' (19). Taylor aptly compares 'the *archive* of supposedly enduring materials (i.e. texts, documents, buildings, bones), and the so-called ephemeral *repertoire* of embodied practice/knowledge (i.e. spoken language, dance, sports, ritual)' (19; emphasis in original). In pursuing the comparisons between these various kinds of embodiments of memory, Taylor reminds us that it is important to consider the 'myths attending the archive' – that it is 'unmediated […] that it resists change, corruptibility and political manipulation' (19). Resituating embodied practices as a system of knowing and transmitting knowledge breaks down binaries that have existed between oral and literary traditions, given the archive's privileged position as a repository of hegemonic power. Instead, for Taylor, these two systems of knowledge and memory are placed in dialogue with one another. Here, hegemonic processes of mediation, among them 'selection, memorization or internalization, and transmission', are profoundly disrupted in relation to the contested and excluded embodied memories of Black bodies, queer bodies, female bodies and disabled bodies, for example (Taylor 21). Taylor's customised use of the term 'repertoire' (19) to speak about narrative memories, and how they interact with embodied memories, is an apt recalibration in the dance context, where the term 'repertoire' is often associated with the endless re-staging, re-rehearsing and re-performance of the 'great works' in (usually) the Western ballet canon. Taylor argues that her idea of an unfolding living repertoire 'enacts embodied memory: performances, gestures, orality, movement, dance, singing – in short, all those acts usually thought of as ephemeral, non-reproducible knowledge' (20).

These embodied (yet often transiently performative) gestures of archiving are significant insofar as they require the presence of those in whom the memory resides, which in turn suggests a greater potential for individual agency to affect and effect the archive than is traditionally associated with 'the archive' as an immutably established site. Perhaps this is where a curated live contemporary dance festival like JOMBA! has the capacity to shift what Taylor so rightly calls the 'myths of the archive' (19) – the idea that an archive is fixed, unmediated and enduring. With curatorial consideration for what has *not* moved within the archive, what work does *not* usually get curated within dance festival platforms, and which artists *are* recognised and seen, my curation of JOMBA! actively calls up and makes visible the presence of those bodies in whom divergent and unspoken cultural, historical, personal and physiological memories are danced.

My own dancing and curatorial preoccupations are an example. In an art form that often subjects the body to exacting standards of training, accomplishment, fitness and perfection, I am interested in how and where the dancer living with intellectual or physical disabilities[2] might sit in dance and in an archive that constructs normative embodiment through often violent exclusionary practices. Dance is about control and the disabled body is often a body out of control (Loots 123). Historically, both choreographic designs and audience receptions have often required a dancer living with a disability to perform in a way that enacts a transcendence of disability, an overcoming of what is perceived as physical limitation, so as to appear to become 'whole', such that, for example, a wheelchair dancer is required to stand up out of the wheelchair at some point in a performance. This must be set against curation that includes differently abled dancers to disrupt perceptions of who can dance and whose embodiment is worthy of the archive. In the 25 years of curating JOMBA!, I have actively made space to curate and support work by companies like Unmute Dance Company (South Africa) and Introdans Interactive (the Netherlands), and dancers like Joseph Tebandeke (Uganda) – such that the gradual curiosity and unease of watching a performer living with a disability dance has reconfigured through consistent exposure. This has moved to the point where JOMBA! now hosts an annual JOMBA! Danceability Focus within the festival's many platforms. It is a small victory that audiences show up, book tickets and engage with dancers working with disabilities in a manner that has seen shifts in the archive. It is here that I again contemplate the idea of curator as archivist, and echo Derrida's idea of an acted-upon and active archive as 'call[ing] into question the coming of the future' (34). Thus, one small curatorial enactment, which includes bodies habitually omitted from mainstream dance archives (that tend to memorialise exceptional physical achievement and physical form) is shifting the future potential for other kinds of excluded and marginalised bodies to be set in motion within an archive that should never be fixed in time and meaning, and that can always be acted upon.

Centring Africa

A most persistent curatorial influence for me is the writing of Kenya's Ngũgĩ wa Thiong'o – in particular, his 1986 work *Decolonising the Mind: The Politics of Language in African Literature*. He writes about the biggest 'cultural weapon' wielded and unleashed daily by imperialism against an artistic collective defiance (3). He refers to the cultural weapon of imperialists – those who seek to rule by creating dependency, for want of a better explanation – as a 'cultural bomb' (3). The after-effect of this 'cultural bomb' is to annihilate a people's belief in their names, in their language, in their environment, in their heritage of struggle, in their unity, and ultimately in themselves. This 'cultural bomb', once detonated, has effected a form of cultural genocide, for it has coerced Africans to see their past as a wasteland of non-achievement, making them want to distance themselves from this history of what seems provincial and thus not worthwhile, and to identify with that which is furthest removed from themselves. This 'cultural bomb' is not a detonation that goes off forcefully; it is an insistent series of small, deliberately muted explosions until, one day, a person finds that they no longer know who they are, or what to think or feel. Thus – as Ngũgĩ implies – the manoeuvrings of neo-colonial international corporate and Northern globalised capital have been allowed to tell African people how to look, think, feel, love and dance. They are left contemplating that they no longer have real memory and history because these endlessly re-written political and cultural versions of who they are, are sold to them as truth.

The effects of this cultural bomb are (perhaps) worse than simply being left out of or excluded from an archive – of not being heard and seen, and remembered – because colonial and neo-colonial processes push people to collude in their own exclusion. Ngũgĩ offers a beautiful vision of Africa returning to itself – through memory and re-education and what he calls 'decolonising the mind' (3). I believe this philosophy is still relevant more than 30 years since he wrote it. While such a belief system is never the full story of a sometimes corrupt and violent independent Africa, it remains true that a postcolonial contemporary Africa still desperately tries to re-evaluate its past across political, social and emotional fronts. Ngũgĩ's ideas of Africans decolonising their minds, speaks movingly to the possibility of changing memory in order to revise African histories of isolation, distrust and negation. Via a curatorial commitment to creating JOMBA! as an innovative archival platform that showcases, shares, partners and collaborates with African dance makers, this Durban dance festival has been unprecedented in South Africa in hosting artists from the continent and for making dance exchanges possible for African dancers and choreographers. To date, JOMBA! has welcomed artists and exchanges from Zimbabwe, Mozambique, Kenya, the Democratic Republic of the Congo, Cameroon, Nigeria, Mali, Senegal, Uganda, Burkino Faso, Madagascar, *Réunion* and Benin. For me, JOMBA! is an expansive, collectively motivated projection of Derrida's call to be open to an approaching future of different and new knowledges via the archive. My exploration of the JOMBA! curator as archivist necessarily engages with feminist, decolonial and intersectional ideas and practices concerning the archive; it emphasises Derrida's idea that the archive is not an immobile, received infrastructure that immutably reifies tradition, heritage and history, and that is determined to set up hierarchical and exclusivist forms of knowledge. Instead, an archive is a process of making, of bringing together into new forms of becoming. This acted-upon archive is a hopeful 'promise of things to come' (34).

Archivist in Mourning

Any curator – working in any context of collecting, choosing and preserving – will face challenges if they are grappling with relevance and context in their curatorial work. The role of the curator, and cognately the archivist, cannot be envisaged as neutral or controlled by a central narrative. Instead,

I am increasingly confronted with the idea that the role of the curator must be that of an activist fighting for those deemed voiceless (Anderson and Hart 28). Michele Pickover also argues that archivists (and curators) are 'agents of change' and that archives (especially those that fall outside of state control) should be 'instruments of empowerment' (2).

Curatorial and archival practices are inevitably politically contested – something is aways left out of the mix. No single annual festival over two or three weeks can represent the experiences of all that a racially violent, gender-exclusive and ableist South African dance history has forgotten, left out, or deliberately not considered. Even the best efforts, then, fall short. Derrida offers a trenchant angle, highlighting a paradox:

> [B]ecause of this very fullness, the hypothetical fullness, of this archive, what will have been granted is not memory, is not a true memory. It will be forgetting. That is, the archive – the good one – produces memory, but produces forgetting at the same time. And when we write, when we archive, when we trace, when we leave a trace behind us [...] the trace is at the same time the memory, the archive, and the erasure, the repression, the forgetting of what it is supposed to keep safe. That's why, for all these reasons, the work of the archivist is not simply a work of memory. It's a work of mourning. (54)

For an archivist and curator, Derrida's idea of 'mourning' is consequential because there is always loss – there are always significant and difficult choices about what is programmed and what is not. Does one focus on engaging all-female choreographers when this means, for example, that some younger Black entry-level dance makers then lose a space? How much international work does one place against local work? Does one programme a company from Europe simply because it comes to the festival fully funded? Does one consider what the work may or may not contribute to a South African dance scene and what form of trace is left by this work? There is a constant interplay of tough choices (economic and artistic) in this search for curatorial relevance – and it is never easy to say no: 'no' to an African artist desperate to bring their work to JOMBA!, or 'no' to a European or American funder, for example, whose offer to support work does not sit within these self-expressed curatorial frames. This archival and curatorial mourning is sobering and it is painful.

Curatorial mourning, for me, is mediated by understanding the larger frame in which my collaborative work with JOMBA! is located. This is an abiding reminder that the JOMBA! initiative has never only been about curating works for stage; it is also about imagining a more holistic space for critical contemporary dance in South Africa. As such, it aims to persuade audiences, dancers and scholars that such dance forms also constitute an archive, but one that moves and performs embodied actions that push back against, remove and disrupt the narrow and entrenched assumptions about 'the archive' as an implacable and sedimented institutional form. JOMBA! is about growing a culture of understanding, support and respect that honours diverse dance as a radical, often marginalised and deeply beautiful art form.

In the ongoing, revisioning search for JOMBA!'s relevance, my curatorial purpose lies in consistently focusing on the making and performing of contemporary dance. Here, the phrase 'contemporary' is a type of instruction to artists, audience and curator to engage and navigate a complex interplay between the confluence and influence of traditional African dance histories and forms, European and American modern and post-modern dance methodologies, and the ever-evolving search for authentic (and multiple) African contemporary dance voices that speak to (among many other ideas) culture, politics, art and identity. There is always an intersectional feminist push to support African women dance makers in a dance environment where their involvement is not consistently on festival agendas. There is also an ongoing push to connect and programme Southern dance makers – be they from India or Brazil, for example. Key on the curatorial agenda are ways to support collaborations that see dancers from different parts of Africa meet and work together in Durban, showcasing new dance works. The festival embraces new technologies and offers platforms for digital dance makers and 'screen dance' to find a home on the African continent.[3] There is curatorial space for invitations to dance makers, and there are also specific platforms for commissioning early-career South African dancers and choreographers. These curatorial emphases are reviewed each new festival against local and global politics to see where JOMBA! may potentially situate itself in relation to who is habitually included and excluded at any given moment in the festival's history.

My work as curator for JOMBA! over the past 25 years has entailed significant learning and self-reflection around my identity and my value systems as a Southern feminist artist-scholar. My own personal and political commitment to an intersectional gender politics has been the foundation from which I continue to ask questions of myself. I have not been allowed to stagnate as choreographic practitioner under the misapprehension that JOMBA! would gradually unfold, reach and bend via a fixed set of curatorial paradigms. The Covid 19 pandemic, for example, tasked me with imagining an innovative digital platform for a live embodied art form. In related ways, my imagination has been pushed to think of dance through multiple embodiment possibilities beyond the normative able body. I am also aware that a time will emerge when I must hand this project on to another curator who will want to find other ways to continue JOMBA! This too is important. After 25 years, JOMBA! is in some sense an established archive, but it must also be understood as a project in motion, since such flexibility – conceptual and embodied – carries the crucial ability to alter and re-imagine the very constitution of archiving as an ongoing, performative dynamic (Yiakoumaki 243). As Yiakoumaki suggests, the choreographer and dance practitioner as archivist is actively engaged in forms of dance curation, having the capacity to shift what is remembered and how, helping to dismantle old ideas of the archive as an inert repository of some unchanged and unchangeable past. Perhaps my role in JOMBA! can be considered 'a curator's intervention' in the archive of South African dance, a form of 're-deposit' within the archival process 'as a means for the archive's potential expansion' (Yiakoumaki 2). My hope is that my work with JOMBA! offers mobile revisions of archiving as an embodied action of re-imagining, a powerful 'promise of things to come' (Derrida 34).

Endnotes

1. For more information (and the festival's archival repository), see jomba.ukzn.ac.za/.
2. Within Critical Disability Studies, linguistic naming is a contested terrain of meaning (see for example, Loots pp. 122-132). I have chosen to embrace the UN Convention (and the human rights disability frame) of naming in this moment. I am aware that this too is a form of linguistic curation.
3. JOMBA! is the only African dance festival to date that offers a curated digital space for dance makers to showcase screen dance works.

Bibliography

Anderson, Steve and Genevieve Hart. "Challenges in Digitising Liberation Archives: A Case Study." *Innovation: Journal of Appropriate Librarianship and Information Work in Southern Africa*, vol. 53, 2016, pp. 21-38.

"Archive Fever in South Africa." *Refiguring the Archive*, edited by Carolyn Hamilton, Verne Harris, June Taylor, Michele Pickover, Graeme Reid and Razia Saleh, Kluwer, 2002, p. 38

Bruchet, Elizabeth Anne. *Curation and the Archive: Entanglements of Discourse and Practice.* 2019. University of Brighton, PhD thesis. www.research.brighton.ac.uk/en/studentTheses/curation-and-the-archive.

Derrida, Jacques. *Archive Fever: A Freudian Impression.* University of Chicago Press, 1996.

Foucault, Michel. "Fantasia of the Library." *Language, Counter-Memory, Practice: Selected Essays and Interviews by Michel Foucault*, edited by Donald F. Bouchard, Cornell University Press, 1977, pp. 87-109.

"Funding Overview". *National Arts Council*, 2023, www.nac.org.za/funding-overview/.

Garuba, Harry. "What Is an African Curriculum?" *Mail and Guardian*, 12 April 2015, http://mg.co.za/article/2015-04-17-what-is-an-african-curriculum/.

Heleta, Savo. "Decolonisation of Higher Education: Dismantling Epistemic Violence and Eurocentrism in South Africa." *Transformation in Higher Education*, vol. 1, no. 1, 2016, pp. 1-8, Oasis Publishing, https://doi.org10.4102/the.v1i1.9.

Loots, Lliane. "'You Don't Look Like a Dancer!': Gender and Disability Politics in the Arena of Dance as Performance and as a Tool for Learning in South Africa." *Agenda*, vol. 29, no. 2, 2015, pp. 122-132.

Ngũgĩ wa Thiong'o. *Decolonising the Mind: The Politics of Language in African Literature.* Heinemann, 1986.

Okri, Ben. "Ben Okri > Quotes." *Goodreads*, 1996, www.goodreads.com/author/quotes/31425.Ben_Okri.

Pickover, Michele. "Negotiations, Contestations, and Fabrications: The Politics of Archives in South Africa Ten Years after Democracy." *Innovation*, vol. 35, 2005, pp. 1-11.

Pink, Sarah. *Doing Sensory Ethnography.* Sage Publishers, 2015.

Taylor, Diana. *The Archive and the Repertoire: Performing Cultural Memory in the Americas.* Duke University Press, 2007.

Wall, Sarah. "An Autoethnography on Learning About Autoethnography." *International Journal of Qualitative Methods*, vol. 5, 2006, pp. 146-160.

Xaba, Wanalisa. "The Black Body as a Moving Ancestral Archive." *Culture Review*, 20 May 2021, www.culture-review.co.za/the-black-body-as-a-moving-ancestral-archive.

Yiakoumaki, Nayia. *Curating Archives, Archiving Curating*. 2009. University of London, PhD dissertation. *Core*, www.core.ac.uk/download/pdf/42387206.pdf.

Writing Body as Land & Land as Body in *Mine Mine Mine*
Uhuru Portia Phalafala

In this essay, in relation to my poetic epic, *Mine Mine Mine*, I consider the embodied political praxis of writing in the wake, which entails the practice of producing philosophy that is harnessed from creative work and lived experience. The essay is written in the wake of catastrophe that reaches through the personal into the structural, and which has upended and continues to end the world for Black people. The wake according to Christina Sharpe is a condition and ritual for communal grieving in the face of ongoing loss; the wake is the logics of plantation and extraction and separate development, brutalities that extend beyond the abolition of slavery, colonialism and Apartheid, into dehumanised afterlives (21); for Sharpe, the wake is an awakening, a critical consciousness (21). In *Mine Mine Mine*, I am concerned with several interlinked ecologies of the procedural, the emergent and the ongoing, a focus borne out of witnessing the struggle to articulate the co-constituted extractive violence on Black bodies and bodies of land, as encountered through my grandfather and my mother.

My project, at once creative and philosophical, implicates historical and ecological crises as being also a crisis of the imagination. I draw on the field of Black studies to learn about living at the end of the world, in the uninhabitable and unliveable. I reimagine an intersecting array of ecologies of crisis by thinking with and through forms of Black radical imagination, since the worlds of Black cultural and intellectual production offer aesthetics, gestures and grammars of survival, resilience, and resistance that imagine strategies of aliveness where we were never meant to survive. I locate *Mine Mine Mine* in this tradition of Black radical imagination, speaking with, from and within the ravages of colonial extraction. *Mine Mine Mine* is a personal narration of my family's experience of the migrant labour system brought on by the gold mining industry in Johannesburg, South Africa. Using geopoetics to map geopolitics, the epic poem connects a number of catastrophic environments, or ecologies of crisis: the effects of gold mining on the miners and the environment; the destruction of Black lives; threats to the institution of the Black family; and the radical reconfiguration of Black sociality. *Mine Mine Mine* also addresses racial capitalism, bringing together histories of the trans-Atlantic and trans-Indian slave trades, of plantation economies, and of mining and prison-industrial complexes.

This essay engages with creative practice, revisiting the methods and principal concepts of writing and performing[1] *Mine Mine Mine*. The epic addresses extraction through the mining industry, presenting it as a systemic removal of that which is commodified – that is, natural resources – from the *body of the earth*. In both the epic and this essay, I demonstrate how this systemic removal of natural resources happened through the simultaneous instrumentalising and mechanising of the Black body as commodity. The aim is to reveal how the extraction of natural resources from the body of the earth is contingent upon the extraction of the Black body from the *body of humanity*. This destructive, colonial approach is framed and powered by the world view of extractivism, a noxious New Worlding cosmology undergirded by the expansion of Western domination, commodification and capital accumulation – achieved through the systemic separation of humans from nature by inaugurating systems of relation governed by conquest, hierarchy and a binary ordering of the world.

I am invested in the Black feminist labour of imagining otherwise, of refusing the terms of a New Worlding cosmology through artistic, cultural and intellectual praxis. I think of *Mine Mine Mine* as existing in this long tradition of 'making' and 'doing' against the commodification of humans and earth construed as property, of working from 'an elsewhere', where we refuse the terms of wreckage, detritus and ruin by experimenting with the poetics of aliveness, possibility, communion, repair and futurity. Inspired by Ashon Crawley's notion of 'aesthetic vitality' (235), among others, this essay is concerned with the *how* of breathing, living, loving, fellowshipping, and insisting on beauty and love in and through and despite the unspeakable violence of coloniality and toxic atmospherics that persist in debasing the lives of Black people. Through and through, Black feminist cultural production provides coordinates to the *how* by lighting within me alternative neural pathways that map the way forward, which is also outwards, within and across. I begin with a personal narrative that is foundational to the conception of *Mine Mine Mine*, an instantiation of the wake: a ritual for communal grieving.

Biography as Biology: In the Beginning is Mother

In March 2019, my parents visited me in Cape Town, and as part of my planned itinerary of things to enjoy with them, we visited a neighbouring gallery to appreciate some art: David Goldblatt's exhibition, "On the Mines". I was excited – I had only seen the images online. But shortly after arriving, as I stood in the foyer reading about the exhibition, I noticed my mother standing alone in the exhibition space, looking distressed. I immediately went to check on her and will never forget the state in which I found her: as if she wanted the earth to open and swallow her, she was attempting to recede into her body, into a shell, or some kind of protective cave. In today's language we might call her 'triggered'. My mother was an army colonel who only retired in 2016. I grew up with a military mom who was heavy footed, wore army fatigues and exercised a particularly disciplined regime, not only in the household but in all that she did. This image of her frozen in the gallery did not reconcile with the image of her I'd held since childhood: imposing, statuesque and unbreakable.

I held her in my arms and asked, 'What is going on?' She glanced at the black and white photographs hanging on the wall, looking shaken and intimidated, and said, 'When I see these photos, I think I might see my father, or encounter among these miners my father at a young age'. I was deeply stirred. Here I was standing with my mother who was feeling the essence of the exhibition in her body, sensing it before even viewing the photographs with intent, seeing them in her being, and being unmoored. I realised that visiting the exhibition was not merely an exercise in formal viewing; the experience had become personal, historical, familial, and embodied. I quickly moved my mother out through the foyer, and we sat outside in the sculpture garden on the grass, leaning on each other.

She then recounted a somewhat disjointed story about growing up without her father, how he only came home every Christmas, for two to three weeks. She spoke from a place I had never witnessed, touching on the pain of having a *lekarapa* as a father, a man who worked away from home, only returning in December. I was moved by her narration;

she spoke personally about how she was adversely affected by growing up without her father, and recounted Hugh Masekela's song "Stimela", which chronicles the experience of miners – the hostels they are subjected to sleeping in; the terrible food they are fed, shovelled with a spade; the families they constantly yearn for. My grandfather: *lekarapa*. So many other Black men in a similar situation: *makarapa*. Our family. Many broken families.

I was captivated by the register of my mother's storytelling. I knew that I would have to write about it, to bear witness. I was completely taken aback by the ways in which the history of mining was lodged in her body. I am quite sure she has never visited the mines: mining is such a hidden and inaccessible industry if you are not a miner. Yet the knowledge of the mines was located within her body. She knew the violence of extraction caused by mining, the extraction of her father from her life at a young age, the extraction of gold from the land, and the extraction of life force from his body. All of these losses she felt. Her body bore witness to the familial and national histories of exploitation in the making of Southern African modernity. In a sense, her body was an archive that catalogued these losses: to borrow from Frantz Fanon, in the making of the wretched of the earth, the earth itself was made wretched. Her personal biography comprised the lived experience of extraction, loss, longing, and yearning by her mother and siblings; her body transcribed that biography, cataloguing it in her biology. The intricate interweaving of biology and biography was brought to the surface by her experience of a body of artwork that focused on extraction from the land, loss of land, longing, and a deep yearning of the dispossessed, the dislocated and the exiled. In witnessing my mother's distress, I could make poetic connections between the body of the mother and the body of the land, conceiving a *geopoetics* that ruptures any perceived discreetness and stability of these bodies, and finding contiguities between them. This produced the language of 'land as body' and 'body as land' in *Mine Mine Mine*, a poetic that attends to both land and body rendered wretched by colonial extraction.

It is from this position that *Mine Mine Mine* takes its approach, as it attempts to reconcile various scales of extraction: from the body to the land, from the private to the political, from the familial to the national, continental and diasporic. In my epic poem, the geopolitical histories that frame colonial extraction are shown to be felt, lived and embodied: there were, and are, humans involved. Geopoetics is thus a troubling of geopolitics – that instrumental abstraction concerned with international relations, diplomacy and economics, based on Gross Domestic Product, devoid of the intimate, complex intricacies of human and earth involvement. Geopoetics 'languages' the impact of geopolitics on human and earth bodies; it shifts the statistical, theoretical, worldmaking paradigm of geopolitics through storytelling, performativity, interiority, and embodiment; it demystifies the sterile, instrumental discourses of diplomacy and legalese using the languages of the body. Geopoetics listens into the emergence of language from bodies in states of emergency – my mother's body, and the bodies of land and earth – and seeks to write from that place.

In speaking about racial capitalism and colonial modernity, my mother's shuddering body at the gallery taught me to speak from the body, to speak of these concepts as embodied phenomena that are not abstract, theoretical or exclusively academic. They live lodged in our bodies and continue to be transmitted intergenerationally in a civilisation built and sustained by rendering some bodies wretched – open to exploitation and extraction: Black bodies, and bodies of land. Where in my mother's body is racial capitalism lodged? Where in my body can I sense this political economy? As the poems in *Mine Mine Mine* show, history contaminated my grandfather's lungs; it 'ruptures my mother's psychic spleen'; 'history is brewing in my uterus' (12). The epic takes stock of the 'archive of loss in our hearts' (24), attends to the abuse of Black women's bodies, braiding the raiding of our grandmothers with the fibroids in our wombs.

In *Mine Mine Mine*, the transmission of an intergenerational trauma of extraction, and the painful wisdom accrued, takes place through blood, sperm, wombs, saliva, sweat and genetics, and the epic shows how this is encrypted at a cellular and genetic level. We have known the land and created rituals of belonging to the land through these genetic structures of relation: through blood sacrifice and afterbirth, through the burial of our dead and the sweat of our toil. The land knows us through the body; we know the land through the body – our biographies and biologies are intricately linked to geography, and these are sounded in our names, our totems and praise songs. They map us to the land, its waters and the cosmos. In my recently published book, *Keorapetse Kgositsile & the Black*

Arts Movement: Poetics of Possibility, I call this dynamic a names-songs-place matrix, in which the language of the body is the language of the ecology, both bodies sounding the poetics of the geography and biology as whole, as one.[2] The land remembers us. The land remembered and witnessed my mother in that gallery, beckoning her at a cellular level. That is one of the vital and vitalising functions of art. Similarly, song is a passage to memory; in the same way that our praise songs transport us into and through time, Masekela's "Stimela" was her soundscape of recollecting, of re-storying her past to me, connecting her story to our collective past and its afterlives – for me, and potentially for other Black people: for us. It was imperative that I sound this sonicscape in *Mine Mine Mine,* even when the poetry is scripted. This is achieved in song, scream, sermon and the rhythms of the mines, of toil – through sibilance, alliteration and repetition, as illustrated in a later section.

Situated Poetics

In Southern African cosmology, also known as Bantu cosmology, all matter is pervaded by the force of 'Ntu', a life force or spirit called 'Moya', which connects all that exists, has existed and will exist – humans, trees, animals, mountains, rivers, air, the skies and earth, as well as other dimensions seen and unseen, known and unknowable. This cosmology is concerned with the principles of wholeness, interconnectivity, interdependency and interrelation within the vast internetworked ecological ecosystem. Within this cosmology, the human is considered to comprise three interlocking ontologies-in-becoming: the living, the living dead, and the yet-to-be-born – what Mogobe Ramose calls the 'onto-triadic structure of being' (236). Further, the self, each other and the world are considered incomplete, and in constant becoming.

In this cosmology, all are unfinished; it invites us to celebrate and preserve that incompleteness, to 'mitigate the delusions of grandeur that come with ambitions and claims of completeness', and to 'be open-minded and open-ended in our claims and articulation of identities, being and belonging' (Nyamnjoh 262). This requires adaptability and dynamism, but more importantly, it calls for 'conviviality', which 'encourages us to reach out, encounter and explore ways of enhancing or complementing ourselves with the added possibilities of potency brought our way by the incompleteness of others [...] to make us more efficacious in our relationships and sociality' (Nyamnjoh 262). The theory of incompleteness and conviviality underscores structures of being, relation, doing and becoming in the Southern African cosmologies in which I was raised and initiated. In this essay and in *Mine Mine Mine*, my approach is guided by these cosmologies of elsewhere, which reach beyond damaging New World, extractivist cosmologies.

I derive my creative and critical lexicon and method from working with the Setswana/Sesotho/Sepedi concept of *boagisani* to speak to 'conviviality'; the two are congruent. The South African poet Keorapetse Kgositsile brought to my attention the multiple aspects of *boagisani* as concept. In his disavowal of the nation state, state-sanctioned citizenry and its concomitant Afrophobia, he states: 'In Setswana there is no word for *citizen*. We speak of *moagi*, resident. *Go agisana/agisanya*, from *aga*, from which *moagi* derives, means "in the same breath", "building together" and/or "living together in harmony or peace"' (Kgositsile 144). *Moagi* is also the root word of *moagisani*, or neighbour, implying a shared and connected vicinity, geographical and otherwise, intimate proximity implied in breathing together, and, ideally, a mutual espousal of civility, generosity and congeniality.

I consider and deploy *moagi* (resident) as a verb – doing the processional and intimate work of being and becoming together, in the same breath, for purposes of efficacious kinship, reciprocity and responsibility for one another. *Moagi* in the register of geopoetics is not only contingent upon living in harmony and peace, interdependently and interconnectedly, beyond human kinship, but also on right relation with all living bodies – bodies of land, bodies of water, celestial bodies and bodies of animals and plant worlds. *Boagisani* thus conceives of being-in-relation as the communitarian work of continuously reaching out to, aspiring together, feeling with, and acting in unison with the collective. *Boagisani* offers 'aesthetic vitality' (Crawley 235); it produces vitalising openings, invitations, processions, open-endedness and possibilities for living otherwise. It is from this place that I unsettle White settler geographies and their temporalities through my poetics of the *unburied* which asserts and affirms continuities and relationalities between the subterranean, celestial and terrestrial worlds, opening potentialities for different forms of being, belonging and becoming.

As mentioned earlier, the root word of *moagi*, is *aga*, which means to build, and connotes building together, not only with humans but, as importantly, with the non-human world. Our ancestors built on the land, in a relationship with the natural world – with earth/soil, cow dung, thatch, wood from tree trunks, pigment from plants to paint the huts and communal spaces, and water, clay and stones from rivers; these all came together, historically, in an assemblage of building materials to construct homesteads for Southern Africans. Fire comes next – the hearth – a fire is lit to illuminate the activities and spirits of the living. This is a fire that is never extinguished; it is the source of life (food, nourishment), light, and warmth, but also symbolises historical continuity in narrating intergenerational wisdom through lore, song and storytelling (around the fire).

The homestead is built in accordance with celestial phe-nomena, which dictates the direction of the architecture; the entrance of the homestead (the family compound) faces the East, where the sun rises (Erasmus 5). In most indigenous architecture, huts were built in alignment with the stars (as were the pyramids). Structures were 'conventionally built on the northern slope of a hill, with the entrance to the house oriented so that you can always tell, every day when you wake up, what time of the year it is based on the position of the stars at sunrise viewed through the entry portal' (Nolan). The skull of a bull, with the horns attached – a bull slaughtered in a rite of passage in which the bull symbolises the bridge between the ancestral and the living worlds – is affixed at the main entrance of the family compound to ground the home through spiritual fortification. The horns also hold metaphysical currency: the horns of a cow are used to mark time, to store medicine, in agricultural practices, and as wind instruments. In terms of *boagisani*, these are all functions of living with and in relation to intersecting bodies and worlds that constitute our spiritual, physical, psychic and emotional well-being.

Co-creation and collaboration with, and receiving guidance from, natural and celestial elements, is antithetical to Western Enlightenment thinking – in terms of which nature is to be tamed, controlled, dominated and extracted. In Ntu cosmology, we return ourselves to nature for it to re/wild us, witness us, form and inform our ongoing incompleteness and becoming. We live through nature; we live because of nature, which is to say nature builds us; our formation and that of our bodies, the architecture of our beings, are the result of our being co-constituted by nature. The tenets of *boagisani* demand living with and by nature instead of fencing it out, because there is no 'out': we are nature. This philosophy has political currency. The names-songs-place matrix that undergirds this phenomenology – using our names in their fullness, as articulated in the praise song – relates us to animals through totems, and to land through the movements of the lineage. My mother, my grandfather, are *babina-tlou*, the elephants: memory keepers. I am of her; I am of him, I am of them. *Mine Mine Mine* harnesses the political currencies of these situated cosmologies through philo-praxis.

Unsettling Geographies

As we awaken in critical consciousness to the histories of extraction of lands and Black bodies by the global White capitalist patriarchy – the instrumentalisation of both bodies, of land and its people – and the routine large-scale loss of life, we grieve. We grieve in community, which in turn becomes our rite of passage into critical consciousness and moves us towards grieving the environmental catastrophe wrought by Man.[3] The starting point for this critical consciousness is somatic work, embodiment, and returning the body to its deep relations with the land. This is something that *Mine Mine Mine* seeks to emphasise, bringing together the life story of my grandfather with bodies of history, rapacious mining practices, environmental destruction, and the decimation of Black families and cultures. As Malcom Ferdinand argues:

> Very often melting glaciers, oil spills, and deforestation, as well as war and racial and gender discrimination, are lamented without calling into question the places, practices, and uses of our bodies that are anchored in these destructions. [This fracture] extends Fanon's incantation directed at making the body the starting point for an interrogation of the world and Giovanna Di Chiro's proposition to 'bring ecology home'

> by committing to *forming a body in the world* [*prendre corps au monde*]. Forming a body in the world consists in revealing the material and imaginary relations through which our bodies are the *trace-bearers* and the *tracers of a world* [...], and in making the body the starting point for an engagement with the world. (205; emphasis in original)

What does it mean to take the body as the starting point of commitment to self, to critical consciousness, and how does this resonate with Sharpe's 'wake' as awakening; what does it look like to take the body and its traces to the world? Sharpe proposes 'wake work', which addresses the paradox of living in an uninhabitable anti-Black world; 'wake work [is] a mode of inhabiting and rupturing this episteme with our known lived and un/imaginable lives. With this analytic we might *imagine otherwise* from what we know now in the wake of slavery' (18; emphasis in original).

In her exceptional book *In the Wake: On Blackness and Being*, Sharpe invites us to undertake 'wake work'. In response to her invitation, I bring my body – my corporeal body and its experiential inventory, as well as my poetic body of work. *Mine Mine Mine* elaborates and extends the Black feminist chorus in two ways: through rootwork, and by extending the three holds that Sharpe argues undergird race-making in the New World. These holds are the ship, the plantation and the prison. I explore their afterlives, and add to these holds the hold of the mining industry, which, it has always been clear to me, is the foundation of South African modernity and which marked for Black people the end of the world as they knew it in relational African cosmologies. Modernity, instead, is built upon and sustained by Black death, the decimation of the Black family, the destruction of Black sociality and the dismissal of Black spiritualities.

Rootwork

Rootwork is my method, concerned as it is with producing otherwise possibilities through mapping history in our bodies. Black people have always been called to be *radical* in our living and breathing, loving and relating, 'in the unceasing labour of producing new experiments in living' (Hartman and Moten), owing to the fundamental difficulty of living and staying alive under systems that seek to eradicate us. The etymological origin of radical (an otherwise overused word but extremely useful here) is 'root'; unburying the root causes is radical in the sense that it goes to the root. I work with the concept of 'rootwork', informed by a section in my epic poem, "Unburied", which captures the process of writing *Mine Mine Mine*. The processes underscored by this section surface in three forms, approaches and methods – namely, excavation, somatic work linked to lineage, and enchantment. I think of rootwork as working with the unseen worlds, in concert with other presences, to arrive at another point different from the given one, in the hope of fostering aliveness in the face of decimation and death.

I have used the concept of the 'unburied' in my book, influenced by a Black feminist practice and methodology that is concerned with overcoming the process of excavation as abstraction of extraction. Excavation is the first instantiation in the rootwork triad. In Black cosmologies as practised outside of colonialism's reach, all manner of digging up the land requires ritual, including but not limited to agricultural labour, mining and exhumation: they all centralise care. As a method for writing *Mine Mine Mine*, excavation is the unearthing and surfacing of my grandfather's life story; it is also excavating (in the sense of uncovering and foregrounding) my mother's and my own body to explore and bring to the surface that intergenerational story's impact. Excavation is divination; witnessing my mother's distress, for instance, prompted many questions; as a witness to embodied complexity, I was compelled to divine answers. In the case of my grandfather, his story moves beyond witness. He with-nessed my questions – for the observer is in turn observed. I felt the presence of his story; I sensed it in the ancestral realm through embodiment and the sensory perception of hearing and feeling.[4] I had to create the space for deep listening *into* that presence. I had to *agisana* – to build together – and co-create the epic with my grandfather. This required particular rituals to receive guidance: the act of excavating both earth body and human body requires presence and guidance from the earth and from humans, on where, when and how to dig and/or unearth that which we seek to integrate in our lives. In writing the epic, I had to adhere to a certain diet to clear my body for with-nessing: awake at 3am for deep listening and co-creating at the altar; and engage in ritual that petitions and supplicates the transferral of what I hear into the 'here', onto paper. In *Mine Mine Mine*, I articulate this in the offering, "Sacraments of Unburying" (55):

Sacraments of Unburying

1. Light a fire (candles)
2. Offer sacrifice (blood, salt)
3. Sing their names (invocation)
4. Burn sage (smoke, incense)
5. Pour libation (water, mqombothi)
6. Make offerings (snuff, sweets)
7. Speak to bones (appease, listen)
8. Unearth bones (Makhosi!)
9. Sing their names (supplicate)
10. Rebury the bones (sing 'Thina Sizwe')

In this poem, the re-claiming of the bones of those who died unacknowledged in the mining industry's hold of the earth, unceremoniously unburied, is a gesture of recovery that centralises the 'wretched of the earth' as well as the 'wretched earth'. Both earth and the Black body are rendered wretched by the same forces, and both warrant a gesture of recovery, of repair. The sacraments are offered to unearth their bones so they may be reburied following the proper burial rites, for their spirits to find peace. These sacraments underscore a continuous expression of relation with the living world through ritual and ceremony; they bring to the fore the crucial importance of aligning ourselves with the elements: fire, water, earth and wind. The ancestral realm is located within these elements, larger and older than us. In excavating bones, we open a temporality beyond one lifetime, and a geography beyond the presence of the currently known world. This requires guidance, the rallying of the past to intervene in the future: the sacraments petition that presence; they are supplication, divination. We return ourselves and sublimate our actions to these wiser planetary phenomena. Rootwork as excavation is premised on understanding the bodies of earth and humans and cosmos as internetworked and agential, thus prohibiting any form of extraction without offerings or ritual. The worlds of the subterranean and the planetary are held in regard, awe and reverence, as are any other worlds – existing as unknown and unknowable, yet in a relationship of with-nessing, constitutive of our total beings and experiences in and of the lives we inhabit and by which we are inhabited.

A Black feminist practice attends to these deep layers of the world beyond the logics of Man (Wynter): the seen and unseen worlds, living and non-living, human and non-human. I know and live these worlds whose temporality, history and future are outside of the machinations of coloniality. In attending to these worlds, I make meaning of our worlds beyond the boundaries of reason and the rational as dictated by Man. Those boundaries are border-keeping roles that have kept Black women on the outside, in the margins and at the bottom. They have also kept out the realm of spirit as real and lived, where Black female power lies and which comprises the source of Black women's assertion of life as creative force – as communal and sustained by care in the face of a loveless world. The power of that realm teaches us that we are abundant and accompanied on this journey, never alone and never entirely inscribed by the capitalist culture of scarcity; that we are entrusted with and guided by intergenerational forces of being and becoming that live through us and by us; that our work is their work; that we are co-creating with them always, for the future us, all entangled in the past and yet-to-come. An honouring of the realm of spirit has the capacity to re-enchant our lives here, now, in this loveless culture of death and extraction – it opens to us other possibilities. It is a love politic, guiding us to clearings and refuge, to rest, renewal, alignment, and relational, living purpose. It underlines a more sustaining and mutually connective life force than the historical vectors of hierarchy, oppression and destruction, offering an imagined realm to which we need to become awake, to fashion liveable lives.

"Unburied" produces a second method in the rootwork triad – namely, somatic work linked to lineage. This is anchored in interiority, in the power centre of the root in our bodies. The body becomes paramount for various reasons: the Black body enters modernity as commodity, as flesh, as an extractible unit of labour. Returning to the body is thus an enlivening praxis – it transforms that which has been rendered expediently illegible, unintelligible and disposable, using a different value system of meaning-making, of creating possibility. It enchants the body by re-sacralising it, being present with the body, listening to its breath through a poetics of *boagisani* – a co-constitutive being and becoming between the mind, body and spirit, which historically have all been undermined by Enlightenment thought. To *agisana* with the body is to resituate the head, logic and reason in contiguity with the wisdoms and knowledges of the body, and thereby engage in the art of being alive. It is this art of being alive that informs our practices of refusal as Black people, as Black women – practices that bring to the surface 'negation as a generative and creative source of disorderly power' (Campt 83). Here, working from the body and its lineages, we are emboldened 'to refuse that which has been refused to us', to reject and disregard colonial legibility and intelligibility (Hartman and Moten; Campt 83). We, the disregarded Black lives, necessarily occupy ungovernable cartographies and multiple temporalities; we are purposefully undisciplined, audacious, and speak in tongues. And this can take place from within our interiority and desires – our languages that are vital and vitalising in unmaking settler colonial worlds and their logics.

If living from a place of interiority, feeling and emotion has been used against us to mark us as instinctual, irrational and devoid of intellectual lives, then we must be suspicious of colonial languages that seek to distance themselves from interiority, feeling and embodiment. Our languages are characterised by poetics as mode of signification, rather than representation – by geopoetics that return the body to the larger living and continuously materialising body of earth. Those languages have complex emotional vocabularies that signal deep appreciation and understanding of our emotional life-worlds, which are always connected to our spiritual lives as the central organising structures of our being, knowing and relating. Our interior life-worlds have the capacity and potential, through re-sacralising the disenchanted worlds of this civilisation, to unmake White settler worlds and their logics of being and relating. We do this through rootwork of the first kind, in its expansion into the power centre of the root in our bodies, to commune with our lineages, our ancestors, our onto-triadic beings. The sonicscape of *Mine Mine Mine* enshrines and embodies memory encrypted in my DNA: my grandfather's story is also my grandmother's and mother's story; their collective genetics live in me. In telling their trauma, their wisdom also surfaces, orally and performatively, in different languages and through different modalities. In writing the epic and subsequently performing it to audiences, I harnessed oralities/auralities from that archive, producing poetics that operate in the emotional and embodied life-worlds of my people, of Southern Africa. In *Mine Mine Mine*, I use songs such as "Abelungu ngoddam, Mississippi Goddam!" (18) and Miriam Makeba's "Khawuleza" (25) to amplify collective love and resistance; the scream gives place to terror; my body in performance – posture, movement, intonation, voicing my grandfather – metabolises racial capitalism in my body; the whistles I deploy on stage invoke trains as in Masekela's song "Coal Train", the police, ceremonial sounds, frequencies and vibrations; the dance summons the collective dance, satirically, in response to President Cyril Ramaphosa's parliamentary invocation of Masekela's "Thuma Mina" (37); rhythms, such as the 'h' alliteration in the sixth movement (43-44) bookend the epic with breathlessness; the sermon, *'lefa la ntate'* (38) invites divination and revelation; and indigenous languages such as *'ke motswetši ke imile ke a hloboga'* (11) harness the sibilance and internal rhythms of our languages. They all encapsulate sound knowledges that are mnemonic devices and coordinates to other forms of being, relating and embodying the individual and communal self that are otherwise to those of the dominator culture.

The third method in the rootwork triad is enchantment. In Black spiritual practices, rootwork is an ancestral form of alchemy that includes herbalism, conjuring, medium-ship and divination. Rootwork was central to the writing of *Mine Mine Mine*, a book that emphasises and brings together dreamscapes, altar work and ancestral practices as ritual portals to other worlds. Enchantment re-sacralises a world whose dynamic agency was flattened by colonial expansion, privatisation, renaming and extraction. As I have said, New World cosmology marked the end of the world for Black and ecological bodies; in comparison, enchantment returns sacredness to these wretched bodies, showing them to be honoured and revered in another cosmology. Enchantment reinvests us and the environs with awe, wonder and curiosity, expanding our sensorial experiences of ourselves to intuit the inner landscape, extending into the deep and infinite vastness of who and where we are. In writing the epic, I used certain herbs at the altar, and I also burn these during the performance of the epic. The field of smell opens areas of feeling, acts as a portal to memory, and invites collective ancestral presence.

In *Nehanda*, Zimbabwean writer Yvonne Vera writes: 'birds fly out of the trees bearing signs that send new hope to the ground. It is always in a state of creation, and of being born: the legend-creating wind gives new tongues with which to praise it, and new languages with which to cross the boundaries of time' (93). The colonial modernity in which we live would have us believe that life is not in a constant state of creation and necessary incompleteness, that we cannot be co-creators of that life, and that we do not have agency. Rootwork hacks and hexes that framework, rupturing linear progressive time to open up a field of life, language, lineage, land and love in fluid flux. It makes possible an experience of the living world at large, of the continuous motion of us as world-in-constant-becoming; it invites us to pay due attention to ourselves as stitched and enfolded in its mutual and co-constitutive becoming. The following excerpt from the "Unburied" section of the epic illustrates this:

> We gravitate toward soil
> sink our fingers deep
> excavate bone and living flesh
> listen to the ground
> for our fathers, brothers
> husbands and sons
> in the heart of dust
> damp, and darkness
> a directive for Black
> pregnant women to eat soil
> and keep sons safely buried
> in their wombs
> away from the tombs of the mines
> Maternal instinct to protect
> mutilation of Black labor
> (*Mine Mine Mine* 57)

In the above excerpt, the relations between the soil as a place of death and birth – life and the loss thereof – and the land and extraction is critical, as is the suturing of the 'fathers, brothers / husbands and sons' to the womb, and of the female body to the body of land, and of the soil/land to the not-yet-born. In *Mine Mine Mine*, as demonstrated above, I am engaged in the poetics and politics of the 'trans*' (Sharpe 30), which cross and traverse boundaries of time and place, as well as the binary orderings of colonial cosmologies: I *trans*gress colonial frames of legitimacy, intelligibility and legibility, and modernity's requirement of *trans*parency – the subterranean, celestial and terrestrial worlds are brought into relation and continuity with human bodies; I assert and affirm a *trans*species sense of being and belonging with the animal and plant kingdoms, who are our *baagisani* and our teachers, as expressed in our totems; I *trans*form the worlds of our discontent and social deaths through enchantment; I *trans*cribe and ascribe ourselves through 'writing as ritual', writing that speaks with, by and from these interpenetrative relations. I deploy ritual to be with, to with-ness, to facilitate repair through return into the folds and principles of *boagisani*.

Incompleteness at the End of the World

It becomes imperative to operate from another place, one with conceptions and value systems concerning land, humans, relations and nature that function outside the damaging logics of property, privatisation and capital accumulation. In "Plotting the Black Commons", J. T. Roane argues that 'Black communities renegotiate the terrain of radical exploitation and totalizing social control' in favour of 'a vision of social-cosmological-ecological integrity outside of mastery and dominion' (242, 261). This essay, embodying my creative and critical energies, speaks from that desired place, rejecting geopolitics that occlude human lives, aspirations and suffering. This essay rejects notions of nation state and citizenship that evacuate some humans and the earth from its regimes of validity, and that limit belonging and rights only to human beings, violating the agency of the non-human. The 'social-cosmological-ecological integrity' on which my work is based has long informed the meaning of our lives-in-relation, as Black people. My scholarship and creative process, then, work with the wake to make place for generative re-turn.

I have drawn from the theories of incompleteness and conviviality offered by Francis Nyamnjoh to scaffold my approaches to language in *Mine Mine Mine*. The language of the epic I have written is a geopoetics of the body and its geography – of biography and biology at the intersections of racial capitalism and colonial modernity. It seeks to disarrange destructive colonial derangements through an unsettling emphasis on the body and interiority, via Black feminist poetics and performativity. This tactic deliberately disorders the dominant New World cosmology that has commodified humans and earth, deified Western reason and rationality as synonymous with White male bodies, and instituted extraction as a fundamental system of dehumanised economic relation, in the process, marking the end of the world for bodies inscribed as extractable and dispensable. For Black people across geographies and histories, the very fact of living otherwise has been a creative force, as the world ended over and over, only to begin again in the morning.[5] Throughout the troubled centuries, the unburying of ancestral memory, enchantment, divination, dreamwork, altar work, and other intergenerational practices tied to rootwork, have made it incumbent upon us to embrace such incompleteness as productive, rather than seeing it as destructive – as New World thinking would have it. In a key sense, then, as embodied in *Mine Mine Mine*, *boagisani* has kept us alive, producing fields of possibility and hope, beauty, community, love, kinship and the vitalising practices and politics of living against this loveless world.[6]

Endnotes

1 Johannesburg launch of *Mine Mine Mine* by Uhuru Phalafala @ The Forge, www.youtube.com/watch?v=80f7ZvUk3UQ&t=55s.

2 What I 'do' in *Mine Mine Mine*, I 'theorise' in my recent book *Keorapetse Kgositsile & the Black Arts Movement: Poetics of Possibility*, which elaborates on the interconnectivity and languages of intersecting bodies in Southern African cosmologies.

3 For Sylvia Wynter, the notion of 'Man' has developed since the Enlightenment, and is everywhere and yet is exclusive. It posits a narrow Western middle- and upper-class ideal, fundamentally racist, violent and constitutive of global exploitation.

4 To listen in my language, *go utlwa*, connotes both hearing and feeling. Elsewhere I call this feel-listening.

5 In the words of Nayyirah Waheed, 'i don't pay attention to the world ending. it has ended for me many times and began again in the morning' (45).

6 A nod to the Palestinian writer Susan Abulhawa, whose novel, *Against the Loveless World* (2019), deeply impacted me. She references James Baldwin's *The Fire Next Time* (1963) in that title.

Bibliography

Campt, Tina. "Black Visuality and the Practice of Refusal." *Women & Performance: A Journal of Feminist Theory*, vol. 29, no. 1, 2019, pp. 79-87.

Crawley, Ashon T. *Blackpentecostal Breath: The Aesthetics of Possibility*. Fordham University Press, 2016.

Erasmus, J. "South African Bantu Kraal." *Bantu*, vol. 22, no. 2, 1975, pp. 1-32.

Fanon, Frantz. *The Wretched of the Earth*. Penguin, 1967.

Ferdinand, Malcom. *Decolonial Ecology: Thinking from the Caribbean World*. Polity, 2022.

Goldblatt, David. *On the Mines: David Goldblatt*, 13 Feb. 2019 -11 Aug. 2019, Norval Foundation, Cape Town.

Hartman, Saidiya and Fred Moten. "To Refuse That Which Has Been Refused to You." *Chimurenga*, 2018, chimurengachronic.co.za/to-refuse-that-which-has-been-refused-to-you-2/. Accessed 20 December 2023.

Kgositsile, Keorapetse. "Race: What Time Is It?" *Democracy X (Imagined South Africa)*, edited by Andries Oliphant, Peter Delius, and Lalou Melzer, Brill, 2004.

Nolan, Dennis Oswald. "Astrologer Monisha Holmes and Artist Nolan Oswald Dennis on the Zodiac and Black Liberation." *Art in America*, 1 January 2020, www.artnews.com/art-in-america/interviews/nolan-oswald-dennis-monisha-holmes-black-liberation-zodiac-1202673932/.

Nyamnjoh, Francis B. "Incompleteness: Frontier Africa and the Currency of Conviviality." *Journal of Asian and African Studies*, vol. 52, no. 3, 2017, pp. 253-270.

Phalafala, Uhuru Portia. "Erotics of Revolution: Mongane Serote and the Black Cosmological Archive." *Literature and the Work of Universality*, edited by Alice Duhan, Stefan Helgesson, Christina Kullberg and Paul Tenngart, De Gruyter, 2024.

---. *Keorapetse Kgositsile & the Black Arts Movement: Poetics of Possibility*. James Currey, 2024.

---. *Mine Mine Mine*. University of Nebraska Press, 2023.

Ramose, Mogobe B. "The Philosophy of Ubuntu and Ubuntu as a Philosophy." *Philosophy from Africa: A Text with Readings*, edited by P. H. Coetzee and A. P. J. Roux, International Thomson Publishing, 1998, pp. 230-238.

Roane, J. T. "Plotting the Black Commons." *Souls: A Critical Journal of Black Politics, Culture, and Society*, vol. 20, no.3, 2018, pp. 239-266.

Sharpe, Christina. *In the Wake: On Blackness and Being*. Duke University Press, 2016.

Vera, Yvonne. *Nehanda*. TSAR, 1994.

Waheed, Nayyirah. *Salt*. Nayyirah Waheed, 2013.

Wynter, Sylvia. "Unsettling the Coloniality of Being/Power/Truth/Freedom: Towards the Human, After Man, Its Overrepresentation – An Argument." *CR: The New Centennial Review*, vol. 3, no. 3, 2003, pp. 257-337.

'What's Up?': Using WhatsApp Group Chat to Teach Undergraduate Creative Writing Workshops during Covid 19

Meg Vandermerwe

The Covid 19 pandemic and subsequent migration to remote teaching created new challenges for me as professor of Creative Writing at the University of the Western Cape (UWC). How was I going to teach Creative Writing remotely when our workshops relied on camaraderie, the energy of the face-to-face and spontaneous group feedback? The situation was made more complex by serious socio-economic constraints. The majority of my students did not have access to laptops at home, nor could they afford Wi-Fi or large amounts of data. This made Zoom or similar face-to-face online sessions impossible. Some also lacked a private, quiet space to engage, as they lived in crowded homes.

This essay discusses how I used WhatsApp Group Chat smartphone technology to try to overcome these challenges in teaching my English 331 Creative Writing cohorts between 2020 and 2021. It explores some of the difficulties I faced, including how I was forced to adapt my curriculum and teaching style. It also discusses some of the unexpected benefits, including the potential opportunities to make Creative Writing teaching more accessible.

In recent years, a number of scholars have discussed the role that WhatsApp might have as an effective pedagogical tool. Its role in Mobile-Assisted Language Learning (MALL) has been well documented by the likes of Sabri Ahmed, a scholar whose work has demonstrated the benefits of MALL for new vocabulary acquisition, as well as supporting a boost in conversational confidence among learners of English as a foreign language (EFL) (62). Similarly, Noor Diana Suhaimi, Maslawati Mohamad and Hamidah Yamat, in their article "The Effects of WhatsApp in Teaching

Narrative Writing: A Case Study" have documented and measured the impact of using technology (versus pencil and paper) on Malaysian primary school students' acquisition of English vocabulary. They noted that 75 per cent of the Grade 6 learners improved by one mark or more (594-595).

Less examined, however, is how such technology might facilitate Creative Writing teaching. Perhaps, this is because of the emphasis traditionally placed upon in-person writing groups and workshops in this area. Creative Writing can arguably be lonely and isolating – and face-to-face human contact with other writers is often crucial to both the writing and the learning. As an academic who has specialised in Creative Writing for more than sixteen years, I have long been a disciple of the face-to-face model. I have 'stuck to my teaching guns' about this even as remote options have grown increasingly prevalent and popular; examples include the online writing schools of Penguin Random House, and Faber & Faber that aim at attracting aspiring authors working outside the academic degree domain.

The arrival of the Covid 19 pandemic in 2020, with associated lockdowns and the subsequent global switch from in-person campus life to remote learning, forced me, radically and quickly, to re-think my previous teaching approach. It seemed I was faced with limited options. Most significant were the accessibility challenges faced by my students – challenges that I felt made relying on video conferencing technology, like Zoom, Skype or even FaceTime, unrealistic. Historically, UWC attracts students from previously disadvantaged socio-economic backgrounds; although our student profile has shifted since I first took up my post fourteen years ago, most students in the Arts Faculty qualify for a NASPA grant, which means that their total household income is less than R350 000 per annum or R29 167 per month. Many of my writing students do not own laptops, have no Wi-Fi access at home and lack a private space for study. These factors were exacerbated during the pandemic, when many South Africans lost their jobs, placing even greater financial strain on already cash-strapped homes; families were also forced to self-isolate together.

I urgently needed to find an inclusive, flexible, accessible and relatively *affordable* means of workshopping with my students, one that ideally drew on resources and technologies they already owned. A quick survey revealed that more than 95 per cent of students already used WhatsApp Group Chat and possessed smartphones. The one or two who did not could at least borrow a smartphone for their weekly workshop. WhatsApp via instant messaging and voice notes (versus WhatsApp video call) also uses relatively little data, making it a far more affordable option than video-link technology. Furthermore, there was capacity for a reasonable group size, and no limit to the duration of a typed chat (unlike Zoom for instance, where a meeting beyond 30 minutes must be paid for). WhatsApp also allowed students not to worry about securing absolute privacy or silence in their environments. Students could find a quiet corner and, if needed, use headphones. So, WhatsApp Group Chat using typed messages and voice notes seemed the ideal solution to the particular challenges faced by my cohort of undergraduate writing students at UWC between 2020 and 2021.

But that begs the question: why workshop at all during such a global crisis? Why not simply switch to working one on one with my students, via email for instance (if such a time-consuming method were logistically feasible given my overall teaching and supervision commitments)? Because writing needs company, debate and pushback, as much as solitary introspection. Ernest Hemingway put things more bluntly in an interview with the *Paris Review*: 'The most essential gift for a good writer is a built-in, shock-proof, shit detector. This is the writer's radar and all great writers have it' (23). However, as many writers know, great or otherwise, when one has been writing for a long time in isolation, one's antennae can attenuate and become unreliable – either too critical or not perceptive enough. Paul Magrs, writer and lecturer in Creative Writing at the University of East Anglia, explains:

> You can learn an awful lot about writing from other people's work. I don't just mean published poems and novels, though of course you ought to be reading those voraciously as well. […] Writers spend a long time alone, working on their own texts. Every writer, I think, needs at some point to belong to a supportive group. You need to have a whole set of people reading your drafts and giving good, constructive feedback. You need it to improve the work, but also as a morale boost, in

> the sense that you need your work to be out there, being read and being inside other people's minds. (315-316)

So, being able to share drafts with a group of fellow writers, monthly or weekly, can be invaluable, not only helping to weed out the muck, but also for vital support and inspiration. This is crucial in university undergraduate course contexts where students, experiencing a taught Creative Writing module for the first time in their academic careers, rely heavily on the guiding hand of a more experienced practitioner. Taught workshops need to be demanding but also thoughtfully structured; students must be led through a series of carefully linked activities, resources and exercises with a view, by the end of the semester, to enabling them to unlock not only their creative potential, curiosity and intuition, but also to produce writing that can be given a grade. After all, they are doing the course as part of an academic degree and they, and I, are thus beholden to the assessment and quantifying gods.

Although I was not aware of this in 2020, other African Creative Writing groups were making use of cellphone chat technology for similar accessibility and inclusivity reasons. It was while researching context for this essay that I came across one such group in Nigeria, the Naija Writers United collective. Created in 2018, the collective's Facebook page describes itself thus:

> Naija Writers United is an exciting and interactive classroom for aspiring writers who are passionate about writing fiction and also wish to belong to an exclusive group of would-be published authors. Naija Writers United was created to inspire a revolution in the Nigerian Entertainment industry by raising a community of writing talents across Nigeria and beyond.

The Facebook page also explains its use of the Telegram social messaging technology:

> Social messaging apps like Telegram are helping in facilitating innovative and interactive ways of learning via group chat, live and interactive sessions, tutorial links, and sharing of

educational materials among group members.

Significantly, the collective also explains that it switched from using WhatsApp to Telegram because its membership exceeded the limit of 256 participants in a single WhatsApp group, showing just how popular the group is. Telegram Messenger has a membership capacity of 200 000.

***

I first communicated with my 2020 English 331 Creative Writing cohort, via email, in August 2020. In this, I set out the course objectives and also gave them the first creative assignment (one that spoke to the main task of the term):

> August 8th 2020
> Dear Eng 331 students
>
> I hope you are keeping safe during these difficult times. In two weeks, we are set to begin our seven-week, 331 prose component together. Attached are the course objectives and the first task, which I would like you please to prepare *before* our first online session on the 21st. I'm sending this to you a bit early so as to give you extra time to make a plan re your interviews.
>
> In the meantime, I'll shortly be sending through a link so that we can establish our WhatsApp Group Chat group.
>
> Take care
> Meg

The following course outline was attached to the email:

ENG 331 Course Outline

Here are the *main outcomes and learning objectives.*
At the end of the prose module you should be able to:

a) write your own prose fiction, applying creative tools such as free-writing to your process;
b) edit your writing in an informed way, using Grace Paley's 'lies' for guidance;
c) reflect on your prose in relation to different writing techniques;
d) locate your prose in relation to historical/literary conventions including South Africa's multi-lingual and multi-cultural context; and
e) read with a new, critical sensibility.

Assessment Criteria

The prose course is assessed as follows:

a) Your creative writing portfolio. This must include your final 'Roots story' plus drafts, and may also include an additional prose piece of your own creation. (50%)
b) A short self-reflective essay. This should be a scholarly and informed account. It should reflect on your writing process whilst doing the Roots task and seek to place your work in its literary and historical context. (50%)

Roots Task 1: Writing in an Authentic Voice

One of the most important aspects of your craft as a writer is your ability to evoke a unique and authentic voice. It is also essential for tapping into your unique story roots (a concept we will discuss more in class). The following is an exercise that will help you. It was taught to me by one of my great mentors (the American short story writer Grace Paley).

a) Please interview the oldest person you know within your own family and get them to tell you the oldest story that they know. So, for example, it could be your grandmother or mother telling you about her grandmother's wedding. It is preferable if the person is from your own familial circle, as this will help you to connect with your unique story roots.

b) VERY IMPORTANT. If their mother tongue is not English then you MUST interview them in that language instead of English.

c) When conducting the interview, you can take as many notes as you like, but the key thing is to listen very carefully.

d) Once the interview is over (of course in the circumstances it is best to do this telephonically or via Skype too), you must then go somewhere where you will not be disturbed.

e) PUT THE NOTES AWAY (so don't refer to them again).

f) Using a pen and paper (no laptops) do a free write for 6-7 mins (use a clock) where you retell the story you have been told in THE PERSON'S VOICE who told it to you, i.e. in first person. Your aim is to capture their voice as truthfully and as accurately as possible. IF THE INTERVIEW WAS NOT IN ENGLISH PLEASE WRITE THE FREE WRITE FIRST IN THE OTHER LANGUAGE and then translate it word for word (i.e. no editing) into English.

g) BRING THIS FREE WRITE TO OUR FIRST VIRTUAL WORKSHOP.

For those of you who are unfamiliar with free writes here are the rules:

The pen must not stop moving for the allotted time. No editing. No crossing out. No changing. Whatever the little voice is saying in your mind, just scribe it down, without judgement.

Yes, it will be messy and imperfect, it is a free write. We will talk more about free writing. It is another amazing tool that can be very beneficial to the author.

If you have any questions re this exercise, please feel free to email me.

***

As the email correspondence shows, from the outset, I was forced to adapt my approach. Usually, I introduce the main creative task of the term in our first face-to-face class. Students are provided with copies of the handouts explaining the 'Roots story' and are given the time and space to ask any questions then and there. Now, with teaching shifting to a remote outlet, I had to send out the task via email two weeks in advance, in order to give students extra time to think about how best to access their chosen interviewee. I also had to leave sufficient time for questions to be emailed and my replies to be made. In short, what took fifteen minutes in the face-to-face workshop was now elongated and had to be absorbed into a far longer pre-course timeline. In addition, numerous emails with questions and concerns from the sixteen students had to be answered and salient information shared with the whole group. This placed more pressure on me as coordinator.

The need to incorporate extra time to achieve tasks remotely became even more apparent at the start of the first WhatsApp workshop, when I began with my usual 'name-story' ice-breaker exercise. An atmosphere of trust and intimacy is essential when running any Creative Writing workshop. If the participants don't feel safe and comfortable with each other, they are far less likely to share their writing, or take creative risks. Each time I encounter a new group of writers, I therefore ask them to perform a short exercise: we go around the room, each of us taking a minute or two to introduce our first name and explain its significance/meaning/origins (if any). This short ice-breaker gives everyone a chance to introduce themselves, warm up their story-telling and reveal a bit more (than just their name) about themselves.

The first time I ran my ENG 331 module via WhatsApp in 2020 I had not considered the extra time it would take for each of the sixteen writing students to share their name stories as voice notes in real time. In a face-to-face workshop, this starter activity takes ten to fifteen minutes. But now, working remotely, each student had first to record their name story then send it to the group. This took ages, with everyone twiddling their proverbial thumbs as they waited for the next student's story to be recorded and shared. The recorded name story then had to be listened to.

So, a two-minute recording chewed up four minutes of workshop teaching time. This seriously impacted momentum and, while a greater sense of intimacy was fostered by the stories, the immediate impact upon student engagement in that first session was terrible. All in all, it was an anticlimactic first session: we never got beyond what was supposed to be the starter activity!

Fortunately for everyone, I quickly learnt from my mistake and asked students to pre-record their work in progress as voice notes so that they could share them instantly when it was their turn. This certainly helped, but overall, a slower momentum while teaching via WhatsApp Group Chat seemed inescapable. Consider all the elements involved: I still needed to give voice-note feedback to students during the workshops and set tasks; and students needed to type and read feedback. All of this took *more time*. Already constrained by having to teach the module in the usual seven weeks (no additional teaching time was incorporated into the university schedule even though we had gone remote), this had an inevitable impact on the creative process and how much could reasonably be achieved.

Although workshops and activities were proceeding at a slower, perhaps gentler, pace, it seemed students' drafts and skills developed more slowly too. This came as a surprise. After all, I was using the same essential activities and tools, and using the same step-by-step scaffolding. So why were students not able to evolve at the usual pace? In addition, I was putting even greater effort into individual and group feedback than usual. Why wasn't the students' writing reflecting this? I cannot 'diagnose' definitively, but speculate that a number of factors played a role.

Distractions in students' home environments probably affected concentration during the workshops themselves, and whereas students could usually rely on a range of senses to stay engaged in face-to-face class meetings, they now had to resort mainly to listening skills, as many essential aspects of the workshopping were done via voice note. The other, more indefinable missing element might have been the invisible and contagious 'buzz' that enters a space when like-minded creatives meet in person, to share, discuss and confide. This collaborative 'vibe' cannot be measured, but anyone who has attended a sympathetic literary salon, jam session or studied at an art school knows what I'm talking about. Without it, perhaps students in the context of the WhatsApp Group Chat were not able to connect to the workshop experience as potently (as least not initially).

Whatever the cause, by the time I taught this course a second time in 2021, I knew to modify the objectives in advance so that students were no longer expected to develop their Roots monologues into fiction pieces, but were instead asked to focus solely on producing their Roots monologues.

There were other challenges. Some students struggled to engage fully with, and even commit to, our WhatsApp Group Chat workshops at the beginning of the course. At the start of every session, I asked each student to raise a virtual hand via an emoji to signal their presence in the class. Overall, attendance was excellent. However, there were certainly instances when I felt that students who had raised their hands to signal attendance were not paying attention for the full duration of the class. Sometimes, when I called on a student to share, or offer feedback, my request was met with silence. The student in question seemed to have exited the virtual room. And why not? With no physical eyes on a student and no way of monitoring who was present (unlike Zoom, for instance, where a lecturer could at least see who was logged into the virtual classroom), the temptation for distraction and to do other things must have been immense.

To overcome this, I became more vigilant about spontaneously directing my attention to specific individuals for feedback, or asking them to share their mini-writing exercises. I also shared more images (as sparks for a free write, for instance), and when students offered to share archive material as part of their Roots writing (family photographs of great-grandparents, for instance, or unearthed birth certificates), this too was shared as a visual via Group Chat. Finally, I made a concerted effort to make my voice notes as concise as possible, so as not to break the momentum.

In spite of these challenges, in my three years of teaching ENG 331 remotely, I found a number of pleasing and even unexpectedly positive outcomes when using WhatsApp to run my workshops. One of the most surprising was that the creative writing produced was generally of a very high standard, comparable to writing produced by in-person workshopping. True, less was generated, and perhaps the writing did not develop as quickly, but the quality of the monologues produced by the English 331 students between 2020 and 2022 was as excellent as anything produced by their peers in prior years, and subsequently, when teaching was once again face-to-face.

Another unpredicted outcome was that by the end of the course, students demonstrated high levels of passion and commitment. So, uptake and engagement took longer in some cases, but the very fact of forced remoteness and the resultant hunger of students for intimate creative contact appeared to have inspired most to push through the veil of disconnect, and ultimately to value the digital workshop experience as a proxy form of human and creative connection. This was evident in the quality of writing they submitted for assessment, but also in their self-reflexive pieces and course evaluations, which tended to be extremely positive.

And there were other benefits. It was useful to have all discussions and drafts captured in one place (the Group Chat platform), both for me as the teacher when it came to assessment, and for students when it came to looking back and gauging their progress and the impact of the course. In a strange way, the Group Chat site became a kind of collective, electronic writing journal for the groups in question – a place for recording their ideas, reflections and spontaneous feedback and suggestions, a resource for future self-reflexivity.

With students unable to meet face-to-face, I was often worried about how the group dynamic would work or what I might need to do to ensure a sense of connection between the writers. I've already mentioned initial attendance and focus challenges and how I overcame them. However, what I also found was that, with time, an alternative, deeply ingrained, almost atavistic sense kicked in – namely, the art of listening carefully and mindfully. The American Creative Writing teacher and short story author Grace Paley often spoke of the essential role that 'good listening' plays in the development of the writer: 'You have to hear how people really talk, and how they act. You have to pay attention. Sometimes it's language and sometimes it's not language. Sometimes it's movement' (37).

Even though we were not physically gathered in one place, I found that students became extremely good at listening with care and attentiveness, not only to the 'voice' that was being brought to the fore by their peers' slowly progressing monologues (remembering that an accurate depiction of voice was an important desired outcome of the Roots task), but also to deeper emotional and literary forces at work behind the shared work – silence, pain, erased history. The depth of feedback and guidance given to their peers' work in progress became more astute and subtle as a consequence. Perhaps being obliged to focus on their listening skills owing to our reliance on the voice-note medium, especially at key moments such as the sharing of monologue drafts, or name stories, prompted an attentive attuning by members of a generation that has arguably become used to not listening mindfully to one another, but rather habitually pays *in*attention, with rapid sensory 'swiping' from one experience to the next.

Finally, one of the most obvious benefits of conducting my workshops via the medium of WhatsApp Group Chat was that no student had to be excluded from taking the course owing to a lack of financial or technological means. Every student and writer deserves the opportunity to explore and develop their own creativity if they so desire; had I not used the WhatsApp medium, there would have been students who simply couldn't attend because they lacked the resources to log in via Zoom, for example. This would have been an unacceptable outcome for me, both as university professor and writer.

So, in summary, here is what my experience of teaching Creative Writing via WhatsApp to undergraduates taught me:

a) Initial tasks needed to be sent out well ahead of the start of the course, in order to give all students adequate time to take additional challenges into account such as for interviews. The convenor also needed to be prepared to answer more email/WhatsApp queries and share useful information with the collective via email/WhatsApp Group Chat.
b) Tasks needed to be simplified and expectations regarding quantity (although not quality) had to be reduced.
c) Students needed to prepare differently – for example, pre-

recording their work in progress before class as voice notes, so that these could be shared instantly during class. Students also had to share documents (if possible) via a Google Drive or via a WhatsApp Group Chat.

d) The number of students invited to share their drafts per workshop had to be restricted (and perhaps group sizes kept smaller than in face-to-face teaching) in order to give everyone enough space and attention to develop their abilities at a more measured pace.

e) Students were ultimately no less passionate and the work produced was often of excellent quality.

f) Attendance and actual engagement had to be carefully monitored, especially initially, and action taken if energies and focus were seeping away from the group.

g) Unexpected skills could be cultivated, such as better and deeper story-listening habits.

h) The medium is highly accessible as most South Africans (and others in emerging economies) have access to a smartphone and WhatsApp.

In conclusion, before my Covid experience of teaching Creative Writing via WhatsApp Group Chat, I was suspicious of such an approach. It seemed completely at odds with so many aspects of Creative Writing teaching that I value, such as the unique and inspirational camaraderie that can spark when writers come together in person. However, I now take a more balanced and pragmatic view. While, in my opinion, face-to-face workshops remain the ideal, I do believe that WhatsApp and other remote-teaching technologies have a role to play, especially in circumstances where accessibility (locational/financial) make on-site workshopping impossible.

The key benefit of teaching Creative Writing via WhatsApp Group Chat, is that, despite not being in person, it *still* allows writers from a wide range of socio-economic backgrounds to experience teaching in real time. Students can share their work with peers and benefit from immediate group and tutor feedback and insight, as well as engage in spontaneous exercises like free writes. In other words, by using the chat function of this free multiplatform messaging app, a Creative Writing teacher can still enable a group workshopping format that is supportive, collaborative and dynamic, albeit in an alternative form. Not only does WhatsApp Group Chat allow discussion and debate, but there are also other potential creative benefits, such as enhanced story-listening skills and the high standard of writing that can be produced, as well as the opportunity to share resource links with the group. In this light, I'm keen to examine future ways in which I might use the medium to teach Creative Writing to those who may need it, but who can't easily access on-site or face-to-face teaching – or even engage with fellow writers, for example isolated writers living in remote areas, or even those in conflict zones or refugee camps who wish to be guided in their writing by a more experienced practitioner, while also sharing their work with fellow writers. In theory, one could even use the medium to transcend international boundaries and borders, creating a writing group with a global reach. I take heart from the positive experience of my English 331 students and the popularity of the Naija Writers United Collective. Here is a medium which, if given careful thought, can, I believe, become a powerful tool for Creative Writing outreach and empowerment.

Bibliography

Ahmed, Sabri Thabit Saleh. "Chat and Learn: Effectiveness of Using WhatsApp as a Pedagogical Tool to Enhance EFL Learners Reading and Writing Skills." *International Journal of English Language and Literature Studies*, vol. 8, no. 2, 2019, pp. 61-68.

Hemingway, Ernest. "The Art of Fiction No. 21." *The Paris Review*, no.18, 1958, pp. 23-27.

Magrs, Paul. "Dynamics." *The Creative Writing Coursebook: Forty Authors Share Advice and Exercises for Fiction and Poetry*, edited by Julia Bell and Paul Magrs, MacMillan, 2001, pp. 315-319.

Naija Writers United. "Posts." *Facebook*, 7 May 2021, www.facebook.com/share/p/n8vrSF7uNNb8fqhH/?mibextid=oFDknk.

Paley, Grace. "Interview with Grace Paley." Interview by Kathleen Hulley. *Delta: Revue du Centre d'Etude et de Recherche sur les Ecrivains du Sud aux Etats-Unis*, 1982, pp. 19-40.

Suhaimi, Noor Diana, Maslawati Mohamad and Hamidah Yamat. "The Effects of WhatsApp in Teaching Narrative Writing: A Case Study." *Humanities & Social Sciences Reviews*, vol. 7, no. 4, 2019, pp. 590-602.

Making *Nagmusiek*
Stephanus Muller

In 2014, I published a three-volume book on South African composer Arnold van Wyk (1916–1983). The project started in 2001, when I embarked on a process of collecting, ordering and cataloguing Van Wyk's voluminous literary estate. In 2004, I joined Marlene van Niekerk's seminar on creative writing at Stellenbosch University, where my own ideas on research and the scholarly nature of my undertaking were fundamentally challenged within the parameters of a master's degree in the Arts. When I left the seminar in 2006, the book underwent further scrutiny and refinement – decisively so when Fourthwall Books in Johannesburg decided to publish it, and a process ensued that emphasised the book as object, and the potential of design and production to extend the creative process. When *Nagmusiek* was published, it received prizes for non-fiction and fiction, an indication that the text could be read – and indeed was read – in ways that challenged the mutually exclusive categories through which the publishing industry recognises writing. After its publication, the book inspired an online series of conversations, creative-writing texts and films in the digital intervention *herri*, edited and curated by Aryan Kaganof.

Over time, one creates fictions of the things one did, and of why. It is impossible for me to recall with any certainty the degree to which my initial project on Van Wyk, which eventually led to *Nagmusiek*, was sparked by a disturbingly overblown hubris, a belief (or set of beliefs) in a thing or things, or a kind of postdoctoral panic. (I completed my DPhil at Oxford in 2000, after which I returned to South Africa, without job or postdoctoral prospects.) All these motivations were probably present in the beginning, in some way or another. Retrospectively, I think that from the start certain foundational concerns occupied my writing and the publication of *Nagmusiek*: the importance to me of writing the book in Afrikaans, and the idea of doing justice to the music of a largely unknown, but very important, White South African composer, without encouraging a nostalgic or reverential homage to Apartheid-era cultural production.[1]

The latter concern manifested in particular in relation to the question of scale, and could be focused in the question: how could a large, monumental scholarly project find a balance between research, scholarly documentation and musicological exegesis on the one hand, and the relativising strategies of fragmentation, insertion, and creative re-imagining on the other? Without much planning, over the fourteen years that the project lasted (and beyond), questions like this gradually became part of conversations with many different interlocutors, several of whom were seminal to the successful completion of *Nagmusiek*, its unusual status as fiction and non-fiction, and its afterlife. Making *Nagmusiek* would not have been possible without a creative process that involved co-creators, with their own creative projects and textual fields of reference. In this essay, I wish to highlight something of the social and literary milieu in which I wrote *Nagmusiek*, illustrating how it was incubated in an academic teaching environment and became an object in the world through collaborative efforts. I understand collaboration in this context as being beyond notions of 'deliberately working together', and extend my thinking to how fields of influence changed and enriched my project in ways I had not previously envisaged.

Marlene van Niekerk's *Kreatiewe Afrikaanse Skryfkunde* Seminar

Marlene van Niekerk's creative writing seminar at Stellenbosch University provided, for two years, a receptive, nurturing and critical discursive context for the first drafts of *Nagmusiek*. Van Niekerk's seminar happened once a month, was structured around the mutual exchange and reading of participants' own texts, formalised written commentary and free-flowing critical discussion. Seminar participants had to submit and discuss readers' reports on recommended novels,[2] and present short versions of protagonists' lives in forms that included a dialogue, an inquisition, a recording of music and mumblings, and a letter to a romantic love (dreamt, hoped for, or real). Theoretical texts concerning technical aspects of writing were prescribed, read and discussed,[3] while in the background, Van Niekerk's own creative work (and that of one or two of the more senior participants) created a force field of suggested readings, conversations and ideas.[4] The seminar profited considerably from the mix of participants. Academic, novelist and translator Michiel Heyns was a constant presence, and the discussion benefited not only from his creative energy and ideas, but from his rigorous and refined aesthetic and scholarly approach.[5] He had reservations about the degree of abstraction that could be sustained in a text like the one I was developing, singling out long quotations from Paul Ricoeur's *Time and Narrative* as particularly obtuse. He identified early on in the life of the text that the three-tiered mimetic framework derived from Ricoeur could be removed (as scaffolding), and pointed to James Joyce's *Ulysses* and its dependence on the *Odyssey* as a possible way to think about this. He sensed the difficulty I had in shaping characters and character relationships, and was very specific in questioning not only the successful creation of these fictive devices, but also in demanding to know why they were required, and what functions they had to perform.

Deon Meyer had a particularly balanced approach to critique that owed much to the pragmatism of his undeniable talent and his ambition to master the detective genre.[6] Meyer's commentary on text was invariably structured into 'What impressed?' and 'What bothered?' responses, and my records show his reservations about things ranging from an overly weighty academic register to unconvincing characterisation. The rest of the writers were mostly younger, and more inexperienced, working on short stories, poems and novels of various kinds. Not all of these projects became publications (some did, and were well received), but I soon realised that I learned as much (if not more) from reading and discussing problems presented by struggling texts, than from reading only accomplished writing.

Van Niekerk's instruction was seminal to the direction that I felt safe to take in *Nagmusiek*, and her influence extended to the period before I formally joined the seminar. Her energy and creative abundance were factors, as was her intuitive technical skill, but in retrospect the most important thing she brought to *Nagmusiek* was her curiosity and enthusiasm, and her subsequent immersion in the material. This meant that she recognised things in the text that I did not, saw possible ways to deploy material that I hadn't considered, and suggested other texts that could serve as models for solutions.[7] Paging through numerous drafts that Van Niekerk annotated between 2004 and 2006 (always in hard copy, sometimes with pencil, sometimes with black pen), I see many instances of detailed technical advice: how to 'colour' the writing without overstatement; comments on timing and tempo; advice on characterisation; detailed criticism of sentence structure.

The very first 40 pages of writing that I presented to Van Niekerk were what I considered to be research – background material for what was still to follow as the proper writing. In her response, Van Niekerk demonstrated how the mechanics of the research already formed the text proper. One could read this response as annotation, but it is more accurately described as insight, explication and recognition – a shaping influence that operated as much through affective engagement as through technical correction, suggestions and running commentary of all kinds. So, before Van Niekerk read and commented upon my final manuscript produced for her writing seminar (my records contain an extensive report dated July 2006, and four bound volumes of annotated writing), she had read many drafts of text sections; crucially, she had conveyed the basic creative insight that the scaffolding of the text was the text proper, and thus had intimated an approach to treating the 'large-scale' in a non-monumentalising way.

The problems of scale and monumentalisation were flagged for me in the remarkable oeuvre of Afrikaans biographical writing by J. C. Kannemeyer. By the time I had started writing *Nagmusiek*, he had published a biography of D. J. Opperman (1986), as well as life and work studies on C. J. Langenhoven (1995), C. L. Leipoldt (1999), Uys Krige (2002) and Jan Rabie (2004). These biographies were uncompromisingly comprehensive, largely untroubled by critical theory, and based on extensive archival research of primary documents. They were part of an astounding sphere of (mostly post-Apartheid) canonisation of an Afrikaans literary tradition that Kannemeyer had mapped in his much earlier, award-winning, two-volume *Geskiedenis van die Afrikaanse literatuur* (1979).[8] In the aftermath of political Apartheid's demise, these books represented, for me, commemoration more than interrogation – monuments to a tradition forged by a succession of literary men during a time when Afrikaans literature stood in a particularly troubled relation to political power. Because my book written about Van Wyk would be the first, and would be based on first-time access to a rich archive of previously unresearched materials, it was clear to me that it would be a large undertaking, more likely than not resulting in a substantial monograph. The challenge, as I saw it in the context of biographical writing during this time in Afrikaans, was to write such a book in a way that could not be hailed as a monument to the nurturing by Apartheid of musical talents like those of Van Wyk, especially as South Africa had begun to dismantle much of the infrastructure that enabled that particular aesthetic and idea of musical creation.

Aryan Kaganof and Fourthwall Books

For years after I had completed the writing seminar in 2006, conversations with Van Niekerk, and members of her writing seminar and circle, influenced my continuing work on the manuscript.[9] Two years after my time in the seminar had ended, I started working with the artist and filmmaker Aryan Kaganof on an unrelated project.[10] Kaganof began reading the manuscript in 2009, and continued to do so until he had finished it in 2011. By that time, it was a consolidated document, which I was submitting to publishers. His meticulous reading, over years, was followed by emails in which comments were structured by page number, and where he engaged with matters ranging from small typographic errors to stylistic advice, indications of what worked particularly well and why, and suggestions for improvement. I printed and cut out these emails, pasted the fragments on blank pages of the ring-bound copy, and gradually worked through everything with close attention. I didn't always have time to follow his instructions on reading rigorously,[11] but, most importantly, he gave me insight into what *Nagmusiek* had become, and what it was about. From Norman Mailer's *The Armies of the Night* (1968), Kaganof sent me this often-quoted passage in an email of 6 December 2011:

> The novel must replace history at precisely that point where experience is sufficiently emotional, spiritual, psychical, moral, existential, or supernatural, to expose the fact that the historian in pursuing the experience would be obliged to quit the clearly demarcated limits of historical inquiry.

This was a different perspective on the more abstract philosophical approach I had taken to structuring *Nagmusiek*, after reading (under encouragement from Van Niekerk) and implementing some of the implications of Ricoeur's *Time and Narrative*, but one that nevertheless confirmed this approach. *Nagmusiek* also benefited from Kaganof's filmic understanding of succession, rather than narrative development. From Van Niekerk's annotated notes, I saw the importance she attached to fairly traditional novelistic devices of communicating information by showing and not telling, by developing characters, and using place. From Kaganof, I learnt that different kinds of cuts and juxtapositions were not inimical to coherence, that the frame was crucially important, and that larger structure could be sustained by, for example, repetition – in place of more conventional techniques like character development.

After he had finished reading the manuscript, Kaganof's involvement with *Nagmusiek* continued. When Fourthwall Books in Johannesburg agreed to publish *Nagmusiek*, its designer Oliver Barstow, set about designing what the book would look like. Already in an email of 29 March 2010, Kaganof had written to me in response to a passage in the manuscript that detailed the protagonist's love of books, and his penchant for smelling them: 'For this reason, and this reason alone, you will have to ensure that *Nagmusiek* is beautifully produced and smells really wonderful'. Kaganof continued to advise me on design and the selection of visual materials to be used in *Nagmusiek*. He was instrumental in the decision, for example, to have the third, blue volume of the book bound flush with its content pages as a high-modernist style statement, setting it apart from the other two volumes, which were bound more conventionally and in grey.

Barstow contributed in fundamental ways to imagining the book as physical object. This included the inclusion of *objets trouvés* strategically placed in the book to be 'discovered' by readers – namely two photographs of Van Wyk with a typed copy of his honorary doctorate acceptance speech at the University of Cape Town. Other features to this end were the foldout of his extended 'astro-analysis' report; the subtle shadings in facsimile reproductions of Van Wyk's scores that highlight particular passages in the music; and the transparent, thin paper of the score reproduction of the piano work *Nagmusiek* contained in a sleeve at the back. The final slip case, altered on site at the printers in China to include a close-up photograph of Van Wyk's hands (because Barstow was unconvinced by the stripped-bare quality of the first version), can be directly attributed to his design sensibility.

In 2015 and 2016, *Nagmusiek* won a number of South African literary prizes for both fiction and non-fiction,¹² the book's reception acknowledging the innovations the project had tried to effect. For instance, in *Nagmusiek*, I addressed the question of monumentality (or scale), by making a book that did not declare itself as history, research, biography, aesthetic object or fiction. The refraction of genre made it difficult to make unambiguous claims about its subject and his art as historical 'facts' or aesthetic validations. A range of strategies had delivered an outcome hailed as both pioneering and ambiguous.¹³ Among these were the conscious inside-out display of the research process that Van Niekerk had intuited would be important, the fragmentation of narrative, clear intimations of necessary narrative incompletion, the erasure of the boundaries between fiction and non-fiction, and overtly aesthetic gestures. The book was reviewed fairly widely, both in the academic and popular press, with surprisingly few reservations. This reception recognised, in some cases, the significance of what had been achieved, and in one particular instance, it sparked writing (and thinking) that developed those ideas further. Willemien Froneman, in her lengthy critical explication of the book for an academic Anglophone audience, concluded by saying that the book 'is a catechism for the marginal, and a lesson in how to theorise at the borders of intelligibility' (194). And yet, if *Nagmusiek* indeed held such a lesson, in the decade since its publication there has been little evidence that its 'ex-centric hermeneutic horizons' have been recognised and engaged with in South African curricula or postgraduate studies, whether as a window onto the study of Van Wyk and/or his music, or onto the history of South African art music during the twentieth century, or as a methodology and theoretical challenge that concerns 'tensions around canonisation, marginality and the geopolitics of knowledge', worked out within 'the apparatus of the book, its formal structure, its metafiction, its narrative development, and its sheer bulk' (Froneman 194).

And yet, *Nagmusiek* has experienced an afterlife among those of my close professional circle. Some of my own postgraduate students have done research work that shows a heightened awareness of the possibilities for archival study to be infused with creative scholarship; some have moved with greater ease between methodological approaches that straddle auto/biography, analysis, ethnography, historiography, and creative non-fiction. *Nagmusiek* has also resulted in a remarkable recording of Van Wyk's mature piano music by Daniel-Ben Pienaar (the first complete commercial recording of this body of music) and, in a manner of speaking, a revelation of Van Wyk to the world, decades after his passing.[14]

herri

A further augmentation of *Nagmusiek* is evident in *herri* (an online digital-arts-based intervention published by the Africa Open Institute for Music, Research and Innovation from 2019 to 2023).[15] Kaganof, who since 2019 has been editor and curator of *herri*, decided in 2020 to devote a thematic section to *Night Music*, the English translation of *Nagmusiek*. It contained a number of highly creative engagements with both my book, *Nagmusiek*, and with Van Wyk's piano work of the same name, but also embedded these in a thematic context that included an essay on Amapiano by Setumo-Thebe Mohlomi, the re-publication of James Baldwin's "Sonny's Blues", artwork by Garth Erasmus, Cornelius Cardew's views on the ethics of improvisation, and a photo essay by Ayi Kwei Armah. This embedding of *Nagmusiek* in the context of wider aesthetic-cultural debate continues to grapple with the conditions under which the work of an Apartheid-era composer becomes legible, and audible, in the post-Apartheid world. Kaganof's curatorial sensibility stretches the notions of 'night' (with its undercurrents of death and mystery), the alienated consciousness, commentary on elitism and Western art music's conceits through the work of authors and subjects materially unconnected with either my or Van Wyk's *Nagmusiek*. With this broadened thematic approach, Kaganof's curatorship continued to ask the question about Van Wyk's enduring importance (or not) 40 years after his death, and about my work about him in *Nagmusiek*.

The commissioned work that engaged directly with *Nagmusiek* (composition and book) in this themed issue of *herri*, did so in more direct ways. I was not privy to Kaganof's reasoning in commissioning artists and writers to engage directly with *Nagmusiek* (the composition and book). However, given my experience of his curation of content for *herri* in the nine issues published to date, I surmise he would have based his decisions on work he had encountered and read, and which could lead to interesting and enriching engagements. Kaganof asked Pluto Panoussis, Tom

Whyman and Leonhard Praeg to contribute to *herri*'s 'Night Music' theme by responding to the composition and the book, and they responded with a film (Panoussis), and essays (Whyman and Praeg). All of this material was embedded in media-rich design on *herri's* pages.

Filmmaker Panoussis writes that his 'project [("*Nagmusiek*")] was conceived as a live performance celebrating the centenary of the birth of seminal South African composer, Arnold van Wyk, and his revered 1955 solo piano work, *Nagmusiek*'. Panoussis describes his film as conceived by several considerations. These included his 'intense dislike' for the genre of the music video, Van Wyk's intention to create a work portraying the night, and the particular choice of recording of the work that was used for the film. My book, *Nagmusiek*, suggested to him 'the possibility of applying a hybrid layering of visual orders' to his film. *Nagmusiek*'s formal experimentation invited from Panoussis and his students 'a desire to strike up an oblique dialogue with that work', leading to an exploration of the figurative and abstract in direct dialogue, the visual tension between the graphic and the textural, animation and live-action sitting alongside each other – moments of visual silence that coerce us towards the music, and moments of visual gasp that steal slightly from the music.'

Philosopher and writer Tom Whyman writes at the beginning of the essay 'The Ghost Has Been Summoned' that Kaganof asked him to write about *Nagmusiek* 'and the philosophical concept of hauntology – which I have just published an article about'. He responded to Pienaar's recording of Van Wyk's *Nagmusiek* as follows:

> [W]hat I hear is [...] very introverted – but also very self-abnegating. It's hard to know what exactly the piece is trying to express, because it seems to be trying to represent an absence – the absence, indeed, of the very self who is doing the expressing [...] It is almost as if the piece is trying to tip-toe around its own subject matter.

Whyman, who cannot read Afrikaans, responded by confronting the beautiful object created by Fourthwall, the three volumes in the slipcase; and he found in the third volume passages in English from which he continued to bring the project into conversation with the concept of hauntology as revived by Mark Fisher in *Ghosts of My Life* (2014), and J. M. Coetzee's *Summertime* (2009). With regard to the former, Whyman considers how Jacques Derrida and Fisher's hauntology is explicitly political, whereas, with *Nagmusiek*, what seems to be at stake is a hauntology of the self. With reference to *Summertime*, Whyman considers effective hauntology of the self as an inevitable violence to the self. For Whyman's essay, Kaganof and his designers made a page consisting of photographs and effects from *Nagmusiek*, but also from the archive and the immense surplus of production that produced the book. Searching for points of recognition in the English sections embedded in the Afrikaans text, Whyman's reading confronts the manner in which the Afrikaans closes the text to the outside, while simultaneously opening it through Fisher, Coetzee and Kaganof's curation in ways undeterred by the text's understandings of itself, delivering on the imperative of a historiography liberated from the taboos of Apartheid's delusions of grandeur.

In the introduction to his extended essay on *Nagmusiek* ('A Melancholy Anatomy'), Leonhard Praeg explains that he was approached by Kaganof as a philosopher, novelist and composer. The essay contains a highly original consideration of the concept of 'tonality', and a complex Afrikaans/English reaction to the bilingual gesture of the book. In writing his essay for *herri*, Praeg also requested more materials from the archive, not provided in the book, to write about classification, transcription and signatures. In a daring continuation of the gambit of *Nagmusiek* (the book), Praeg turns its historical invasiveness onto myself as the author providing me with a fictional masturbation chart deduced from the text 'to codify the (auto)biographer's ecstatic experiences', like the one I had abstracted from Van Wyk's diaries; Praeg proceeds to write himself into the essay not only via a taxonomic interpretation of how language thematically relates to tonality, but by grappling with the foundational philosophical and psychological issues raised by melancholy, and death, as it concerns his own life and work.

Kaganof's contribution to this page in *herri* includes fragments from a filmic engagement with the Van Wyk material, for which I had done voice recordings from some of Van Wyk's correspondence and notes. The larger film from which these fragments are extracted, entitled *Nagmusiek for You Alone* (2015), was filmed in Stellenbosch, Pretoria and London in 2014 during the various launches of *Nagmusiek*, and has never been released. Importantly, these fragments place *Nagmusiek* (the composition), which was dedicated to the memory of Van Wyk's one-time lover Noel Mewton-Wood, in a history of Twentieth-century artistic engagement with homosexual love and sensuality, most notably through its use of images from Jean Genet's 1950 *Un chant d'amour*. During his lifetime, Van Wyk's sexuality was a source of considerable anguish for the composer, whose sense of alienation and vulnerability was intimately connected with this 'open secret'. Kaganof's 'setting' of fragments of Genet's film to the sound of *Nagmusiek* affords a hearing of the piece through images that celebrate the homoerotic and evoke it as a latent quality in the music. In this way, together with Pienaar's 'rediscovery' of Van Wyk in his 2020 recording, Kaganof's filmed fragments continue with a kind of 'recovery' work regarding Van Wyk, for which the book, *Nagmusiek*, functioned more as prompt than destination.

Concluding Thoughts

This documentation of collegial, scholarly and artistic engagements with the book I published in 2014, *Nagmusiek*, shows something of the richness of the collaborative gains of working within a community of scholars and artists where generosity is the norm, and courage to take risks the result of a confidence instilled by support and nurture. The instruction from Marlene van Niekerk was crucial to the directions I felt safe to take in writing *Nagmusiek*; and her seminar procedure of text discussions opened the manuscript, in its formative stages, to a wide variety of important insights and feedback. This collective engagement with a piece of writing, directed by a strong and hugely creative artistic voice within an academic context, suggested a form and register for the writing that would never have occurred to me if I had worked on the text in any other context. Often, creative work is seen as extending the possibilities of academic writing and research, yet *Nagmusiek* benefited in numerous ways by invoking the academic frame even as it challenged it. These benefits included the rhythm of seminar discussions and text completion deadlines, the kinds of literature introduced as contextual reading, the assumptions of rigorous critique that are stabilised by academic conventions in discussion, and the taken-for-grantedness of theory and philosophy as discursive contexts for considerations of storytelling, narration and the poetics of writing.

Similarly, the design phase of *Nagmusiek*, involving the publisher, Fourthwall Books, and the artist, Aryan Kaganof, functioned as an interpretation of the text rather than merely its finalisation as a printed book. This hermeneutic of the object that is *Nagmusiek* was dependent less on the author than on the collaborative creative energies of Oliver Barstow and Kaganof. After publication of *Nagmusiek*, a series of engagements with the book by Kaganof, Leonhard Praeg, Tom Whyman and Pluto Panoussis continued a digitally curated, media-rich reflection on the music and philosophical concerns at the centre of *Nagmusiek*. Importantly, in the digital space, these interactions go their own way, identifying – in the givenness of the subject matter (and its material manifestations) – things of importance that had either not been explicated, or understood or known by the text. I like to think of this as an affirmation of the openness of the text, and its contribution to addressing the challenges of scale and 'the monumental' in post-Apartheid historiography. The interdisciplinary, post-publication reflections in *herri* extended the boundaries of the text in unscripted ways, instantiating an *ex post facto* collaboration in the project that is *Nagmusiek*.

Endnotes

1   I remember a conversation with Van Niekerk about Hermann Giliomee's *The Afrikaners* (2003), in which she made the point that the author (generally) is responsible for the readers that identify with the book. Giliomee's project, and this conversation, stayed with me throughout the decade I worked on *Nagmusiek*.

2   I do not have a list of these novels in my records, but remember John Banville's *The Sea* (2005), Tom Wolfe's *A Man in Full* (1998) and a book that became very important for the development of a register in *Nagmusiek*, W.G. Sebald's *Austerlitz* (2001).

3   Basic texts for the seminar included Mieke Bal's *Theory of Narrative* (1985), André P. Brink's *Vertelkunde* (1987), Peter Brooks's *Reading for the Plot* (1984), Joseph A. Kestner's *The Spatiality of the Novel* (1978), Susan S. Lanser's *The Narrative Act: Point of View in Prose Fiction* (1981), and Patricia Waugh's *Metafiction: The Theory and Practice of Self-Conscious Fiction* (1984). Also included on this list was Paul Ricoeur's *Time and Narrative*, vol. 2. (1986), a book that had a profound influence on my project.

4   At the time, Van Niekerk had just completed *Agaat* (2004) and was working on *Memorandum* (2006).
5   Heyns had just published *The Reluctant Passenger* (2003), and in 2005 published *The Typewriter's Tale*. During 2006/7, he also translated Van Niekerk's *Agaat* and *Memorandum*.
6   Meyer was working on *Infanta* (2005) at the time, which was already his fourth novel.
7   For example, reading an early draft of a scene between the main character and his mother, she directed me to Pedro Almodóvar's film *Talk to Her* (2002); in the Doppelgänger strategy between fictional biographer and his subject, she recommended Martinus Nijhoff's *Awater* (1934); with regard to melancholy, Robert Burton's *The Anatomy of Melancholy* (1621) and Patricia de Martelaere's *Het Verlangen Naar Ontroosbaarheid* (1993).
8   After 2004, Kannemeyer would also complete biographies of Etienne Leroux (2008) and J. M. Coetzee (2011).
9   Most notably, the work was read and commented upon with illuminating insight by Lou-Marie Kruger, who was able to see in Van Wyk's material (the diary entries, for example) and the construction of the fictional protagonist Werner Ansbach, invaluable potential for fictional representation of historical detail.
10 This was the film *An Inconsolable Memory* (2014). I write about this creative partnership in 'Scholarship, traumatic histories, and the boundaries of the personal: The making of *An Inconsolable Memory*' (2018).
11 Kaganof recommended many more sources than I can list, but these included Milan Kundera's *Immortality* (tr. Peter Kussi, 1991) as a possible inspiration in dealing with a certain section of the book, especially a sexually charged scene; the music of Tom Waits and the album *Swordfishtrombones* (1983) to illuminate the obstinacy of the piano in the imagination of the protagonist; and his own brilliant writing and films that led me to discover work by Elias Canetti, George Bataille, Joseph Roth and Guy Debord, among others.
12 The Eugène Marais Prize for an early belletristic work, awarded by the Suid-Afrikaanse Akademie vir Wetenskap en Kuns (2016); the kykNET-Rapport Prize for non-fiction (2015); the Jan Rabie Rapport Prize for debut fiction (2015); and the University of Johannesburg Debut Prize for Creative Writing in Afrikaans (2015).
13 In this regard, see especially Joan Hambidge's review in her blog *Woorde Wat Weeg*.
14 Many of the works on Pienaar's recording can be heard at herri.org.za, which also contains an interview between myself and Pienaar about Van Wyk's piano music, and his recording of this repertoire.
15 I am the Director of the Africa Open Institute.

Bibliography

Armah, Ayi Kwei. "Night Music 8: The Final Sound." *herri*, issue# 03, herri.org.za/3/ayi-kwei-armah/.
Baldwin, James. "Night Music 6: Sonny's Blues." *herri*, issue# 03, herri.org.za/3/james-baldwin/.

Cardew, Cornelius, and Garth Erasmus. "Night Music 7: Acceptance of Death." *herri*, issue# 03, herri.org.za/3/cornelius-cardew/.

Froneman, Willemien. "Ex-Centric Hermeneutics in Stephanus Muller's *Nagmusiek*." *Royal Musical Association Research Chronicle*, 8 June 2017, pp. 179–194.

Hambidge, Joan. "Stephanus Muller – Nagmusiek (2014)." *Woorde Wat Weeg*, joanhambidge. blogspot.com/2014/11/stephanus-muller-nagmusiek-2014.html.

Kaganof, Aryan. Email correspondence. 29 March 2010 and 6 December 2011.

---. *Nagmusiek for You Alone* (unreleased film). Directed by Aryan Kaganof, 2015.

---. "Theme: Night Music." *herri*, issue# 03, herri.org.za/3/sections/theme/.

Kruger, Lou-Marie. "Nagmusiek deur Stephanus Muller." *LitNet*, 19 August 2014, www.litnet.co.za/article/nagmusiek-deur-stephanus-muller.

Muller, Stephanus. *Nagmusiek*. Fourthwall Books, 2014.

---. "Scholarship, Traumatic Histories, and the Boundaries of the Personal: the Making of *An Inconsolable Memory*." *Challenges in Contemporary Musicology: Essays in Honor of Prof. Dr. Mirjana Veselinović-Hofman*, edited by Sonja Marinković, Vesna Mikić, Ivana Perković, Tijana Popović Mladjenović, Ana Stefanović and Dragana Stojanović-Novičić, Faculty of Music, Belgrade, 2018, pp. 455–471.

Panoussis, Pluto. "Music 2: *Nagmusiek*." *herri*, issue# 03, herri.org.za/3/pluto-panoussis.

Pienaar, Daniel-Ben. "Arnold van Wyk – The Mature Piano Music." *Africa Open Institute*, 2020.

Pienaar, Daniel-Ben, and Stephanus Muller. "Night Music 4: Finding Specific Meaningfulness in Arnold van Wyk." *herri*, issue# 03, herri.org.za/3/daniel-ben-pienaar-and-stephanus-muller.

Praeg, Leonhard. "Night Music 5: A Melancholy Anatomy – Notes on Arnold van Wyk's *Nagmusiek*." *herri*, issue# 03, herri.org.za/3/leonhard-praeg.

Ricoeur, Paul. *Time and Narrative*. Translated by Kathleen Mclaughlin and David Pellauer, Chicago & London, University of California Press, 1984, 1985, 1988.

Whyman, Tom. "Night Music 3: The Ghost Has Been Summoned." *herri*, issue# 03, herri.org.za/3/tom-whyman.

Concert Note – Remember Who You Are
Liesl Jobson

> The great malady of the twentieth century, implicated in all of our troubles and affecting us individually and socially, is 'loss of soul'. When soul is neglected, it doesn't just go away; it appears symptomatically in obsessions, addictions, violence, and loss of meaning. Our temptation is to isolate these symptoms or to try to eradicate them one by one; but the root problem is that we have lost our wisdom about the soul, even our interest in it. (Moore xi)

At an online twelve-step meeting, Thomas Moore articulated how, in his experience, a loss of soul often expresses itself as yearning and compulsions, which then manifest in addictive attachments to substances or processes, which, oddly, often feel like love. I recently revisited my much-underlined copy of Moore's *Care of the Soul*, a gift from my mother when the book was published in 1992. That year I gave birth to an extremely premature infant and greatly needed whatever guidance was on offer to steer me through the ensuing upheaval.

At the online meeting, Moore also described the soul as

> the essence of who we are […] beyond our emotions, beyond the mechanics of our daily lives. It's deep deep down. We encounter it in our dreams with those images and those narratives that we find ourselves in at night. It's such a mysterious place, but the soul itself is quite mysterious. […] the best way to relate to it is to honour its mystery instead of trying to explain it or control it. (Moore and McA 00:03:58-00:04:31)

Creative practice enables me to tap into the Self that is smarter, kinder and wiser than the small self that shambles through my days, cooking, crafting, completing assignments and that battles to come home to myself.

My personal creative practice has taken various forms that sustain and promote healthy and engaged living, and that return me to the essence of who I am. They include the vital act of writing against self-erasure and self-destruction; music-making for the silenced and wordless parts of myself; and making images that remind me who I am and where I've been. In writing, I access the healing mystery in which ink flows through my fountain pen, a lifeblood with a pulse. In playing a musical instrument, I keep life's beating heart alive. This is my practice: to write life's long story and to sing its song.

***

In 1981, I played the flute in the Summer Theatre of the New Canaan production of *Hello Dolly*. We had moved to America for eighteen months for my father's work in New York City. I was fifteen and unbearably homesick, yet my country was not a place I was proud of, and I had no desire to return there. Our family home was chaotic and unpredictable. I was an outsider who didn't belong at New Canaan High any more than I did back at Westerford High in Cape Town.

The conductor, Chris McCormick, was the first person to help me understand how orchestral accompaniment worked. He taught me that I could count the bars and follow the cues to enter precisely where I was supposed to play. He taught me how to move with a beat that accelerated in places and then slowed to a pause. I learnt that when I did this, it impacted what he was doing and contributed to the overall success of the show.

My fingers lifted and closed into each note, and I was alive to hear it. I formed the embouchure and focused my airstream across the mouthpiece, striving to make the purest sound I could. I became one with my instrument, watching the baton, listening to the singer, counting rests until my entry, and then, finally, leaning into the musical phrase. I learnt that my nerves had a purpose – they were needed by the actors and musicians, conductor and director, stagehands and technical team. I merged with something bigger than myself. I had found my tribe.

This holy encounter confirmed what I had already intuited from attending symphony concerts with my father: I knew I wanted to play in the orchestra forever. The hollow ache that threatened to pull me under was quietened in rehearsals where there was so much to learn, to practise, to perfect. When I practised alone at home, I sensed that I was in service to a tradition. There was always a destination – not literally, as in a lesson or a rehearsal, but a sense of placement in the music. By shaping the apex of the phrase so that I could arrive at the high point and release into the end of it, in the acquisition of a tricky technical passage, and in arriving at the sonorous centre of each note in tune and in time, I was aligning myself with a concerted reality that stretched back through the millennia. Making music was about keeping time and about a timely reunion. It was about belonging.

That summer I also fell in love with Larry because of how he held his double bass. As he took it towards himself, his own belly merged with the huge body of the bass. He drew the bow across the strings with a deft and precise wrist. His fingers plucked the strings with a resonant depth. Larry gave me a tiny maple leaf during one of the breaks that I put in my Bible, which sits now between *Roget's Thesaurus* and Oswald Mtshali's *Fireflames*.

I turn the delicate pages looking for the leaf. My eye lands on an underlined section: Matthew 12:31 cautions against blasphemy against the Spirit. I remember trying to decode this verse. What, precisely, was the unforgivable sin? Suicide? I couldn't really ask anyone because I didn't want to alert anyone to how much time I spent thinking about ending my life. In case it was indeed the unforgivable sin, I would have to stay alive. Music had already become the lifeline that would help me do that. If I could remain in that enchanted circle where words were not necessary, I sensed I could probably endure.

The leaf is gone. I turn to Mtshali's first poem in *Fireflames*.

***

The richness of the soul

> The depth of my soul is fertile
> at its most profound level;
> everything thrives on it;
> wild carrots and wild lilies
> enrich the life of the soul on this earth;

the earth rings with the song of great singers,
who are dressed in loin skins of gemsboks.
I offer this poem as a sacrifice.
(Mtshali 1)

***

That autumn, the school drama department at New Canaan High put on *Alice's Adventures in Wonderland*. I played the Red Queen, wearing a scarlet gown and a satin crown. As Alice transforms into an adult, the Red Queen calls out a mantra, 'Remember who you are! Remember who you are!'.

It was a pertinent warning. In the intensity of my loneliness, I forgot quickly. I was an awkward stranger with an accent frequently mistaken for Australian. I wore silk shirts and long linen skirts that were better suited to the wealthy matrons who'd donated them to the village thrift store. Other sophomores emulated Brooke Shields in their Calvin Klein jeans. They wore sneakers. I wore black cloth slippers from Chinatown that were hopeless in the snow.

The sense of disconnection that has been a lifelong struggle started with many moves – from school to school, jumping up a grade in junior school, and repeating one in high school. Intense loneliness and bullying led to a bout of pre-teen depression that didn't get better with the transcontinental move to a posh East Coast town. My letters home described the peculiarities of American life, but not that I fantasised about ending my life. I was intrigued by what I'd written, not yet fully aware that articulating my dislocation gave me a concrete way of knowing that the bizarre and nonsensical experiences were real.

There was a babysitting job, which included mending clothes for an alcoholic whose children went hungry and fought each other while she stared listlessly out of the window. There were flute lessons with a Japanese teacher who ate his grandmother's noodles with chopsticks. One day I lugged a double bass home from school through the woods so I could teach myself to play. Did I imagine standing beside Larry at the next summer theatre production? The bass soon lost its appeal when I bought a clarinet with my babysitting earnings at a yard sale. The next purchase was a clarinet method book with a fingering chart from Merritt Music.

I worked as a night aide once a week for an elderly woman who was paralysed from polio. Her mechanical rocking bed kept her breathing while she slept. It was my job to slip the female urinal in between her legs when she called me. It was a perilous manoeuvre that had to be carefully timed. It was a job that paid well.

I told nobody about that distressing intimacy. Instead, I wrote about learning to make snacks for her bridge pals, and the astonishing town library, the church choir and the eccentric school conductor, Mr. Krenecky, and the Baskin-Robbins that sold 31 different flavours of ice cream. I wish I had those letters now. They were my first experience of narrating – and thereby creating – my own reality. Whatever I wrote went into an envelope in the mailbox with the red flag. The mailman arrived in his small truck and exchanged my outbound letter for whatever had come in.

After the first couple of replies from school friends, I was disappointed. Despite compliments on my beautiful letters, their own accounts of the friendships I'd left back home were insipid. The correspondence was uninspiring, but the major discovery was that I could tell a story. I could, indeed, remember who I was.

***

It is 40 years since the production of *Alice's Adventures in Wonderland* at New Canaan High School but, like Alice, I am still finding my way. The sense of loss and being lost is seemingly permanent. Perhaps that is the experience of all who sit on the margins of a society with materialistic values? Perhaps that is just how it is for those with addictive tendencies or mental health challenges? But when there is an outlet that transmutes the loss of meaning, serenity and equilibrium are possible.

To make sense of creative practice, we must address how to earn a living. After studying music at Wits University, I played in chamber ensembles that performed at weddings, and in amateur and professional orchestras while teaching music part-time. With two babies, I needed to relinquish the night-time orchestral work, so I ventured into nursery-school teaching and later professional writing. I worked in journalism, copywriting, editing and photography. After the beginning of the Covid 19 pandemic, I switched to teaching music and writing online.

My entire professional life has been piecework. Scraps and threads. Here and there. Now and again. Occasionally an employee. Sometimes a contractor. Mostly freelance.

I'm an artist, though, not a businesswoman. I have little interest in marketing and invoicing, yet somehow, despite disorganisation, I have earned a living from these creative skills. Fortunately, there have been husbands. Could I have survived financially on my own? Probably not.

Creative work is time-consuming and generally poorly paid, but the additional administrative tasks and following up of unpaid invoices garners no extra remuneration. When a university administration department takes more than a year to pay an artist's fees, resentment grows. Sometimes a gig offers only petrol money – a meaningful gesture in the absence of sponsors. I typically join such an orchestra, glad to be part of the greater community, but know I am always scanning for another opportunity. Networking and being seen. Hustling and hopeful.

The money one makes in the orchestra is a cruel joke, really, because the freelance rate only just covers transport, bassoon reeds, instrument maintenance and insurance. It's an expensive hobby and a curious paradox – earning so little after spending so much money and time. Nobody can buy the musical competence that is the entry ticket into a permanent post. As a beginner, there are lessons to pay for; as a student, the costly access to institutions of higher learning. Getting one's own instrument and the never-ending challenge of sourcing and acquiring suitable reeds is another dreadful expense.

After practising for years and mastering the skills, there is still no guarantee of a seat in a working professional orchestra, where a player is likely to earn less than a private school teacher. And, unsurprisingly, the precision, stamina, subtlety, flexibility and performance under pressure that are integral to successful music-making are skills that cannot be bought.

With various sources of income and unpredictable performance opportunities, my finances are often strained. My last royalty cheque from a major educational publisher that uses my work in a high school textbook was for 37 cents, with the following qualification: 'Please note that it is not feasible to pay amounts less than R100.00. Such payments will be carried over to the next financial year'. If I earn 37 cents a year it will take 270 years for my money to come home. However, I think it's a lump sum, and the interest calculations don't bear contemplation.

I'm immensely fortunate that my father, who was a corporate executive, generously bought me a good second-hand professional model Püchner when I was a third-year student. It has served me well and is insured under an all-risks policy. To replace it would cost about EUR25 000. How a young person without such privilege acquires their own instrument is beyond comprehension. The finances of being an artist simply don't add up.

These accounts serve to remind me that, paradoxically, I am exceptionally lucky to have had three books published – flash fiction, poetry and short stories – and three children's books via Book Dash, a not-for-profit South African publishing initiative. There are so many who aspire to be published, who long for a book of their own, yet never see their name in print, so I am keenly aware of my good fortune. Publication is a profound validation; it says to the world: this person is an *author*. It is, quite literally, a stamp of authority.

One day, you cross the divide and join the elite circle of authors. It feels good. Momentarily. The fanciful notion of being an author often holds a raft of imagined promises of a magical future replete with literary awards and finances restored, book tours and glamorous parties. In reality, publication in South Africa might yield readings at literary festivals, book launches, hybrid collaborations with cross-disciplinary artists and other new projects. It has not paid my bills, however. Is that why I struggle to say aloud that I am an artist?

> 'Who in the world am I? Ah, THAT's the great puzzle!'
> (Carroll 15)

***

As a teacher of piano, flute and recorder, I learnt that engaging with my students involved deep listening. Teaching them to hear themselves was gratifying. As the teacher, I held the memory of how they had played a piece in previous lessons and noted their progress over the course of weeks and months. I also held an imagined possibility for them, reminding them that it was likely that they could soon play the piece with confidence and competence, experiencing joy in their own mastery of the skills and sharing that experience with an audience – whether at a school concert, an eisteddfod or a gathering of friends in their home or church.

My work was to empower them. It was to develop their awareness of the lyrical lines, their tone colour and dynamics, the articulation, phrasing and rhythmic stability. My job was to enable a student to progress independently, to read, to interpret, to self-assess. Stimulating this perception was always helped by recording their performance and playing it back to them. As soon as they heard themselves objectively, they could transfer the knowledge and remedy any instability in their playing.

In the days before mobile phones, this was a laborious process. At Wits University in the 1980s, Professor Mony showed me how to record myself on a reel-to-reel tape recorder, playing back in real time and then at half speed. In real time, I heard where the problem was generally, but when slowed, I heard exactly which finger lagged or what note sequence dragged. I knew how to remedy the errors, but I didn't know whether my fingers and tongue would ever be smooth enough or fast enough. Now I write flash fiction about this, an attempt at repairing what might never be fixed. I offer this work as a sacrifice.

***

Etude #2 – Practice Video

I set my phone up on the music stand to video myself practising Milde bassoon etudes on the contrabassoon, aiming for clear articulation and smooth fingers. The idea is to self-identify the trouble spots before the rehearsals begin. Long grey strands of hair are escaping my plait. The heavy curve to my arms never used to be there. I'm trying not to judge my appearance harshly.

In a short skirt and a cross over t-shirt with an itchy label at the neck, I look like a schoolgirl, but who is watching this video? Only me. The sound is muddy, though the phrasing is musical. I remind myself: don't judge too harshly. I reply to myself: but how will I improve?

I've just returned from Durban where I played Brahms's first symphony with limited success. Or so it feels. So it always feels. Something about playing the contrabassoon always feels vaguely fraudulent, like anybody could do it, but nobody does.

I'm due to play Brahms's third with the Cape Philharmonic and Bernhard Gueller will conduct. I can't remember how to finger the high notes on this instrument even though I played this work last year under his baton. I need to find the trick fingerings for this instrument, but it's like driving in another country. The one in KZN is again different from the UCT instrument. The variation is slight: differently shaped keys, a millimetre to the right or the left – enough to disorient me under pressure. My geography is insecure. The fingerings are not the same. The phrase slips – because I am tired and losing focus? Because I have not practised enough? Can one ever practise this instrument enough?

I angled the contra into the car with the back seats folded down, then drove home from the Artscape Theatre in rush-hour traffic, worrying about getting rear-ended, imagining the contra crushed. This instrument costs the same as a small flat in the suburbs. How does one justify the expense of such an instrument? How does one insure against damage?

I dreamed of dancing a contrabassoon ballet while playing it, making a gorgeous otherworldly sound. Listening to the video now, my upper register is flat, and the lower notes do not have a solid centre. In my dream, I had high arches and wore a tulle skirt. My upper body was strong as I whirled across a stage with a deep burgundy instrument. I turned *en pointe* spinning the instrument on its spike. Each footfall was in time. Not a step was ungainly.

***

With a dream like that I cannot but keep going. Writing about the contrabassoon is a way to comprehend my musician self, focusing on the sound register of the instrument and the monotony that practising requires. It permits – perhaps even honours – the fretfulness and the conflicted pleasures of playing 'the buffoon'. Writing about anything defines it – aesthetics, emotions, experience – taking it from a shimmery abstract realm, making it definite. It enables me to recognise the warring internal states where obsession competes with addiction. Transforming distress into poems or stories rewires and releases the anxiety precisely because it has been beheld. Writing makes things whole. It composes. It notes what is holy.

***

When the Covid 19 pandemic shut down all orchestral work, I segued into running my own small media consultancy. I promised myself always to do my work with love. I promised only to do work I love. A rash promise that isn't financially savvy, but it is how I want to be in a world that is hurting and broken and warring. I want to rise up and salute the sun. I also want to make enough money so that I can stop wading through the night fog of money worry. I took on clients: a township educational trust, a security company, a firm of engineers. They needed websites and newsletters, social media, marketing plans and tenders. I edited and posted and tweeted. I interviewed people. I liaised, trained youth, coached people.

When the orchestra manager called me, I always said yes, rescheduling meetings and taking on extra freelancers to cover me while I attended rehearsals. I juggled deadlines, kept time sheets, tracked developments, listened and advised, followed through and checked up. I reminded myself to do these tasks with love, because I chose this path. My daughter reminded me that if somebody paid me to juggle Fabergé eggs standing on a bar stool in pointe shoes, I'd give it a go. I arrived late to rehearsals, unprepared and scattered. I left a crook behind, then dropped my reeds through the cracks in the stage to the depths of the theatre below. I missed entries because I was trying to placate a client on my phone. I didn't socialise with other players during the break because I was decoding spreadsheets in the cafeteria. I made more money than I ever had before, but I had no heart for the work.

When I was in primary school my father bought us tickets for a symphony concert. We sat in the tiered stand behind and above the orchestra. Looking down, I watched the flute follow the conductor, awaiting his cue. The oboe section breathing together. The tune looping from horns to clarinets to bassoons, lilting into a seamless whole. Each note threading from player to player. The beauty grew. The sonority was so intense that all worlds and all time met and married. Each instrument's ecstasy took shape. It was perfection. It was where I belonged. If I could get there, I would always be home.

**

The contrabassoon rests against the grandfather clock that came from my parents' home. I'm practising for the Summer Symphony Season with the Cape Philharmonic. My colleague Simon Ball has lent me his crook, which shines on the dining room table, which also came from my parents' home. Debussy's *La Mer* is first on the programme. I'm thrilled to be asked to play. I am also anxious. To prepare, I listen to the pieces on *YouTube*, following the score, familiarising myself with the part, so I won't be completely at sea when rehearsals begin.

The grandfather clock escaped the borer beetles that created a fine lattice of pathways through the Oregon pine floors of my childhood home – a late nineteenth-century Georgian construction. With thick walls and high ceilings, it was cool in summer, but cold and damp in winter. My feet were permanently wet inside my socks. By spring each year, dark shadows of mould had formed in the crevices and curlicues of the pressed steel ceilings in my parents' bedroom.

I practise the contra, fumbling with the spike, adjusting the music stand, soaking the reed, and settle down. I trust that I will find a way into the music, that I will form a solid platform on which the rest of the wind section will be able to build each chord, and weave each intertwining melody. The anxieties that undermine me are like the borers that weakened the floor of my childhood home. Intrusive thoughts arrive and suddenly I'm fretting about beetles and mould destroying the contrabassoon. I listen to the recording on my phone on my music stand. Counting the bars,

I breathe and blow into the solo. I record myself. I dislike the clatter and burble and delayed beginning of each phrase.

***

The phone rings and the senior sister at Murambi House is calling me to my mother's bedside. She has had a stroke, and the doctor is on the way. My mother declined over ten years before she entered the dementia ward at the height of the Covid 19 pandemic. The care facility is around the corner from my parents' home of 50 years. I sat beside Mom, knitting a sleeveless pullover in her favourite colour, something between turquoise and teal and duck-egg blue. Would you be proud of me? Am I turning out just fine? Do you know how much I love you?

I go home to teach a dentist who plays all the woodwind instruments and has rented the contrabassoon from the Cape Philharmonic for a concert in the Winelands. I show him where to hold the instrument, how to adjust the spike and crook for optimal comfort. I show him the plumber's tape trick to seal the crook. I find a decent reed and lend him my copy of *The Contrabassoon: A Guide to Performance* by Cornelia Biggers. I listen to him play. I suggest sitting on a high chair to help with deep breathing. We talk about teeth and bite and the musculature of the mouth. We do resonance exercises to open the throat and drop the jaw. He finds his way around the instrument. He has conviction and focus. He's enthusiastic and with his chosen profession, he might in future be rich enough to buy his own instrument.

I encourage him to play and to be playful. It is not lost on me that his devotion outweighs mine. I envy his passion and, momentarily, his lifestyle. I want to be that enthusiastic again and that free. Why am I no longer playful? When did my musicianship lose its lustre? Did it really ever have any – back in New Canaan, as a student at Wits? Will I never cease to be anxious and self-critical when I perform? How do I put the joy back into performance?

***

Mom sleeps through most of my visits. In the pale sunshine that falls across her bed and onto the visitor's chair, I slip four stitches onto a cable needle at the centre of the pattern. I think about the twisted places of my creative urges, which often come to nothing. Once, I could have voiced this failure to her and she would have listened. She would have understood that it was not self-pity or self-accusation, but a genuine question, an attempt at a reckoning. If I can follow this line to the end of the account, will it show me what is due? What is the debt I owe, and can I pay the price? I would like such an insight then to free me to complete some … finish a … make something like … something more … more than …

The right word to complete that sentence swims beyond my reach. Something between worthy and beautiful and substantial. Something like a novel, or an opera, or even a poem that throws someone a lifeline. Something more than a knitted jersey that anybody who cared enough to read a pattern and buy the yarn could complete.

What is the yarn I've bought? What unravelling will enable me to un-tell myself the unwelcome stories that plague me? I knit the next four stitches, passing the cable needle to the front. The next twist of the cable appears. Over and over. Row by row. The pattern is predictable and rhythmic, a fresh and friendly obsession. I sink my fingers into the weft of the fabric that is forming on my needles, weighty and soft. The squishy texture is soothing.

My creativity seems to have withered. I feel trapped in a wasteland. But that is demonstrably untrue. I have authored three books and three children's books. I have edited manuscripts and collated poetry anthologies. I have performed as a poet and musician at local and international literary and music festivals. I have played with symphony orchestras around the country. Yet, I am troubled by my problematic and persistent underperformance. I need to account for the nature of my professional failure, to weigh it against whatever success there has been, and to examine my conflicted obsession with being an artist. Perhaps I want to figure out how I might redeem myself. Such redemption could only be in my own eyes, as nobody else is concerned with my particulars.

***

This yarn wears me down. I need a better story. When the wool runs out, I hunt for the centre pull of the next ball. I prise the ball open at one end, insert a finger, probing for the pull skein, the start at the centre around which the entire ball is wound. When I get this right, the yarn flows easily as it unravels without effort from the inside. Today, the ball remains stable and does not roll around, catching shoe buckles and winding around table legs. Sometimes the ball collapses in on itself, reduced to a giant knot that gets progressively more difficult to untangle. I debate whether to unpick the whole lot and start something new.

***

It seems to me that when I try to distil what creative practice actually means, I am reckoning with the inevitable and intractable anguish of living in this age. I want to account for my own disaffection with life, but I don't have an answer. Is it lassitude that prevents me from starting or is it procrastination? Am I stuck in worn-out memories that, like a gramophone, can't pop out of a scratched groove? It's hard to tell, in the same way that it is easy to mistake anaemia for depression, or to confuse post-Covid malaise with the drugged feeling one gets with taking sinus medication during allergy season. Could this emptiness be a fallow field from which new forms of expression can grow?

The experience of being a working musician, writer, arts journalist, literary editor, music and poetry teacher, life coach, rowing coach and recreational crafter remains elementally weird and refuses neat categorisation. I am not this or that. I am both/and/all. I do many different things. I have specialist skills, yet I'm a generalist. I can't explain easily or adequately define what I do. I don't have a singular identity, yet I yearn to be exceptionally good at the various things I take on. That's before I consider who pays me. As a freelancer, financial planning has eluded me. Utterly. The anxiety of paying my way drains my energetic freedom. I long to submerge myself in what I call 'my real work'.

I remind myself that I'm also caring for my father, 81 (who has just had his fifth eye surgery), for my friend Chris, 74 (who underwent cardiac surgery), for my husband Tim, 64 (who had three hospital visits), and my partner Jim, 80 (who is regaining his balance after a hip replacement).

***

In the weeks after Mom dies, I buy many balls of yarn. Merino, cotton, flax, silk. I buy more and more. I know it's an obsession, but Mom's favourite shades call to me: teal, aquamarine, turquoise, sky blue.

My mother grew up in the dust and heat of Kimberley. She loved swimming in the sea more than anything. In my early memories, she carries me into the surf at Addington Beach. She holds me in her arms as she jumps over the waves, wading deeper and deeper. Her joy was complete in the water. Her delight filled my small body. This was my first experience of exploding bliss with the light bouncing off the water, all ripples and shimmer.

I buy hand-dyed bamboo yarn with names like 'watershed' and 'ocean', 'seashell' and 'mist'. I already have enough yarn to last me the rest of my days, but still I look at colourful skeins on the yarn websites.

I finish the sleeveless sweater and begin a shawl. I finish the shawl and start a hat: cast on and rib, pick up a stitch. I insert the needle, wind the yarn over, and bring the stitch through. Over and over. Time after time. The watery colours sparkle. Loops and speckles form swirls of light. I am knitting up the sea. My hands have the same shaped nails as my mother's. They never grow long. I now have her arthritic knobs on my knuckles, the same strong thumbs.

As I write this essay, I'm reaching for a sense of how to define the power of lived and remembered connections, wanting to find where and how these aspects belong together. My fingers slide across the keyboard, reaching for the words I choose, the words that choose me. I want to tie together the threads and strands of memories that have made me who I am as an artist. Since that first time I looked down into the orchestra and experienced the interplay of sound and movement, direction and spontaneity, with my father beside me, my life's course was set. The memory of him showing me how to play the recorder by closing the tone holes properly is close to me each time I pick up my bassoon. If my finger joints bend much further, will I be able to close the tone holes on the bassoon? Recollecting how Dad taught me to read music as a six-year-old tells me of my earliest excitement at being able to respond to instruction. This explains why I enjoy teaching. Unlocking another's potential is such a pure experience of love. It is soul work without regrets.

How will I knit and knot the vital elements of money and time, keystrokes and compulsion into something rich and meaningful? There is nothing single-minded in this combination of care and process, imagination and potential, entanglement and unravelling. I do not know how to comprehend my place in the world, yet I show up. I chant to myself: 'Do the work. Do it with love, even when it hurts, even when it makes no sense'.

***

Seldom organised and predictably messy, my life has been 'colourful'. It is also a privileged life. Order is elusive and guilt is a daily neurosis. All too often, I feel like the talentless servant in the scriptural parable who invokes his master's wrath because he buried the gold in the ground. Where do such terrible self-assessments come from? Teachers who beat out the rhythm on my body with rulers? Parents unable to contain their own sense of unworthiness? Living in a time where individual success is your personal responsibility?

There was an overwhelming sense that with great privilege comes great responsibility. It was my job to live up to my potential. I owed it to the God who had given me the talent to become a writer, a musician, an artist. There's a lot of muddled theology deeply wired into my neurology, and it's taken years of psychotherapy to unpack and defang that.

The creative outlets that came my way have placated some of the emotional turbulence that threatened to overwhelm me. Much of my life, I have tried to rearrange my face to avoid standing out in public. The despair and frustration that came with each failed audition, lost publication opportunity, missed boat or consolation prize was substantial. My underperformance was fertile soil for a lacerating internal critic who would banish my artist self to perpetual outer darkness. Sources of regret have been both external, with rejected submissions and unsuccessful orchestral auditions, and internal, with my own inability to generate new material and meet deadlines, my reluctance to practise my instrument, and my non-participation at events where I would probably be welcomed.

Despite the uncertainty and disappointment that is an inevitable part of being a working artist, there are wonderfully complex developments that open the way to deeper experiences and new creativity. Being an artist means entering a crucible, where the heat and compression and effort of surviving transform one's whole being. The fractured, fragmented experiences are still arduous and unwelcome, but after all this time, I know that a benevolent light suddenly, unexpectedly illuminates the darkness and a new possibility is briefly, but irrevocably, perceived. When Simon pats his leg after my solo landed well, I know I have been heard. There is a point to it all. When an editor says, 'Complex, brave and original work', or a reader says, 'Your story gave me goosebumps', I have been seen and I can go on.

Being an artist – whether you claim the title or not – is a complex and multifaceted existence, often baffling and unmanageable. I hope this exploration comforts those who yearn to realise their talent even as they doubt it, those who await recognition of their talent from external sources, that might or might not arrive – but Lord, when it does, I bow down and kiss the ground.

***

Plácido Domingo takes the podium slowly at the Operalia competition. He wears sneakers and gets confused about the repeats that are in and the cuts that are out. The assistant conductor explains again.

As each soloist in the opera competition walks on stage, he greets them with an immense smile. 'Welcome! How are you?' The competitors' voices are liquid gold. Sweet as honey. They are soaring, gliding, birds of light. The flute mimics the soprano. The tenor duets with the bassoon. The melody swoops and bounces from flute to oboe, clarinet to horn. How can I adequately describe this exquisite tension, this dance of sonority? What words can ever sufficiently convey the sensuality of the xylophone solo, the deep visceral resonance of trombones and tuba in tune, in chorus?

After each aria, Domingo looks at the singer on stage as if they were the one for whom he has waited his entire life. He touches his heart and says, 'Lovely singing. So lovely!' He thanks each soloist sincerely. He is unaffected and genuine. He is affectionate. I wait behind him as he exits the pit. He takes the stairs slowly. As we exit the theatre, I say, 'Thank you, Maestro. A lovely rehearsal'. He touches my arm and looks me in the eyes. He says, 'Beautiful playing. Just beautiful!'.

***

There's still something missing from my exploration of creative practice. If I pursue this line of enquiry, it will probably come through. If I can stay sane enough, long enough to do so, I might emerge. I might stay sober. What is sanity? What is sacred? I read. I listen to podcasts. I attend twelve-step meetings. I pray.

Perdita Finn speaks about storytelling in her book *Take Back the Magic: Conversations with the Unseen World*. In an interview with Ayana Young, Finn says:

> It's very hard to experience mercy and justice and love inside the short story of the single life. It's impossible to make sense of most lives within a single life [...] But for our ancient ancestors, for most Indigenous Peoples, they live inside the long story of their souls, which is not a linear story, with a beginning, a middle and an end, but a story that's about birth, death, and rebirth.

The impossibility of making sense resonates. These words encourage me, give me hope. By showing up for the process, be it art-making or conversation, teaching or listening, even though, and especially when, I don't know where I'm going, I can tolerate non-linearity and unknowing. I find myself led inexorably and inevitably to a kind of redemption where I sit with my despair and rage and befriend them. Embedded in the universe as a hologram, my questions and quarrels, risks and revelations are inverted and reinvented.

Could this be how we recover wisdom? By allowing and encouraging our creative urges and professional performance to merge and emerge from memory, from silence? In this earthly environment, society's multi-dimensional fractures and fragmented sensibilities can, perhaps, co-exist as sane and sacred chants, prayed incantations of possibility that are fractal repetitions of truth and hope and purpose.

Show up. Do the work of the soul, without trying to explain it or control it. Do it with a willing heart so that you can remember who you are ... Could it be this simple?

Bibliography

Carroll, Lewis. "Alice's Adventures in Wonderland." *Open Books*, 2007, www.openbks.com/alice-15-16.html.

Finn, Perdita. "Transcript: PERDITA FINN on the Long Story of Our Souls /353." Interview by Ayana Young. *For the Wild*, 25 October 2023, https://forthewild.world/podcast-transcripts/perdita-finn-on-the-long-story-of-our-souls-353.

Moore, Thomas. *Care of the Soul: A Guide for Cultivating Depth and Sacredness in Everyday Life*. Harper Collins, 1992.

Moore, Thomas and Patrick McA. "The Soul of Recovery." *YouTube*, uploaded by Friendly Circle Berlin, 22 December 2023, www.youtube.com/watch?v=f1Aknui-DqI.

Reviewing as Attentive Praxis
Wamuwi Mbao

In this essay, I consider the generative capacities of public prose, which is the term I use to hold in close consideration a wide range of reading, writing and speaking activities. Examples of public prose include literary journalism, book reviews, literary non-fiction (particularly in essay form), podcast discussions, book salons, festivals, and other forms of gathering. While this essay's focus is on reviewing, my broader proposition is that when we understand public prose as an experimental form of attentiveness, we reshape how we think about it as a literary practice that brings what is interpretable, contestable, or arguable in public life to the fore. I will discuss the possibility of an imperceptible but meaningful shift from regarding public prose as 'elevated seeing' – a kind of elitist framing activity practised by individuals who have been recognised publicly as being 'good' at what they do – to regarding it as a form of position-taking that recognises the need to create a space for listening, for giving time, and for holding other attentional practices that sustain or create alternative lifeworlds. If we understand that the public space afforded to talk, to express opinions, to critique and to confer value upon literature, has traditionally been dominated by privileged voices at the expense of the marginalised, then my sense is that thinking through what goes on in that critical sensibility might enable us to better understand what is at stake. If reviewing is to have any social relevance, then it needs to be available differently and for more people than those who have traditionally been able to afford the time-consuming labour and other attendant costs of paying close attention.

We might think of attentiveness as a praxis of storytelling in the following way. You read a review of a book you are planning to buy, or a book you have read and whose central ideas are expounded upon by a noted reviewer. As you read, you take note of the style, how the reviewer parses detail, the clarity of their argument, and whether they give away too much or too little of the book in question. Your position in relation to what you are reading may lead you to spot weak points, areas of omission, or other gaps that are themselves a factor of the author's position in relation to their subject. For instance, in a review penned by prominent South African writer Sisonke Msimang, she notes that the book, written by a White American author, is closely concerned with the intimate lives of two Black women. Msimang's reading robustly critiques the moments of narrative inattention that serve to reproduce racialised imbalances, and she uses her review to draw attention to the limits of the author's position as a White person in relation to what she was writing about.

I find Msimang's review a helpful one to think about, because it highlights that being a reviewer is to perform a certain kind of storytelling. That telling doesn't mean rehashing or paraphrasing the story under review. It means telling a story about why the book matters, and how it succeeds or fails in what it sets out to do. Reviewers often don't get this right, which is why many reviews tell you nothing you couldn't learn yourself. The work of conveying understanding in a review is essentially to create space for the capture and transfer of your positioned sense of your encounter with the book, while also ensuring space for your reader's attention in relation to the book you are reviewing.

My task here is to reflect on reviewing as a form of creative practice, embedded in the twinned activities of listening and attentiveness. I view the function of a literary review as something that, while elucidating the cultural value and social worth of a literary text, tries to make visible the various relationships of meaning that encircle and activate the lifeworlds to which the book speaks. These relationships of meaning exist between members of the imagined community of authors, readers and publishers (the latter category enfolding both production and marketing). My thinking here takes its energy from Les Back's work on sociological attention,[1] but focuses on understanding book reviewing as a form of attentive practice that brings what is interpretable, contestable, or arguable to the fore by refusing to reproduce the taken-for-granted as the Real (*The Art of Listening* 1).

To be a reviewer, a close reader (with all the historical weight that term implies), for a literary publication is to participate in a trade that has, often unfairly, struggled to justify its instrumental value. Outside of a handful of major, well-funded publications (*The New Yorker*, *Granta*, *The London Review of Books*), contexts for public prose are plentiful but precarious. However, public-facing literary criticism is also a low-prestige business, poorly recompensed (if at all), as *n+1*, a print and digital magazine of literature, culture, and politics, observed in a pithy editorial:

> The pay? Maybe $250 for a shorter piece or if she's lucky, $600 or more for something longer. If she's never been a staff critic (and odds are she hasn't), and if she cares (and of course she cares!), she will undoubtedly toil for a poor wage-to-labour ratio. For starters, she has to read the book—or books, if she's assigned more than one to cover in the review. Then there are the author's previous books, and if she's really thorough, reviews of the author's previous books, as well as interviews, early work, and other miscellany. For a 1,200-word review, it could take a week to write, maybe two if she tends to over prepare. For a career survey, or a review essay in one of the big publications, it could take months or a year to finish (and to get paid). Then factor in self-employment taxes, the unreliability of assignments, delays in payment, and cost of living. (The Editors)

This anxiety-provoking picture is immeasurably less rosy for writers based on the African continent, whose access to comparatively more lucrative and attention-generating publications based in the Northern hemisphere is relatively poor. The local publications that have held sway for the last two decades – *The Mail & Guardian*, *LitNet*, and the *Timeslive/News24* conglomerates – pay comparatively poor rates, and most of these have substantially reduced their page share for reviews in recent years.

By most accounts, book reviewing in its traditional sense is taking strain. The locus of the 'literary-intellectual-commercial space', to use Lee Siegel's compound phrase, has shifted away from newspapers and other print publications towards digital media. Literary outlets willing and able to devote space and resources to complex reviews of literature have dwindled in recent years. Internationally and locally, publishing sites have shuttered their doors, gone on hiatus, or been rationalised into near non-existence as funding dried up. In 2022, the New York–based *Astra* literary magazine – launched to great fanfare, with high profile contributions from

Elif Batuman, Ottessa Moshfegh, Mariana Enríquez, Raven Leilani and other illustrious names, and rave reviews on social media – was suddenly defunded and shut down before its third issue. Meanwhile, in South Africa, the leftist digital platform *New Frame* proved a bright-burning space for well-funded longer-form writing and intellectual critique, before it too folded amid ignominious squabbling and pulled funding. The website is at present no longer online, meaning that a valuable repository of recent writing on South African sociopolitical happenings has potentially been lost forever.

The picture is not unremittingly dire, however; there are still sites that hold a space for public-facing writing. Many of these sites straddle the artificial divide between academic journals (with their tethering to idiolect and disciplinary structuring) and journalism sites that cater to a wider readership. Online-facing platforms such as *herri, The Johannesburg Review of Books, Africa is a Country,* the *Los Angeles Review of Books, Brittle Paper, Doek* and *Lolwe,* among others, are public contexts that constantly wax and wane in the practice of paying attention to texts that shift the terms on which social difference is understood and engaged. In other senses, that the present is hyper-online has also meant that many of the former delineation points between 'high culture' and 'middlebrow' spaces have dissolved. If this dissolution has threatened the cultural high ground of the professional critic (many people are more likely to get their literary news from *BookTok* than from the **Insert-Your-City-of-Choice* Review of Books*), it has also broadened the terrain. As Merve Emre points out:

> It is not unusual to stumble upon an essay on Goodreads or Substack that is just as perceptive as academic or journalistic essays, which, no matter how many rounds of revision they undergo, reflect the *déformation professionnelle* of their respective spheres. Nor should we limit the domain of criticism to writing. Anyone who has taught students knows that the best critiques are often produced in the classroom, through conversations in which one is trying to demonstrate how a poem or a novel works to many different readers, few of whom aspire to write or to join the professoriat. ("Everyone's a Critic" 62)

Having outlined this context, I will situate my experience by way of an extended story about my teaching. Much has been written over time about the shifts in the role and place of public prose in its various forms and manifestations. I tend to narrow the focus of my teaching to public-facing literary criticism, a vocational mode of critical thinking that includes literary journalism, book reviews, radio programmes, panel discussions and podcasts. My use of the anecdotal element in what follows below allows for the plotting of certain through-lines within a model that is attentive to the world, while acknowledging it as partial in its notation of events.

Reviews as a Classroom Tool

Over the past three years, I have been teaching a semesterised course to second-year students. The course draws from a selection of other courses I have taught, primarily (but not only) at undergraduate level, for almost a decade. In these courses, I require my students to engage theoretically and creatively with the book review as a genre of public thought, by asking a simple preliminary question: what is this writer doing? I may phrase this question differently according to the requirements of the course, what I want to impart, what I consider it salient for students to grasp or grapple with, or where I want to lead a discussion. What I always strive to convey is that the discipline in which we are working has to do with the history of stories, why we tell them, and how we might learn to tell better ones by learning to listen differently to what is placed before us.

The concept of the story is a building block for all my teaching, and works particularly well in this second-year module. I remind my students that stories are everywhere: we bring them with us wherever we go, and they circulate around or between us. Some stories radiate or preserve or sustain or give credence to particular ways of being in the world. Other stories interrupt harmful attachments or draw our notice towards what has been overlooked or elided. Over our time in the classroom, we work towards an understanding of how stories shape the popular imagination in interesting and important ways. Stories guide us on how to respond to events – catastrophes, calamities and the like – when they happen. But we can only make sense of these stories when we give due and patient attention to them. As Rebecca Solnit proposes, 'Attention itself comes from attend, which means to not just show up but to stay, and attention is at least the beginning of respect'.

From this launchpad, we can then begin to coagulate an idea of the book review as a model for how we might pay attention. I present students with examples of reviews that I have curated, drawn from both local and international sources. I don't limit the objects of review, initially: reviews of television series, or music albums, or films, can be literary in their expression, just as well as traditional book reviews.

In my discussions with these students, who have committed to being trained by us in the expression and rigour of 'professional' reading and writing, some – who feel themselves in the pull of a collective free-falling – want to know what avenues exist for them to place their ideas in the world. (In other words, what will arrest that fall.) This is a vexing question to which the answer is always partially unsatisfactory – in the context of the Capitalocene, the rapid decanting of value from the Arts, the widespread (euphemistic) rationalisations, the redirection of students toward more 'useful' subjects, and the overall increasing precariousness of the humanities as a discipline. The sense of an inexorable garbaging in the face of an increasingly disordered higher education system, which students approach in an instrumentalised how-do-I-use-this-to-get-that way, has conversely meant that it is rewarding to teach world-expanding forms of reading/writing that scan as 'practical' to them. I always frame my response by pointing out that the years they spend with us constitute a training in critical literacy, and that this training is helpful for seeing and hearing beyond the unhelpful fantasies the current configuration of life is still directing them to follow.

I anchor my pedagogical approach in Edward Said's trenchant assertion:

> An imprecise, not very concrete hold on language and reality produces a more easily governable, accepting citizen, who has become not a participant in the society, but an always hungry consumer. Literate, critical education has an extraordinarily important role to play in providing the instrument of resistance to this and, it must be said plainly, in providing a means of self-defense. (11)

Thus, for as long as books remain part of the public sphere, there will be a need to attend to them as being important contributions to the transformative circulation of ideas in the social environment. In class discussions, I tell students that, while in many senses, the economy of attention has moved towards other forms with quicker circuits of interest and payoff, book reviewing (and other forms of close attention) persist and should be encouraged as genres that make available different, more patient models of engaging with the world.

My classes proceed from the starting point that there are phenomena in the world that might be interesting to historicise and find meanings for, through absorption, speculation, discussion, debate and play. I am interested in thinking about these phenomena because I believe they generate challenging conversations about reading and paying attention, in relation to which students can position themselves. In these classes, the book review becomes a particularly useful way of engaging the students' sense of the ordinary world, because through performing the kind of reading we do for a review, in which some of the things we take for granted are defamiliarised or given new textures, we learn to think about the ongoing ordinary in more complex ways.

In one class, for example, we read sections of Joan Didion's *The White Album* alongside contemporary reviews of the collection that appeared in the public press, in order to see where we might find congruences between how contemporary critics often unfavourably perceived Didion's account of the long dissolution of the optimism of the 1960s' in the wake of radical social change, and how critics today unwittingly express their alienation from a world that refuses to cohere. We could ask what it would mean for Martin Amis, writing in 1980, to describe *The White Album* as 'a distinctly female contribution to the new New Journalism', or what significance we read into the contemporary *New York Times* review spending an inordinate amount of word space linking Didion's physicality to that of her various characters:

> Wearing a faded blue sweatshirt over brown corduroy levis, Didion at 44 strikes anyone who sees her for the first time as the embodiment of the women in her novels[:] like Lily McClellan in "Run River", she is 'strikingly frail' (Didion is 5 feet 2, and

> weighs 95 pounds); like Maria in "Play It as It Lays", she used to chain-smoke and wear chiffon scarves over her red hair; and like Charlotte in "A Book of Common Prayer", she possesses "an extreme and volatile thinness … she was a woman … with a body that masqueraded as that of a young girl."
>
> There is a certain sadness in the face that indicates a susceptibility to what she calls 'early morning dread'; even indoors, she wears oversized sunglasses to protect her light-sensitive eyes. An almost Southern softness lingers in her voice – she identifies it as an Okie accent picked up in Sacramento high schools – and bright laughter punctuates her unfinished sentences. It is a voice so soft, so tentative at times, that one frequently has to strain to hear her. (Kakutani)

In another class, we read Lauren Oyler's hatchet-job review of Jia Tolentino's essay collection *Trick Mirror*, as a way into the meaning of virality in the literary world. In each case, we are taking as our starting point a review, and using it to model a scene that is more familiar, whether that be a question about how women are perceived in the public sphere, or what the role and authority of the literary critic is in the online age.

In a sense, I am asking my students to think together about literary journalism as a way of being attentive to the present world. In some of these classes, we break down what happens when we read from a reviewer's position: I posit that the reviewer, in their writing, tries to situate the reader's attention by paying attention to the dispositions, attitudes, tones, or modes of address that appear in the work. I suggest to the students that to read like a critic (such as a book reviewer) is to be decisively present, to listen for what is worth drawing out, what is worth conveying, what might be of interest, in relation to the current world. As we discuss in class, this kind of literary criticism isn't always about shining a light on what is new: it may be about creating an intellectual conversation between an older work and our present-day context. Or it may be about reading something against its own grain: if the text inclines towards a brisk, superficial read, or seems to be saying something obvious, then what does a slower, more considered read reveal? If we read differently and more attentively, will what we read communicate something else?

With that in mind, what would it mean to think about reviewing as the craft of responding politically to a text? Thinking this way means treating the review as a genre of public thought that makes meaning through attentiveness. That meaning-making is often a privileged position is clear: the reviewer's view is elevated; the reviewer assumes a particular authority to make decisive claims about the newness of a given work, how it hews itself to convention or what has been overlooked in the readings of others. We talk about reviewing as a way to tell what might be general in things that read as specific: a review like Msimang's, say, is also a way to talk about the dearth of discussion on post-Apartheid racialised intimacies.

Students in these classes are from diverse academic backgrounds in which the ability to read for meaning might be wielded to different ends. Many of them are primary readers, by which I mean that history has crafted their reading habits as peripatetic and motivated primarily by available time, energy and inclination. These things might be affected by the insistences of their classes and other scholarly activities, or aided by works they have recently enjoyed during their secondary school years, or that enabled escapism from the demands of the present. In many cases, they are incurious readers who have been socialised into viewing reading as a minor utility, rather than something of public value. Some students confess to not having read a complete book, or to being unsure if they could recognise that the kind of reading enacted in a review might be helpful in other contexts of the lived world. In most cases, they are not inattentive students, but rather students whose reading has been configured by an attention economy pitched towards rapid, surface-oriented consumption.

By reading together, we cultivate new attention practices. In shorter class-bound experiments, and in longer exercises that encourage them to extend the work beyond the classroom, we practise thinking about what it means to read with attention to the world. We look for and engage different examples of reviews, including those that praise and those that damn. We read and discuss together, sharing what we find surprising or unexpected, what we learn or what confounds, delights or perplexes us as we read. A typical class will see us read a piece together, often repeatedly, always out loud, or in smaller groups. I outline to the students the various ways in which the reviewer gives time to the book's formal choices and decisions. We work together to try and recognise how a reviewer enlists our attention as readers. By the end of the class, if things go well, we should have some sense of how to read both critically and fairly, and what robust criticism looks like.

This last point is important because it is possible to expose students to a kind of critical literacy they can use to grapple better with the rules of attention that structure their worlds. I am aware that in doing this, I risk creating a kind of false equivocation – what Emre, citing Nabokov, parses as the 'bad reader' (the students) compared to the aspirational 'good' reader (the critic). Initially, students tend to respond to being presented with examples of 'good' reading/writing by trying to figure out the performative conventions of what they are engaging with. In other words, when asked to produce their own reviews, they invariably produce anodyne summaries of the books they are 'reviewing', or they hesitate to bring their own knowledge to what they are writing – perhaps out of reluctance to untether themselves from the book under review. They usually prefer to defer authority to the text, and in many cases are unsure about what to extract from the displays of subjectivity they have witnessed in the reviews that I provide to them. In other words, presented with a review by James Wood, for example, they try, with varying degrees of skill, to replicate the high seriousness they registered in his work, rather than seeing the far-reaching elasticity of Wood's writing.

Over the course of a semester, we think in various ways about how to build the kind of self-reflexivity that makes a book review less wooden and formulaic. In one exercise, we read a short story quickly, and then write a time-limited response. Then the students are given more time to read the story again, and more time to write a more meaningful response. It has been insightful to observe students learn that complexity is a desired outcome, that it is okay not to have pat answers or quick summaries for what one has read, and that the working through of the thoughts one has in relation to a text can itself be a creative thing. By seeing how a review becomes an infrastructure for understanding the world, many of them begin to grasp the importance of complex, expansive reading, and the possibility of arriving at conclusions that are, in Back's terms, 'historically situated, reflective, contestable, uncomfortable, partisan and fraught' (*The Art of Listening* 22).

The task then, is to understand this sort of reading as an interruption that calls the ordinary into question. I have, in seminar workshops, asked students to write their own partial review, of the introduction to *The White Album*. As they write, I ask them to consider why they think Didion chose to say, 'we tell ourselves stories in order to live', rather than just saying, 'life is made up of stories'. This question sets up a moment of intellectual risk where the answers are at first tentative and incipient, then more confident – and we build a conversation about cultural capital and how our apprehension of intimacy, vulnerability and the personal has shifted in an age of precarity.[2] Because Didion is an obvious example, she is also proof that even obvious examples may be leveraged for their bridge-building: in this case, a bridge between the abandonment of the inherited writing register with which students have been inculcated (witnessed always as a hewing towards the bland impersonal passive voice), and the lively self-conscious first-person used to such good effect in Didion's work.

A constant point of reference in these classes is that our modern sociality occurs in an information-saturated context – one that demands coherent (and often over-simplified) narratives. A key theme carried across many of the contemporary book reviews we read in class, concerns the ways in which the extant stories no longer seem to have a necessary traction. We think together about how a certain kind of story has often been told about South Africa's transition to democracy, and how trying to live that story (with its familiar placeholders – the Rainbow Nation, post-Apartheid) has resulted in the scenes of disaffection we see today. My hope is that students exiting the course understand how attention can be – to borrow from Lauren Berlant – 'a mode, resource and effect of how worlds are built' (Demeyer 96).

Reviews as a Way to Follow Literature

For those of us who do review work, while also being practitioners of literary studies in institutions of higher learning, our outputs are often received with indifference: 'at best, they're a "public service"; at worst they could raise suspicions that [you're] not "serious"' (The Editors). Book reviews are largely excluded from the stocktaking research output infrastructures that universities operate. Writing public prose, with its different configurations of taking and giving attention, is often accorded the same value as having a hobby. As Freeden Blume Oeur argues, 'the academy valorises talking above listening. You must *assert* yourself in a conversation. One must clearly carve out space for oneself and state one's *intervention*. We're encouraged to *force listening upon others*, to make sure that we are heard' (496; emphases in original).

In this context, reviewing books is attentional labour that falls outside of all the meaningful remunerative frameworks: within the professionalised world of university service, one is never paid when one reviews for academic journals (whose funding may be poor or ringfenced and subsidised in ways that don't include rewarding those who do the work); and review work, both within and without the university, rarely counts for the point-accruing or subsidy-accessing frameworks that structure the academy's conservatively defined auditing processes. As Keyan Tomaselli avers, '[i]n South Africa, only "full" research outputs count: reviews, review essays, research letters, editorials and commentaries are often considered distractions'. However, because literary criticism was professionalised within the university, my day job as a university lecturer bestows a particular kind of legitimating energy upon what I do in the world of public prose: my opinions on books are validated by my professional training, despite there being a canyon separating the two modes of writing. Being tethered to a department grants one a captive market – a limited public – for one's work product, which is a kind of thinking with/thinking about language distributed primarily for the engagement of other people similarly employed. In this sense, the public prose work I do is a helpful counter to the siloing effects of university training.

By my count, I have written over 60 long-form book reviews for *The Johannesburg Review of Books* since the publication was established in 2017. These reviews represent rigorous, scrutinised performances of creative critical reading that are widely read and shared (in most cases, greatly more so than the research articles I publish in scholarly journals). They have provided a valuable space for trying out different kinds of writing, for experimenting with form and address, and for generating ideas in proximity to new literary works. As a participant in the paraliterary economy of which reviews form an important part, my reading contexts are enlarged by the work that goes into reviewing:

a) Reviewers receive books from publishers for potential review selection. It is helpful to maintain a sense of what is in the market in order to establish whether a work under review is groundbreaking, or merely echoing a trend. One year, for example, may produce a slew of historical fiction novels, and this context matters if you're exceptionalising a book in your review.
b) Knowing what's flying off the shelves, what's going viral, or what the prevailing mood is seizing upon, is an asset for teaching, allowing one to structure a discussion using the contemporary as a scene of relation, or to test out ideas using sustainable models and examples that have purchase for students.
c) An immediate, if unintended, benefit of occupying a different temporal frame in relation to the release and distribution of books is that one can bring an interesting book into a course syllabus with much lower lag-time than would otherwise be the case. Most of the courses I teach in my academic work involve recent texts that I initially encountered not in my institutional work, but in my role as a reviewer.

To be a literary reviewer is to follow books around in a way that acknowledges the quiddity of the book more closely. It is also to access books in different scenes, and to pay attention to them in contexts not structured by the imperatives of a controlling academic discipline. Of course, one need not review books in order to read attentively, or to put it another way, reviewing is but one of numerous possible ways of paying attention to the world through literature. But as a reviewer, I now necessarily read more widely and more consistently around what's current, and I am more than ever aware of the ways different publics might encounter a book, and how this compels one to read and practise for more than just academic readers (or those we are training to become academic readers). Reading in this way untethers one from the primary goal of a professionalised discipline, which is to establish conventions for repeatability and citational reference. Before I took up reviewing in earnest, my syllabus content was self-regulated rather clumsily around the unspoken imperative of this goal: what my colleagues teach, what is convenient to fit into the infrastructure of teaching and studying for two or three years, how I secure a niche for myself (thus justifying my value), and so on. But working as a reviewer turns one away from these deadening demands and imperatives, and orients one towards different arrangements and understandings of what's vital, resonant or emergent in what passes as conventional.

Conclusion

When pausing to consider the idea of attention as a kind of transformative infrastructure, my sense is that only in the most provisional of ways is it possible to position the book review as a useful hinterland, framing the kind of artful attention I have in mind. But this very provisionality is what permits an elastic stretch and slowing-down that allows us to read feelings and ideas that are still ongoing, still unfinished, still subject to change. It is not my desire to install reviewing as a device that ameliorates crisis or acts as a lever against the corrosive logics of society. What appeals, rather, is the notion that we can see in public prose more generally, and in reviewing specifically, a shared project of critical literacy that is inventive and accessible, and that calls attention to falsely or reductively cohesive scenes of living. As Emre puts it, such a project 'would touch our ordinary activities and conversations; our habits, our routines; the well-worn fabric of our lives' ("The Function of Criticism"). By paying attention this way, we create the infrastructures for the world we want to live in.

Endnotes

1. Back argues for paying attention to 'the fragments, the voices and stories that are otherwise passed over and ignored' (*The Art of Listening* 1).
2. Judith Butler explains precarity as 'the politically induced condition in which certain populations suffer from failing social and economic networks […] becoming differentially exposed to injury, violence, and death' (*Frames of War* 25). Precarity names the condition in which some groups of people are exposed to greater risk than others.

Bibliography

Amis, Martin. "Joan Didion's Style." *London Review of Books*, vol. 2, no. 2, 7 February 1980, www.lrb.co.uk/the-paper/v02/n02/martin-amis/joan-didion-s-style.

Back, Les. "Attentiveness as a Vocation: An Interview with Les Back." Interview by Ruiz Rafico. *Seachange*, vol. 1, no. 3, 2012, pp. 98–113.

---. *The Art of Listening*. Oxford, Berg Publishers, 2007.

Berlant, Lauren. "Lauren Berlant on Intimacy as World-Making." Interview by Hans Demeyer. *Extra Extra*, no. 16, 2021, pp. 90–100, extraextramagazine.com/talk/lauren-berlant-on-intimacy-as-worldmaking/.

Butler, Judith. *Frames of War: When is Life Grievable?* London, Verso, 2009.

Emre, Merve. "Everyone's a Critic." *The New Yorker*, vol. 98, no. 46, 23 January 2023, p. 62. *Gale Literature Resource Center*, https://go-gale-com.ez.sun.ac.za/ps/i.o?p=LitRC&u=27uos&id=GALE|A735244734&v=2.1&it=r&sid=summon.

---. "Good Reader, Bad Reader." *The Boston Review*, 27 November 2017, www.bostonreview.net/articles/merve-emre-good-reader-bad-reader/.

---. "The Function of Criticism at the Present Time." *Vinduet*, 6 September 2023, www.vinduet.no/engelsk-versjon/the-function-of-criticism-at-the-present-time-lecture-by-merve-emre/.

Kakutani, Michiko. "Joan Didion: Staking out California." *The New York Times*, 10 June 1979, www.nytimes.com/1979/06/10/books/didion-calif.html.

Msimang, Sisonke. "No Justice, No Peace." *Foreign Policy*, 27 November 2022, foreignpolicy.com/2022/11/27/south-africa-trc-reitz-ufs-jansen-race-justice-reconciliation/.

Oeur, Freeden Blume. "The Art of Listening: Notes on Feminist Book Reviewing." *Contemporary Sociology*, vol. 52, no. 6, 2023, pp. 495–500. *Sage Journals*, doi.org/10.1177/00943061231205662.

Oyler, Lauren. "Ha ha! Ha ha!" *London Review of Books*, vol. 42, no. 2, 23 January 2020, www.lrb.co.uk/the-paper/v42/n02/lauren-oyler/ha-ha!-ha-ha.

Said, Edward W. *The End of the Peace Process: Oslo and After*. United Kingdom, Pantheon Books, 2000.

Siegel, Lee. "Burying the Hatchet." *The New Yorker*, 25 September 2013, www.newyorker.com/books/page-turner/burying-the-hatchet.

Solnit, Rebecca. "Respectfully." *Center for Humans and Nature*, 28 September 2020, www.humansandnature.org/respectfully.

The Editors. "Critical Attrition." *n+1*, 21 July 2021, www.nplusonemag.com/issue-40/the-intellectual-situation/critical-attrition/#fn1-13668.

Tomaselli, Keyan G. "Book reviewing should be a measurable academic output." *University World News Africa Edition*, 21 April 2022, www.universityworldnews.com/post.php?story=20220418043931171.

The Writer as Reader: Reflections on Poetry and the Avant-Garde
Simon van Schalkwyk

When I was invited to contribute an essay on the subject of 'The Writer as Reader', I initially wondered what it would mean to imagine a writer who did not read, readers who did not write, and writing that resisted being read. This seemed like a useful approach: consider the limits of writing and reading to set the conditions for what it might mean to write and to read in a clearer light.

I found myself thinking about Jorge Luis Borges's Pierre Menard, a writer who set himself the task of reproducing exactly a partial duplicate of Miguel de Cervantes's *Don Quixote*, but without reading, re-reading or copying the original text (62-71). By immersing himself so completely in the contexts familiar to Cervantes's world, Menard wagers that undertaking any act of writing would inevitably produce a fragment of the Quixote. Menard, as Borges's story wryly suggests, manages to succeed and fail at the same time. I also thought about Woody Allen's film *Bullets Over Broadway*, in which a hapless dramatist, David Shayne, finds that an illiterate mob-enforcer, Cheech, is probably the greatest playwright of our times.

Eventually, I thought about poetry – a form of writing that, for any number of reasons, I have always laboured to read, understand and write – and I thought about the history of a poetic version of the avant-garde, intent upon testing the limits of the legible.

***

The idea of writing something that looked like script but was actually scribble, can be traced back to two Chinese calligraphers from the Tang Dynasty. Zhang Zu and Huaisu (or 'Crazy Zhang' and 'Drunken Su') were apocryphally known to produce visually arresting but semantically impenetrable (or *asemic*) calligraphic forms – Zhang using his own hair,

Huaisu deploying banana leaves – while under the influence of alcohol or high artistic inspiration (Fenstermaker). Writing that minimises or obscures clear semantic content – meaning, information or sense – invites the reader to reflect upon stylistic aspects of the letter, word, phrase or sentence: their auditory qualities and visual dimensions, their potential as image, metaphor, symbol or sound.

A similar interest in exploring *how* a medium operates – whether this medium be written or spoken language, sound or music, paint, sculptural materials, video or, say, the Internet – rather than focusing primarily on that medium's communicative potential informs the practices of any number of contemporary avant-gardes flourishing in the blasted ruins of early- and mid-twentieth century Europe. Consider, for example, the calligrammatic word-pictures of concrete poetry, which drew attention to language's potential to form mimetic images of its subject. (John Hollander's "Swan and Shadow", a poem in which semantic content imitates the visual content, is a recognisable example.) The automatic writing of the Surrealists, Dadaist cut-ups, and the late-blooming Lettrist intervention, are similar examples of mid-twentieth century attempts to liberate letters from what were regarded as the restrictive limitations of semantic imposition so as to release their asemic value as sound, shape, mark or glyph.

As if in response, the Oulipo movement emerged to investigate how written meanings might be contrived via the application of 'constraints' (Terry xix) – an inventive series of rules ranging from the Algol poem (which uses only the 24-word vocabulary of the computer language ALGOL (Algorithmically Oriented language)) to the well-known equation n+7, which replaces each noun in a poem or other written work with the seventh subsequent noun in any given vocabulary.

My interest in poetic writing has been and remains informed by my awareness of these and other procedures designed to disrupt or dislocate language's primarily semantic function, in large part because I have always regarded poetry as that form of language in which the boundaries between sound and sense are particularly porous.

In my weaker moments, I find myself thinking that the easiest way to understand Lettrism and its aftermath is by googling 'Mall Art' (or actually visiting a mall) or listening to an ASMR podcast. For Oulipo, I imagine playing any kind of rule-bound game, reading an IKEA instruction manual, or doing whatever it is you're meant to be doing at work. Eulogies for the death of the avant-garde are far from uncommon, especially for an avant-garde that, hoping to seize the power of novelty for itself, frequently dances on the grave of its immediate predecessors. Yet, far from representing some thrilling alternative to bourgeois complacencies, and far from being an exhausted enterprise or aesthetic dead-end, what had once been recognised as the avant-garde is arguably so familiar by now, so ingrained and assimilated into the fabric of everyday middle-class life, as to seem entirely unremarkable.

David Lehman makes a similar point in *The Last Avant-Garde: The Making of the New York School of Poets*, suggesting that the avant-garde itself has been absorbed into the machinery of commerce and consumption, such that it has long since lost whatever capacity for shock it might once have had. 'The survival of the avant-garde as a vague term of approbation', he writes,

> confirms the suspicion that avant-garde art – the real embattled underground thing – has lost the force it formerly had in our cultural life. The avant-garde is dead, we're told, because there is no longer any significant resistance to artistic innovation. Everything is instantly accepted, absorbed, glorified, bought, sold, copied, recycled, trashed. Such is the fate of artifacts in an age of electronic transmission. The time-honored bohemian battle-cry, 'Shock the bourgeoisie', requires the existence of a middle-class capable of being shocked and shamed, but Court TV and supermarket tabloids have rendered that impossible. (287-288)

John Ashbery, a central subject of Lehman's study alongside his fellow New York School poets Frank O'Hara, James Schuyler and Kenneth Koch, takes a more clearly despairing view of the matter. 'It is no longer possible, or it seems no longer possible', he glumly complains, 'for an important avant-garde artist to go unrecognised. And, sadly enough, his creative life expectancy has dwindled correspondingly, since artists are no fun once they have been discovered' (qtd. in Lehman 283).

Lehman's and Ashbery's remarks continue to inform my thinking about reading and writing. The questions they raise about the avant-garde remain useful. How, I wonder, does one position oneself in relation to an avant-gardist sensibility that, because it seems paradoxically both dead and alive, holds the same fascination as zombies and viruses? How, in other words, might readers and writers position themselves in response to the etiolation of the avant-garde's familiar oppositional role with respect to tradition and dominant contemporary forms of writing, and to the markets and marketplaces – once 'global' and now increasingly virtual – of late-stage capitalism?

I find it more convenient to think about the idea of 'positionality' in terms of 'attitude' or 'comportment'. If it is possible to detect a note of lament in both Lehman's and Ashbery's remarks, I wonder what it would mean to respond to the framing of the avant-garde as a spent force, not with despair but with relief or even joy. From this perspective, the writer or artist may find themselves unburdened of the avant-gardist obligation to remain always combative, oppositional and innovative – in other words, free to adopt a more relaxed, casually knowing, and perhaps even wryly bemused stance in relation to the more bombastic, splenetic and grandiose claims of various traditions – including, now (and for quite some time, in fact), the paradoxical 'tradition of the avant-garde'.

As someone who has found both reading and writing difficult, more provisional than practised, I have always regarded the avant-garde with decidedly mixed feelings. This essay therefore provides me with a timely opportunity to reflect, in a more personal way than I am usually accustomed, upon my own investment in a particular expression of avant-garde writing and art.

"At North Farm"

In my third year of undergraduate study, I attended a lecture on Postmodernism that focused on Ashbery's poem, "At North Farm" (301). The lecturer, a professor from England's 'grim North', would sometimes mention his working class aspir-ations and his investment in the New Left's neo-Marxist mash-up of dialectical materialism and Freudian psychoanalysis. Ashbery's poem, he suggested, was typically postmodern because it demonstrated the breakdown of causal links between one sentence and the next, one line and the next, one word and another. I understood the basic principle: every word, line and sentence of Ashbery's poem were slippery signifiers whose relationship to their referents – the world, other words, the sound-images, and concepts that comprised signs, signifiers, and signifieds – if they did not float entirely free of one another, were at least troublingly loosened from their conventional referential moorings.

"At North Farm", with its indefinite spatial referents and deictic pronouns, demonstrated the first part of the lecturer's claim plainly enough: 'Somewhere, someone is travelling toward you', the poem begins, 'At incredible speed' (301). Who is speaking? We do not know. Where are we? We do not know. Who is the traveller? We do not know. As for that 'you', does it refer self-reflexively to the mysterious and anonymous speaker of the poem's opening lines, or some unnamed addressee occupying the poem's imagined (if frustratingly indeterminate) setting? It is entirely possible that the 'you' refers to the poem's reader, but who is that, exactly? 'You' may refer to any of the poem's many readers; it may refer to 'me', one of those readers and also the writer of this essay; or it may refer to 'you', the person currently involved in the act of reading this essay.

The poem's fuzzy logic gets even fuzzier. Who, for example, is the mysterious traveller? What does it mean to travel 'furiously'? Is it possible for intransitive verbs to be invested with adjectival properties? That the traveller travels 'day and night' through all kinds of terrain and weather seems both vaguely possible and vaguely implausible, and the imprecision of 'incredible speed' only serves to complicate the matter further – 'incredible speed' in relation to what, exactly? What, precisely, is 'speed'? And does 'speed' even matter? As the speaker of the poem suggests, the traveller may not even know where he (she? it?) is supposed to be heading, or who she/he/it is travelling to meet. If the traveller is meant to deliver something (some indeterminate 'thing') to the poem's 'you', this 'you' is given little in the way of knowing what, exactly, it is they are meant to receive. The traveller may not know either.

The poem's second stanza is similarly bizarre. Silos of grain stand in a desert that is nevertheless bursting with water, fish and birds. Someone wonders if it is 'enough / That the dish of milk is set out at night / That we think of him sometimes, / Sometimes and always, with mixed feelings?' (301). The milk dish has been a particular point of interest for critics of Ashbery's poem, an opportunity to fill in a poetic blank, potentially rich in tantalising literary allusion: some have suggested, with unfounded pragmatism, that it might be for a cat; others, showily displaying their familiarity with Irish folklore, have argued that it is for a goblin (a more interesting but similarly baseless claim).

A more practical consideration, given the opening stanza's investment in keeping things as vague as possible, would be to wonder whether the speaker of the second stanza is the same as the speaker encountered in the first, or whether the pronoun 'we' should be understood as a collective pronoun or a paradoxically singular one. In the editorial sense, in other words, 'we' might suggest that the speaker – far from being the coherent, self-present and agentic subject valorised by Western liberal democracy – is actually little more than an instrumental spokesperson or representative for some shadowy collective or institution. But if the 'we' happens to be a royal 'we', it should be understood to refer self-reflexively to a figure of singular, supremely elevated status.

The fact is that there is simply no way of knowing how the pronoun should be understood. The same goes for the pronoun 'him' that enters the poem in the final couple of lines: does the third person pronoun here refer to the poem's inaugural 'someone', the mysterious traveller, or the frustratingly indefinite 'you' of the first stanza? Or does it refer to someone else entirely? It comes as a relief, perhaps, to find that we (or perhaps only some of us, or maybe just I) can at least understand what it means to think about others 'sometimes and always, with mixed feelings' (301).

If Ashbery's poem seemed clear as mud, the ways in which it elegantly evaded definitive meaning was at least easy enough to see. What I struggled to understand, however, was what any of this had to do with the lecturer's concluding salvo: 'Ashbery's poem', he declared, pausing dramatically as he prepared to deliver an Eng. Lit. Prof.'s best impression of a mic drop, 'mobilises semantic indeterminacy in ways that are inimical to the reifying forces of capitalism'.

… wait, what?

At the time, I could not possibly have known that an answer (of sorts) to the mystery of the professor's concluding statement would soon be travelling toward me, albeit at less than incredible speed …

The Horseman

Midway through my Honours degree, the English Department hosted a visiting scholar named Steve McCaffery. McCaffery, was part of a Canadian sound-poetry collective known as The Four Horsemen (the other three agents of the apocalypse were Rafael Barretto-Rivera, Paul Dutton, and bpNicol). I looked forward to his arrival because McCaffery's work overlapped with the L=A=N=G=U=A=G=E (or, more simply 'Language') school of writers and poets for whom the disjunctive lexical arrangements of Ashbery's first collection, *The Tennis Court Oath* (1956), represented an influential precursor of their particular and decidedly avant-gardist literary interventions.

By this time, my interest in Ashbery's work had begun to expand into a larger investment in mid-twentieth century American poetry. I was familiar with the poetic debates between so-called 'Formalist' and 'Confessional' poets that had come to characterise the field, and which had been memorably described by Robert Lowell in his 1960 National Book Award acceptance speech: 'Two poetries are now competing,' Lowell began,

> a cooked and a raw. The cooked, marvellously expert, often seems laboriously concocted to be tasted and digested by a graduate seminar. The raw, huge blood-dripping gobbets of unseasoned experience are dished up for midnight listeners. There is a poetry that can only be studied, and a poetry that can only be declaimed, a poetry of pedantry, and a poetry of scandal.

The argument alluded to by Lowell was central to the so-called 'poetry wars' of the American 1950s. As Marjorie Perloff explains, these 'wars'

> produced lively and engaging debates about the nature of poetry and poetics. What made a lineated text a poem? Did poems require some sort of closure, a circular structure with beginning, middle, and end? Should the poet speak in his or her own person, divulging intimate autobiographical details? ("Poetry on the Brink")

Ashbery (along with a third group of artists and writers referred to as the 'New York School') managed to occupy a position somewhere off to the side of these debates. By contrast, the Language writers appeared to press the conditions of the argument between Formalists and Confessionals to the limit. The arrival of Language poetry in the 1980s, Perloff continues, not only renewed but introduced new, more specialised contexts into the Raw vs. Cooked debate, 'demanding an end to transparency and straightforward reference in favour of ellipsis, indirection, and intellectual-political engagement' ("Poetry on the Brink").

***

In George Hartley's *Textual Politics and the Language Poets*, McCaffery is quoted as saying that Language poets generally share 'a community of concern for language as the centre of whatever activity poems might be' (xii). These 'language centered' concerns, Hartley explains, 'grow out of the rejection of the dominant model for poetic production and reception today – the so-called voice poem', which, he adds, 'depends on a model of communication that needs to be challenged: the notion that the poet (a self-present subject) transmits a particular message ("experience", "emotion") to a reader (another self-present subject) through a language which is neutral, transparent, "natural"' (xii).

Language writers, in other words, had little interest in whether a poet could express their feelings, attitudes and moods, whether formally or informally, and they had little time for poets who committed themselves to the task of producing formally pristine sonnets, villanelles, rondeaus and sestinas. Even the idea of a poet commenting self-reflexively in a poem on the limits of the sestina as a form would seem *infra dig* to a Language writer. The point wasn't so much that writers used language in order to produce various modes of writing or various expressions of subjective experience; by contrast, language already produced the conditions according to which such literary forms or personal expressions might occur in the first place. Language poets, as Charles Bernstein explains, hold that it is a 'distortion to imagine that knowledge has an "object" outside of the language of which it is a part – that words refer to "transcendental signifieds" rather than being part of a language, which itself produces meaning in terms of its grammar, its conventions, its "agreements in judgement"' (qtd. in Perloff, "The Word as Such" 219). Plainly stated, this means that we are all already coded by a language – a set of discursive rules, conventions and assumptions of a grammar that we cannot help but understand and, worse, that we all too frequently ignore or disavow.

The Language movement also held that such linguistic programming was deeply implicated in the similarly occulted operations of (whisper it) C=A=P=I=T=A=L=I=S=M. Its project, therefore, was simultaneously to disrupt and demystify the terms upon which the status quo rested. Ben Lerner, following Ron Silliman's early polemic on the matter, puts it this way:

> [T]he program of Language poetry was a kind of deprogramming, a weapon in class warfare: disjunctive prose poems would both illuminate and interrupt the linguistic norms of capitalism. [...] This short-circuiting of our reading habits was important [...] because absorptive texts that conceal their own production, texts that depend upon conventions of a unified voice or realist strategies of depiction, are the means by which 'capitalism passes on its preferred reality through language itself to individual speakers'. [...] For the Language poets generally, a smoothly written lyric or narrative poem might have progressive or revolutionary content, but it would nevertheless be reactionary in its reproduction of the norms of bourgeois representation. Laying bare the device was part of anticapitalist struggle. (18-19)

Accordingly, like the sleeper-agents in John Frankenheimer's *The Manchurian Candidate*, we have been brainwashed by a language that has been surreptitiously coded into us, and we act, unthinkingly and without any agency or will, in accordance with pre-programmed linguistic directives. The Language writers promised at least to reveal the programme's operative code.

***

In 1977, McCaffery led a symposium titled "The Politics of the Referent" in which he claimed that 'what Marx exposed as the fetishism of the commodity is the same mode of mystification that is enacted in the fetishism of the referent' (60). He carries on to say that, by 'eliminating [the] grammatical armament[s]' (67), Language-centred writing consequently managed to disrupt a normative poetic (and capitalistic) hegemony geared toward the uncritical consumption of ordinary-language linguistic fantasies. For McCaffery, it seemed, language itself *was* capitalism and to destroy language was to strike a blow on behalf of exploited workers across the world.

McCaffery and many other Language poets soon dialled back the force of the analogy they hoped to draw between commodity fetishes and poetic objects. This arguably occurred because their pronouncements struggled to pass muster in the crucible of intellectual and academic debate spurred by their initial provocations. As Timothy Kreiner explains, the emergence of Language writing coincided with the precise moment at which previously marginalised poetic voices reliant upon language's semantic potential were beginning to emerge. As a result, Language poetry, despite the value of its theoretical insights, could easily be regarded as a conservative retreat into a generic politics of form. For Kreiner, then, Language poets as much as their bourgeois antagonists, traded in a form of high theoretical literary elitism in ways that were surprisingly disarticulated from more politically pragmatic poetic alternatives.

***

All this is not to say that I didn't like the avant-garde or, more specifically, the particular expression of avant-gardist intensity focalised on Language writing. Language poems reminded me of my own efforts at 'poetic experimentation': perfectly acceptable poems that had come to seem despairingly, prosaically dull, clichéd and unoriginal and which, during long periods of uninspired creative torpor, I had decided to subject to a process of creative dismantling. My writing practice during times like these was frequently guided by the application of some half-baked Oulipian rule:

a) Make creative use of the TAB function and spacebar.
b) Use MS Word's strikethrough function to place certain words ~~under erasure~~.
c) Place parts of words in parentheses to form trenchantly new (s)words.
d) Delete adjectives/nouns/verbs/in/definite articles/commas/all punctuation
e) Apply only lower case or, during a Bidartian phase, ONLY CAPITALIZATION.
f) .epyt eht fo noitcerid eht htiw sgniht driew oD
g) Redact words like a deeply ▮▮▮▮ yet also ▮▮-crazy and ▮▮▮▮ racist ▮▮▮▮-era censor working for the ▮▮▮▮▮▮ Board.
h) Combine the worst part of one poem with the worst part of another.
i) Translate and back-translate idiomatic English expressions and colloquialisms like 'lifðu og lærðu' using English and Tagalog as translational media.
j) Substitute for the law of *le mot juste* the radical alternative, *le mauvais mot* (or, more radically still, *le mot de gauche*).
k) Replace ordinary, boring, everyday words with words derived from Theory: *aporia, chrestomathy, einfulhen, hamartia, shivering fragments.*

Sadly, there was no guarantee that my best efforts at 'experimentation' would make my writing any less terrible than it already was.

Still, I didn't mind McCaffery's efforts at Language, Concrete and Visual poems – phonemes of varying sizes and orientations that seemed to have been Spirographed across the page, or misprinted, the way photocopiers on the fritz sometimes overlay letters and words in combinations of magnetic color – cyan, magenta and green – like stereoscopic pentimenti designed to be looked at through 3-D glasses.

The poems weren't the problem; the inflated (or, perhaps, reductive) claims McCaffery and other Language poets made for them were. While I could see how Language writers foregrounded the reader's part in the production of the writing's potential meaning, I struggled to see how this was especially different, in kind, from a reader's more general co-production of the meaning of any text. And if foregrounding such readerly co-production was the point, I struggled to see how doing so could be regarded as a sort of revolutionary act, a kind of class warfare determined to undermine the extractive, exploitative and reifying forces of capitalism.

Would McCaffery be able to explain? Would I, by attending McCaffery's reading, somehow be inducted into the Revolution?

I hoped so.

S=P=I=D=E=R=S

I remember waiting outside the office that had been offered to McCaffery for the duration of his visit, for a consultation that he had kindly agreed to offer students interested in his work. I didn't have as much time as I would have liked because he spent an hour talking to a young man with long hair and a backpack filled with dried, long-stemmed flowers. When I finally entered the room, I must have asked all the wrong questions because he seemed slightly distracted, evasive, even bored. It turned out that he had to attend a reading in a few minutes' time, so he suggested that I buy copies of his books – *North of Intention* (a collection of selected essays) and *Seven Pages Missing* (a selection of previously published and uncollected poems, including examples of his concrete and visual poetics, sound poems and performance scores, and extracts from chapbooks).

As the reading began, another of the Department's professors – a lapsed Marxist and poet in his own right – set down a stack of exam papers which he proceeded to mark, loudly flipping the pages of each script, sighing audibly, and scribbling extensive marginal notes with surprisingly indignant force. Despite this distraction, I did my best to listen to McCaffery and Karen MacCormack – a neat woman with a fashionably complicated haircut – intone a series of words deliberately designed to seem as disconnected from each other as possible. When MacCormack enunciated the word $C=U=T$ – pausing to look at the audience as if to emphasise the significance of not just the meaning or the sound of the word but the phonic vitality of each individual phoneme – the lapsed Marxist impatiently gathered up his student papers, abruptly scraped his chair against the floor, and left the room. A brief, mildly embarrassed silence ensued before the reading continued to its end.

Later, I overheard McCaffery discussing the minor scene with another professor who remained committed to Classical Marxism's investment in the material bases for superstructural ideological symptoms. 'Sadly, yes,' he said, nodding gravely, 'the conservatism here is quite extraordinary'.

Later that week, I tried to visit McCaffery again. I found him in deep conversation with his host and another professor, a Classical Marxist who retained an anti-New Left commitment to the social base. McCaffery seemed concerned by a rash that had broken out on his left arm. The Neo-Marxist tried to reassure him that it was probably nothing. The Classical Marxist, however, looked at the rash over the bridge of his spectacles and said, 'Spiders'. This troubled McCaffery deeply. 'Spiders?' his voice quivered, and all three men bowed their heads in unison to inspect the rash. 'Spiders,' said the Classical Marxist, 'definitely, definitely spiders'.

A compelling scene, I thought, replete with dramatic irony: three professors so deeply invested in the finer points of Marxism that, like their predecessors in Paris, 1968, they failed to see the writing on the wall. McCaffery, who had made it his life's work to unhinge words from the doors of perception, seemed anxious enough to suggest that the phonemic chain 's=p=i=d=e=r=s' corresponded to the word 'spiders' which, in turn, corresponded to the creaturely thing capable of producing the stuff called 'bites', and that these words, those creaturely things, that stuff, shaped a perception of the body which, in turn, shaped that particular cast of mind capably represented by a series of phonemes capable of sound-imaging an abstract concept conventionally understood to mean 'c=o=n=c=e=r=n'.

But perhaps I had misconceived things. Perhaps the situation was more meta than I initially imagined. Who could possibly know what McCaffery thought of his predicament, or what he understood by words like 'superstructure', 'base' or 'spiders'? Who was to say that the three professors were not engaged in a kind of improvisational theatre, each of them deadpanning their way through a routine in which they recognised themselves with the sharp self-awareness familiar to a certain type of postmodern literary critic, once widely praised, as knowing participants? It was entirely possible, in other words, that the joke was on me, reading a scene for its effect as an unselfconscious irony when I should have recognised that the scene playing out before me was little more than a performance by three theorists of language who understood, with an air of dispirited resignation, that they were once again going through the motions expected of them by a language over which they had no control.

Returning to North Farm

In her account of "At North Farm", Helen Vendler avoids any attempt to link the poem to theoretical abstractions that might mobilise its anti-capitalist potential. Yet by reading the text in relation to a set of specifically poetic, linguistic and cultural values, I wonder if Vendler is any less guilty of the charge of setting poems within contextual matrices that are similarly abstract, similarly unpersuasive.

Describing the poem as a unique combination of cliché, poetic and folkloric allusion, and American plain-spokenness, she argues that the poem is significant *as poem* because of its relationship to a particular poetic *tradition*: 'We register at first the clichés', she begins,

> as we read 'incredible speed', 'desert heat', 'narrow passes', 'granaries … bursting', and 'mixed feelings'. These trip so easily on the tongue that we understand this drama to be something 'everyone knows' […]. No pleasure is sweeter in the ear than something new done to the old. Ashbery's deep literary dependencies escape cliché by the pure Americanness of his diction. (Vendler)

Using Ashbery's almost deadeningly colloquial 'Nothing grows here' as an example, Vendler reflects on a long poetic tradition in which drought and desolation have been described – from the 'stubble-plains' of Keats's "To Autumn" to 'the barrenness / Of the fertile thing that can attain no more' in Wallace Stevens's "Credences of Summer". These phrases, Vendler argues, are 'words used so memorably that they cannot be reused'. Nevertheless, she continues to suggest that it is impossible for a particular reader – Vendler identifies this reader as a 'middle-aged American', suggesting, perhaps, an American still capable of some proximal relation to the Dust Bowl and the Great Depression – not to recognise the quintessential Americanness of Ashbery's idiom: the flatness and despair of the most plain-spoken statement of fact, 'Nothing grows here' (301).

For Vendler, in other words, Ashbery's achievement lies in his ability to recast words so overcharged with the familiar meanings of poetic memory as to seem oppressively meaningless with a surprising (and surprisingly national) familiarity. Ironically, it is this familiarity that Vendler, drawing on the terms of the avant-garde, associates with the 'shock' of Ashbery's novelty.

Poems are commonly read in relation to other poems or poetic traditions. There is nothing especially *wrong* with this, but it is worth noting that a troubling spectre haunts this endeavour, threatening to cast the poet, if not all writers, into a potentially agonistic contest with canonised predecessors. Harold Bloom describes this contest as one in which a prospective poet or ephebe struggles against, swerves away from, revises and reclaims, the work of ancestral authorities in relation to a series of obscure terms: *clinamen*, *kenosis*, *tessera*, *askesis*, *apophrades* and *daemonization* (14-15). Following Bloom's theory, we should imagine the poet or writer as a slightly frazzled paranoiac behind the wheel of a car that must constantly swerve out of the way of yesterday's traffic.

Despite their differences, Vendler and the Language poets may be less different from one another than they first appear: they both read poems in relation to theoretically abstract concepts, contexts and received ideas – an idea of language as an irredeemable symptom of late capitalism on the one hand, a selective idea of American poetry on the other – that ultimately reflect their respective, curiously personal ideological preferences. Put differently, both Vendler and the Language writers may be understood as unacknowledged Oulipians, introducing their own rules to the game of poetic reading and writing. Anyone willing to follow the rules is allowed to play, and each player is rewarded with the satisfaction of arriving at meaningful conclusions about the game's success, value and worth. Sometimes, players familiar with one game might get bored and decide to form a breakaway faction, modifying familiar rules or inventing new rules for the game. It may even turn out that a key condition of the new game, one that allows it to be played at all, requires some dismissive acknowledgement of the rules of the games that have been left behind. Some games may even require the player to cast aspersions on the rules of a game played by others. But perhaps there are some versions of the game capable of recognising the game's history and how its self-satisfied confidence in its own terms and conditions has necessitated not only alternatives but, perhaps, also animosity.

Yet why should we think of reading and writing as a narrow

confrontation with a prior author, text or genre? Why should poetry always be *about poetry*? Why, similarly, should we think of language as slavishly implicated in the inescapable web of capital? Why not, instead, follow the cue of Bernadette Mayer, another writer associated with the New York School, who, during her involvement with the St. Marks Poetry Project, conducted poetry workshops that opened the field of allusion and resource to non-literary texts? As Mayer realised, 'poets were "starved" for other information' to the extent that '[i]t was a dream, that all the disciplines could enter into a dialogue' (qtd. in Champion). From this perspective, it is entirely possible to read the final line of Carol Ann Duffy's "Prayer" – 'Rockall. Malin. Dogger. Finisterre' (48) – as a platform from which to launch further inquiry into the broader historical and cultural or ecological significance of the shipping news, rather than to fuss over the question of how it demonstrates some kind of anxiety of influence when read in allusive relation to the opening line of Seamus Heaney's earlier "Glanmore Sonnet VII" – 'Dogger, Rockall, Malin, Irish Sea' (115).

***

It is obvious that words conventionally carry sense.

Yet in poetry, as has frequently been noted, lines never reach the end of the page; sentences break off unexpectedly or rejoin each other at the level of a line, disrupting more conventional notions of syntax; end-words echo each other as rhyme while sounds carom off earlier sounds. All this serves to foreground the artificial nature of language that is set to artistic rather than functional or plainly communicative purpose.

As for communication, in poetry, semantic meanings dissolve into ambiguities and musical phrases; assonance and alliteration draw our attention to sound as well as substance; simile claims that unlike things represented by words – ravens and writing desks, to use Lewis Carrol's well-known formulation – are more alike than they may seem at first glance; and metaphor insists, against all conventional logic, that the particularity of one thing is exactly the same as the particularity of something entirely unlike it.

I feel as if I have always retained the vague suspicion that the relationship between words and meaning, far from being plainly self-evident, was in fact haunted by the spectre of ambiguity, paradox and contradiction. Language is always prone to parapraxical Freudian slips of tongue and text (like 'when you say one thing but mean your mother'), or the mondegreen of a misheard song lyric such as Taylor Swift's 'all the lonely Starbucks lovers'.[1] If these examples seem trivial, they nevertheless hint at the vibrancy of potential meanings echoing within the chamber of the word, and which, for the most part, we pretend not to hear or mishear, pretend not to read or misread.

Far from the frustrated and lamentable tone of T. S. Eliot's memorable suggestion that '[Words] strain, / Crack and sometimes break, under the burden, / Under the tension, slip, slide, perish, / Decay with imprecision, will not stay in place' (194), there is something thrilling about the idea that words mean *more* than they are conventionally taken to mean. I always struggled to take seriously the modernist attempts to 'purify the dialect of the tribe' (Eliot 218). Instead, like the Celtic idea of the 'thin place',[2] poetry was for me always that form of language where the boundaries between words and the potential words they might evoke are more permeable than elsewhere.

Austral Languages[3]: A Tentative Conclusion

In a series of lectures eventually collected into the book *Serendipities: Lectures on Language and Lunacy*, Umberto Eco presents a similar understanding of language. Eco's essay ranges across various well-known theories of language, from Noam Chomsky's concept of Universal Grammar, Wilhelm von Humboldt's Epicurean hypothesis by which one invents a sort of private language to deal with one's own experience, and the notorious Sapir-Whorf hypothesis according to which language does not simply give form to, but reductively determines, our experience of the world.

Tellingly, Eco remains non-committal about each of these theories and their respective claims, embarking instead upon a lengthy reflection on an eighteenth-century preoccupation with establishing universal laws for ideal or utopian language imaginaries. Ranging across Swift, More, Godwin, de Bergerac, de Foigny and Lull, Eco notes that all of these figures hoped to 'postulate a priori a system of semantic universals' by assigning 'to each semantic atom a visual character or a sound' in their attempts to arrive at an ideal 'universal language' (78). Focusing on de Foigny and Varais's novels about 'journeys in the Austral Land' (80), Eco proceeds to investigate how such 'Austral languages' aspire to ideals of linguistic precision before inevitable lapses into ambiguity, or what Eco regards as the 'double articulation' familiar to all natural languages (88). As Eco concludes, '[e]very attempt to establish an architectonically perfect system of ideas composed of mutual dependences and strict classification from the general to the particular would prove to be a failure' (92). By the same token, however, this failure only proves that 'the utopias of the a priori philosophical language, [...] instead of constructing perfect linguistic systems, have demonstrated how our imperfect languages can produce texts endowed with some poetic virtue or some visionary force' (95).

Eco's investigation of the limits of Austral languages, their misguided attempts to lock markings or sounds to things, ideas, concepts, meanings, has a happy correspondence with many older understandings of what it might mean to write and to read. The word 'write' is also of Germanic origin and can be traced to the Old English word *wrītan*, meaning to 'score, form (letters) by carving, write' and to the German word *reissen*, meaning to 'sketch, drag'. The word 'read' is of Germanic origin and derives from the Old English *rǣdan*, to the Dutch *raden*, and the German *raten*, meaning to 'advise, guess'. Early senses of the word meant to 'advise' or to 'interpret (a riddle or dream)'. However much writers may drag, carve and score words into the material of the world or the mind, their meanings remain closer to sketches than finished products, dependent upon the participation of a readerly dreamer who, however much they may interpret or advise others about the riddle of what has been written, are in actuality involved in a kind of guesswork.

Eco's rehearsal of Austral languages, and his concluding remarks about the potential of natural languages not only to accommodate but invent the Austral languages he has been discussing, suggests that it does seem possible to adopt a pragmatic position in the spaces between more reductively determined and deterministic points of view. This option admittedly doesn't always pass muster – it is difficult, for example, to read a poem like Chris van Wyk's "In Detention" as anything other than a presentation and critique of the extent to which the Apartheid regime, in addition to its more obvious crimes against humanity, deployed euphemism, syntactical distortion and doublespeak as it waged a proxy war on the fabric of grammar itself.

Reflecting on the history of avant-garde writing has and continues to inform my own writing, investing it with a measure of provisionality rather than any clearly defined or practised method. My thinking about writing (and reading) now tends to oscillate between a recognition of language's fundamentally slippery significance, and the necessity of its referential force. Still, I prefer to think of poetry as the space in which even the worst linguistic excesses might be critically, and perhaps even playfully, framed and reflected at its abusers, as through a glass darkly.

Endnotes

1   The word 'mondegreen' refers to Sylvia Wright's 1954 confession that she misheard the phrase 'and laid him on the green', the last line of "The Bonnie Earl Moray", a seventeenth-century ballad, as 'and Lady Mondegreen' (48-51). The Taylor Swift mondegreen is from the song "Blank Space", where the phrase 'got a long list of ex-lovers' has been misconstrued to mean 'all the lonely Starbucks lovers' (Rosen).
2   'In Ireland', explains Kerri ní Dochartaigh, 'these places are often referred to as *áiteanna tanaí, caol áit* – thin places. Heaven and earth, the Celtic saying goes, are only three feet apart, but in thin places that distance is even shorter' (48).
3   "Austral" refers to the Southern hemisphere. The French Austral Lands and Seas comprise the largest of the emerged landmasses in the southern Indian Ocean: the Crozet Archipelago, the Kerguelen Islands, Saint-Paul and Amsterdam Islands as well as 60 small sub-Antarctic islands. Eco may therefore be referring to C17th-18th voyages of discovery leading European writers to invent fictions about exotic foreign lands and their equally exotic, if not entirely fantastical, languages based on travellers' reports about these distant spaces.

Bibliography

Ashbery, John. "At North Farm." *John Ashbery: Selected Poems*. Carcanet, 2002.
Bloom, Harold. *The Anxiety of Influence: A Theory of Poetry*. Oxford University Press, 1997.
Borges, Jorge Luis. "Pierre Menard, Author of the Quixote." *Labyrinths*, edited by Donald A.Yates and James E. Irby with a Preface by André Maurois, Penguin, 1970, pp. 62-71.
Champion, Miles. "Insane Podium: A Short History." *The Poetry Project*, web.archive.org/web/20140222195214/http://poetryproject.org/history/insane-podium/.
Duffy, Carol Ann. "Prayer." *Meantime*. Anvil, 1993, p. 48.

Eco, Umberto. "The Language of the Austral Land." *Serendipities: Language and Lunacy*. Translated by William Weaver, Columbia University Press, 1998, pp. 77-95.

Eliot, T. S. "Four Quartets." *T. S. Eliot: Collected Poems 1909-1962*. Faber and Faber, 1963, pp. 177-209.

Fenstermaker, Will. "Mirtha Dermisache and the Limits of Language". *Paris Review*, 2018, www.theparisreview.org/blog/2018/01/30/mirtha-dermisache-limits-language/.

Hartley, George. *Textual Politics and the Language Poets*. Indiana University Press, 1989.

Heaney, Seamus. "Glanmore Sonnet VII." *New Selected Poems 1966-1987*. Faber and Faber, 1990, pp. 109-118.

Hollander, John. "Swan and Shadow." *Poetry*, vol. 109, no. 3, December 1966, p. 77.

Kreiner, Timothy. "The Politics of Language Writing and the Subject of History." *Post45*, no.1, 1 October 2019, post45.org/2019/01/the-politics-of-language-writing-and-the-subject-of-history/.

Lehman, David. *The Last Avant-Garde: The Making of the New York School of Poets*. Doubleday, 1998.

Lerner, Ben. "Past Imperfect." New York Review of Books, vol. 69, no. 3, 25 February 2021, pp. 18-20.

Lowell, Robert. "National Book Award Acceptance Speech." *National Book Foundation*, November 1960, www.nationalbook.org/robert-lowells-accepts-the-1960-national-book-awards-in-poetry-for-life-studies/.

McCaffery, Steve. *Seven Pages Missing: Volume One: Selected Texts 1969-1999*. Coach House, 1997.

---. "Politics of the Referent**.**" *Open Letter*, no. 7, 1977, pp. 60-99.

Ní Dochartaigh, Kerri. *Thin Places*. Canongate, 2021.

Perloff, Marjorie. "The Word as Such: L=A=N=G=U=A=G=E Poetry in the Eighties." *The Dance of the Intellect*. Cambridge University Press, 1985, pp. 215-238.

---. "Poetry on the Brink: Reinventing the Lyric." *Boston Review*, 2012, www.bostonreview.net/forum/poetry-brink/.

Rosen, Christopher. "Even Taylor Swift's Mom Thought It Was 'Starbucks Lovers'." *Entertainment Weekly*, 25 May 2015, ew.com/article/2015/05/25/taylor-swift-starbucks-lovers-mom/.

Terry, Philip, editor. *The Penguin Book of Oulipo*. Penguin Classics, 2020.

Van Wyk, Chris. *It Is Time to Go Home*. AD Donker, 1979.

Vendler, Helen. "Making It New." *New York Review*, 14 June 1984, www.nybooks.com/articles/1984/06/14/making-it-new/.

Wright, Sylvia. "The Death of Lady Mondegreen." *Harper's Magazine*, vol. 209, no. 1254, 1954, pp. 48-51.

Academic Writing: Starting, Stopping and Coming to Grief
Sally Ann Murray

Straw women are easy to torch, so I had better get off on the right foot. Let me start by stating the obvious: there are many ways to write in academic research contexts, and many of these have proven effective, over time. Perdurable. Many writers have managed to make entrenched conventions work for them. While this chapter deals with elements of so-called innovation in academic writing, it does not toss convention. Labels are just that: useful for labelling. My intention is to remark some writing modes and methods that welcome an openness (and open-mindedness) towards the latent creative or hybrid potential of research writing. This could prove invigorating for those researchers (especially in the arts and social sciences) who chafe against the inherited, normative authority of historically disinterested 'scientific' models of presenting research findings that tend to efface person and perspective, and often give short shrift to interesting forms of expression or style.

***

Toril Moi admits that she has 'often given up on reading academic' writing because it is 'too deadening, so awfully dry, boring and turgid, with sentences that fall apart and never-ending paragraphs. Even if there's a good argument lurking' further down the line, 'I just don't think I can get to it' (Moi).

***

Portrait with Keys is Ivan Vladislavić's slantwise, formally inventive 'Joburg & what-what' of relational citiness, creative self-searching and city selving. In the opening section, Vladislavić recalls the pleasure taken by the narrator's father in sharing old-time directions. A stranger might pull up in his car outside the house and ask the way, reaching out over the low wire fence. Instead of a gruff 'get lost', the dad would 'pass the time of day' (13), unfolding a map on the bonnet of the stranded car, pointing in word and gesture, caught up in the happy happenstance of a meaningful close encounter between unfamiliars who were willing to risk the vulnerable intimacy of asking, and guiding. 'No lost soul was ever turned away from our door without a set of directions that would take him to his exact destination', writes Vladislavić (13). Such directness is precisely what the man hoped for, after all.

It can be helpful to know your route precisely. It certainly saves time and trouble and minimises risk. And yet, as Vladislavić remarks, cannily cueing the indirect method he prefers for *Portrait with Keys*, 'experience has taught me, and a host of writers have confirmed, that getting lost is not always a bad thing. One might even consider misdirecting a stranger for his own good' (13).

It seems almost impossible, these days, to get lost (and yes, thank goodness for Google Maps), but some form of getting lost has become key to my academic writing practice, disorientation enabling me to feel where it is that I and my ideas are going. I must go here, and there, and somewhere else again. I must turn and return via a *détourné*. Ply, play, ploy, *plooi*, deploy, pla, *plié*, plu ... It is not an efficient method, agreed. It's not for everyone. You risk losing the thread and rabbit-holing. You can seem to be stalling, unwilling to reach The End – not knowing, frankly, when this ending might be reached. But along the way, the serendipitous discoveries of unexpected dis/connection allow me to shape an academically acceptable paper in which established conventions morph (for mere moments or through more extended metaphor) into the animation of the poetic, where thought and content and style are all shared components of the poiesis.

***

Taking a cue from Leslie Jamison, we could find an interest in unusual forms of academic writing that borrow from the personal essay and the autoethnographic (see Murray). In such writing, we follow 'the infinitude of a private life toward the infinitude of public experience', being 'wary of seeking this resonance by extracting some easy moral from the grit and complication of personal particularity: *love hurts, time heals, always look on the bright side*' (Jamison; emphasis in original). Instead, we could find ourselves drawn to write academically in ways 'that allow the messy threads of grief or incomprehension to remain ragged, to direct our gazes outward' (Jamison; emphasis in original). A crucial question becomes, how does 'personal experience create something that resonates beyond itself?' Jamison suggests that if your writing 'honor[s] the complexity of your own life – if you grant us entry into moments that hold shame or hurt or heat, and if you're willing to follow that heat, to feel out where all the small fires burn, then your readers will trust you'. If, as sceptics protest, the 'contemporary essay's ideas tend to foreground intimate, emotional experience rather than those honed through the production of knowledge' (Kingston-Rees), advocates of essayistic writing believe that

> the electricity created between erudition and flesh is something fierce. You can move from the rigors of scientific inquiry to […] vulnerability […] in a sentence – if curiosity demands it, if the sentiment can hold it […] There is so much outside the false cloister of private experience; and when you write, you do the work of connecting that terrible privacy to everything beyond it. (Jamison)

***

I am writing my chapter. He is dying
I am supposed to be writing. He is not supposed to be dying
I am not writing. He is still dying
Starting. Stopping. Stops and starts
This chapter gives me grief
Stop. Please don't stop

***

Living. The things people do for a living. To make a living. And how to do 'living', beyond a job, a career? What does it mean, to live, to be alive, to have lived? How long is long enough, before it's done? How to make a dying? What does it mean to make a good end of things? What matter matters, and what is wasted? What counts as life wasted? Is there some golden ratio of profession and poetry that eludes me, or is poetry always to mean but a meagre, mendicant's ration in the professional world of metrics and ir/rational demands, creativity clinging to the edges, or wedged precariously betwixt and between?

***

As a postgrad, I had a misguided respect for status and authority, including the authorised status of genre. My own distinction was poetry, and I had won the Arthur Nortje Prize and the Sanlam Literary Award. I never considered writing fiction (who could match Gordimer and Coetzee?); autobiography was a shameful no-go (the life story of a White girl?); and except for glimpses of 'The New Journalism', creative non-fiction seemed another, unnamed universe altogether, a barely distinguishable island still rising amorphously into being. So, poetry it was. Until a nascent academic career demanded robust scholarship, in an appropriately scholarly register. Young (lacking courage, determined to impress, ignorant or supercilious of other ways), I aced the unwritten rules of professional academic voicing, while playing on the side with personal, creative things. It took me way too long to appreciate that my lyrical, embodied impulse, lodged in an avidity for the thrilling shapes and soundings of language both within and beyond the university, was a fantastic resource that need pay no obeisance to the prescriptive categoricals of genre as they had become sedimented in academia and in publishing. Instead, 'the poetic' was a lived and living disposition, a dynamic cast of visceral mind that was able to bring poetry, ideas and life writing into the exhilarating potential of poiesis, whatever the discourses.

***

Outnumbering the restios and arums in the neighbouring scrap of vlei is slangbos, a plant established in my mind as 'bankrupt bush'. I'd once remarked the tough blueish foliage to an Australian acquaintance, and she'd scoffed: 'In the Outback, that's the last ditch plant alive, your final bloody chance when everything else has been grazed to the ground. The only thing coming next is the bank, when your bond is foreclosed'.

Slangbos is starting to encroach in this part of the world too, helped by fire, though I, admiring, carry a torch for its blend of loveliness and hardiness. Determined to survive. As if everlasting. Here, there, and again: abundant, scrubby aromatic mounds, silvered and sprawling and intricately branched, growing in remnant pockets of the Renosterveld. (I also like that this is a variably described biome, both shrubby grassland and grassy shrubland. Take your pick, depending.)

Seriphium plumosum.

From 'seriph', the line or stroke of a letter.

Belles-lettres: a category of literary writing that is artistically fine and beautiful; a label for literary texts that fall outside the conventional genres of poetry, fiction, and drama.

Belletristic: pertaining to rhetorical styles that engage the aesthetic characteristics of lyricism, beauty, sublimity and wit to affect the reason and emotion of a reader. (Both words used variously to praise or sneer. Depending.)

Seriphium plumosum.

From 'plumosum': feathery. Imagination's flight flocks to birds with sleek, airy plumage, though even a scrawny chicken qualifies. Then the mind swerves, turns, the slightest sleight of hand moving light up and dark down through a child's clumsy cursive learning curve to the spare mechanics of an old century quill, a goose's flight feather cut and stripped and tipped for the writing task at hand.

A man of letters pens a letter. Signs. Ends with a flourish. Such individuated script is an anomaly, now, with the scan and click of digital signatures, and DocuSign, albeit that both are to an extent executed 'by hand' and count as binding. Barring a will, I think, which must be physically signed by the testator, and witnesses, and executor, all dated in the presence of …

***

He lies in bed upstairs, his will subdued, the dying scholar of the long dead eighteenth and nineteenth centuries, of South African colonial literary history, unable ever again to walk the dogs out into their vital daily delight. Scarcely able to breathe. Sorely unable to bath, and bank, and sign with anything but the most exhausted hand, despite his intermittent presence of mind.

> Gently, I try to touch his arm in comfort.
> He pulls away as if burnt.
> Stop it, he says, you're hurting me.
> Then it's my pained turn to recoil.

***

My early career dedication to Literary Culture earned me cultural capital as both scholar and poet. Yet as Merve Emre remarks, 'Any kind of occupational training imparts to its recipients both a sense of mastery and a certain obliviousness to what this mastery costs – namely, the loss of other ways of perceiving the world'. That's one way to interpret the emptiness I felt despite apparent success, an ennui incongruous in a young academic on the rise, an out-of-bodiness that left me no nearer the genuinely thoughtful attentiveness and true-to-self voicing I craved; no closer to being able to engage, reflexively, the cultural forms and subjects and practices that pressed against my life. My passion for Literature came to seem hubristic, a con, and me a fool for having been a groupie in the Emperor's cult. So then. Slowly.

Slowly, in the stead of imitative male mastery and hyper-confident, superlatively executed (glib?) displays of the high-minded manner I believed were necessary for excellent literary academic writing at the time, there came a tentative sense of how to write otherwise. Ideas messily unformed but increasingly insistent. Persistent. The ordinary (or, perhaps, 'the practices of everyday life', as Michel de Certeau theorises) started to claim my attention, mingling with the mysteriously poetic, and with mundane words, and the materialism of a feminist politics, and the alluring otherworlds of stories and re-storying. The corporeal began to feel as warranted as the cerebral, the equivocal meta-processes of meaning-making becoming more intriguing to me than balanced, considered praise and blame applied to 'the work' or 'the text', whether artefact, product, or system of signs. (I cannot elaborate, but of course there were debts to South African history and literary history being written from below, to nascent versions of cultural studies, and to feminist arguments around phenomenology; to the politicised semantic swerves of *écriture féminine*, and to South African female academics' research on women's life writing …)

A chastening lesson had been a doctoral year (mis)spent on the South African short story, a project that stumbled, faltered and fell because it never felt my own, however cogently it had been suggested by a leading scholar as a major gap in the field. Gradually (twists and turns, dead ends and blind rises, and cul-de-sacs), I found myself originating another doctoral study – uncomfortably located within an English department, a project that depended on a disruptive agglomeration of transdisciplinary questions on contemporary consumer culture. This oddity excited me. The melee of ideas and methods morphed my mind away from its timid fudging, making me magpie and myriad, willing to risk an outlier doctoral project that would demand from me both intellectual and experiential truths. It would be a female-centred PhD in which the skills and approaches of literary inquiry were brought into generative, questioning contact with some of the forms, environments, practices and uses of contemporary consumer culture, an embattled field typically razed by cultural progressives and radicals alike. Theme parks, shopping malls, magazines. What could my skills in literary critical reading enable me to 'do', in terms of thought and application? How might they allow me to refocus my imagination's attention on these apparently banal cultural expressions, beyond mere critique or facile celebration? As it turned out, my method would engage an ingenious array of transdisciplinary tactics that verged on the peculiar – veering from familiar, literary text-based analytical strategies and corroborating citation to life writing, fiction, poetry, art, fictocriticism, field work, reverie. This project incubated the syncretic, autoethnographic approach I would come to favour as a scholar, in which critical candour could co-exist with professionalism, intimacy with the intellectual, emotional with documentary truth.

Granted, this doctoral dérive was not synonymous with *easy*, and my rough plan didn't reconcile with the method I'd been taught to respect, that of antithetical thinking, the dialectic in which an outmoded thesis is overturned by the rising argument of an anti-thesis before resolving into a newly gathered thesis assumption. In this method, despite the *provisional* quality of the reworked thesis idea (itself always waiting to be countermanded), there seemed to lie a latent binarism that made me feel trapped, unable to hold the desired both/and. So all I knew – and also *felt* – was that I wanted to lean into learning how to write in a scholarly context by exploring connections between lifeworlds of idea and body that academia had persuaded me ought to be kept professionally discrete; to find ways to wordwork via circuitous and divergent poetic associations, rather than evident and overt referentiality and critical analysis; to find routes into thinking and expression via lacunae as well as bridges; to position myself with sensory acuity instead of supposed objective distance; to discover how uncertainty, speculation, even purposeful equivocation, might persuade into being presently unseen paths other than confident assertive knowing.

***

Still, I've done it myself, as an ambitious, if obedient, student chasing the certainty of high marks. Written rote. Student writers turn to (churn out) the five-paragraph essay. Statement-development-return. Objective voice. Formal register. Claim, illustrate, critically corroborate.

But let's imagine that a diligent well-schooled writer of conventionally excellent expository academic prose wants to become more self-aware about seemingly immutable academic writing practices, even Procrustean conformities. (Where might s/he learn this, when there is no rhetoric and composition – scant explicit teaching of essay writing beyond first year English modules? Osmosis? No wonder many scholarly writers don't deviate much from the given flow, in their papers.)

For my own graduate students, Sean Sturm is indispensable. He maps the 'narrative cartography' of 'point first' academic writing, the habituated essay and article-writing model of the 'academosphere' (3). He renders visible the 'unspoken and unexamined' assumptions of this rhetorical model and epistemic method – among them, ease of marking, forensic examination, and the preservation of specialist authority (3). Let's unpack some customary features of point first (PF) and point last (PL) essay structures. As Sturm notes, quoting Hahn, 'the standard formula is "tell me what you're going to tell me, tell it, then tell me what you told me"'(4). The PF model of academic writing is 'seemingly native' to 'the academy'. It is an expository writing method that aims to *'display knowledge*: it stakes its claim at the outset and then sets out to prove it' (1; emphasis in original). The PL model is less common in university research writing, although it is 'truer to the origin of the essay', in that it is *knowledge discovering*, 'a *heuristic* […] and thus *exploratory* writing technology' (1; emphasis in original). It works via a willingness to present open-minded routes and processes, even though it does arrive at some claim towards the end. Sturm continues:

> These different aims also imply different rhetorical and stylistic objectives: the PF essay aims to express a single voice and to achieve transparency, namely, plain speaking and plainness; the PL essay, in contrast, is able to express multiple voices (or a multiple voice) and to achieve a certain idiosyncrasy, that is to say, complexity and a stylistic 'complex'. (2)

A single voice: premised on the writer's unequivocal assertions? Multiple voices: a more circumspect, provisional treatment of subject matter from various angles. A paper which, while focusing on X, draws G and M and Q and C into its atypical ambit, using discrepant discourses and registers? Perhaps, even, a writing method that, in its content, style and form, grants the polymorphous *multiples* of a writer's mind, drawn to this, *and* that, *and* that too, finding value in apparent contradiction. (The echoes are of John Keats's 'negative capability'.) I think of Mikhail Bakhtin's dialogism ('two voices' are 'the minimum for life, the minimum for existence') and heteroglossia (a term describing the incorporation, in the novel, of varied speech genres, languages, dialects, to convey textually the multiplicity of sociolinguistic relations) (252). In South African higher education contexts, there is an urgency for academic writing that embodies multiple, previously marginalised voices, that personalises and humanises, since the old master knowledge and denigrating epistemes must be decentred, transformed, shown for the power plays they have masked. Without naïvely idealising, perhaps essayistic expository academic prose can sometimes serve as 'a form of transgressive symbolic action in which intellectual freedom is enacted as a movement across ideological boundaries and borders' (Heilker 181). Sturm writes:

> This critical mobility is embodied in the various forms of critical-creative writing, like the performative essay, the creative non-fiction or fictocritical essay, the lyric essay and so on, that inhabit the margins of the academosphere. [...] These forms are not only vehicles for critique (critical in their *content*) but also implicit critiques of the essay as mere container for content (critical in their *form*). (14; emphasis in original)

Dare I say, too: talk to yourself, as a writer, even before you communicate with others. This ventriloquising internal cacophony can be selectively externalised in a managed way in the space of your academic writing; it is potentially a precursor of your paper as a heteroglossic space in which many voices co-exist. They might do so with difficulty. With noise and rebuttal, rather than studied or complacent ease. But in thinking about academic writing, I deliberately avoid metaphors of competition even while envisaging dialogic voicing as a mobile, sometimes disjunctive range of tones and values and intensities.

The hope is that my writerly expression is enlivened by varieties of inflection, affect, vantage, subject and approach, instead of being a masterfully monologic insistence that mutes challenge or demurral. At the same time, I try (fail?) not to fall into the trap of figuring multi-voicedness as some polite conversation, where I pretend that every voice has equal say, only because I am unwilling to face the inequities of the power relations that are inevitably at stake. How does the 'I' get heard, become present, without silencing and effacing the 'I's of others?

***

Come the day he said to me, in despair, that he wished the cursed neighbour would stop his endless banging. What the fuck was he even *doing*? That guy was either yammering 'Sweet Caroline' as if life was a drunken karaoke or hammering away night and day like Mr. Fucking Fix-It. Fucker should get a life. Read a book, for a start!

Listen: he cocked an ear; raised a slow, halfway hand to summon the racket into the ambit of his own growing stillness.

I listened. Intently. Heard nothing.

We stayed quiet like that for a while, he lying in the living death bed, I standing alongside, on barely breathing pause, both trying to hear the same imperceptible thing by acutely earing.

And then subliminally it came to me: the sound of the life-giving oxygen machine, puffing as heavily as a man with terminally compromised lungs. Whuuuph whuuuph whuuuph. Relentless. Life flailing, beating on as hard as it could, resounding in the echoes of a mind coming loose, losing its hold.

Impossible, he said. What I'm hearing is much fucking louder than that. *Much.* Until I turned the machine off, and we leaned in close, again, listening again, now to the sound of nothing.

Not that this brought peace. After a few hopeless tries to hear properly with his entire wasting body, he conceded, chastened. So it was me, all the time, that horrible, wretched noise?

***

Perhaps academic writing, in some sense a professional, expertly specialist instance of the novice's undergraduate essay, can borrow from the impulses of 'the essay' as practised in more popular journalism. Consider Brian Dillon's *Essayism: On Form, Feeling, and Nonfiction*, a book in which the indefinable process and quality of essaying are valued above 'the essay' as a dogmatic, deterministic genre checklist. As a description of *Essayism* by Fitzcarraldo publishers puts it, drawing on Dillon's ideas:

> Imagine a type of writing so hard to define its very name means a trial, effort or attempt. An ancient form with an eye on the future, a genre poised between tradition and experiment. The essay wants above all to wander, but also to arrive at symmetry and wholeness; it nurses competing urges to integrity and

> disarray, perfection and fragmentation, confession and invention. (Fitzcarraldo)

An essay, as a form (says Dillon), depends on the writer's ability to imagine connections. It is 'a kind of *conglomerate*: an aggregate either of diverse materials or disparate ways of saying the same or similar things' (48; emphasis in original). An essay tends to 'perform [...] its mode of attention', aspiring with 'polish and integrity', a 'simultaneity of the acute and the susceptible', to 'express the quintessence or crux of its matter', even while emphasising 'that its purview is partial, that being incomplete is a value in itself for it better reflects the brave and curious but faltering nature of the writing mind' (85, 11, 8, 11). This entails a skilled performance of both mastery and the tentative – an 'experiment in attention' that resists being pinned down, or contained, since an essay is necessarily 'diverse and several – it *teems*' (86, 10; emphasis in original).

***

Across the Humanities, it has become acceptable, even methodologically necessary in a research culture that endorses collaboration, for academic research to venture beyond disciplinary silos. But an under-examined implication of this reach is that research writing across disciplines extends a tricky relational invitation: How am I thinking through my subject (and its adjacencies)? How do I handle the buts, and abutments? Where am I placing myself in this subject relation, allowing the manifold inflections through which 'I' and its many others can be voiced: singular, subjective, dispassionate, informal, expert, personalised, intimately confessional, remotely distanced? How do my personal habits of thoughts – linear, whirling, teleological, tessellated … – correlate with (or unsettle) habituated methods of scholarly inquiry in particular disciplinary habituses? How might the very processes of thinking lead me to write across a broad span of writing modes, variously familiar and strange in my disciplinary home, so as to engage my readers?

***

An academic research writer could consider livening up her scholarly writing through judicious combinations of

> creative non-fiction   scholarly citation   confessional account
> autoethnographic vignette   poetic lyricism   documentary realism
> critical explication   statistical data sets   visual diagramming
> theoretical questions   narrative scenes   juxtaposed summaries
> epigrammatic quotations.
> (Browning, Freedman and Stephenson, in conversation)

And what else?

… analysis, lists, diary entries, dramatic dialogue, definitions, oral anecdote, recondite fact, interview snippets, archival texts, descriptions of objects and processes, life stories, etymologies, weather reports, poetry forms, letter extracts, mundane found materials, object histories …

***

So many possibilities. As Jamison cautions, though, 'one of the central imperatives of combining personal material with history or criticism or reportage' is that 'each thread must do some work that isn't being done by another; that *can't* be done by another'. Here, an academic writer might envisage the subject of her writing as a tangible 'object' of intellectual inquiry that she is crafting, each element quilled to scale. This is to position the scholarly writer less as magisterial master of existing knowledge than as a maker of a conceptual-creative work.

Clearly, this is about ways of *thinking through* your subject matter, as much as writing up your 'findings'. When I teach graduate workshops on writing, I recommend that writers *show* their struggles, rather than pretend that they have magically arrived at mastery. This processual kind of scholarly writing not only helps with anxieties about word count (that false, facile metric) but functions as an ingenious vehicle that enables the thinking-writing to move – forwards, backwards, sidewise, slantwise – all in the emergence of the paper's becoming. This method is a device – a *devising* – through which you, as writer, take pleasure in, and responsibility for, the idiosyncratic yet purposeful shapeliness of how you communicate your ideas. The difficult to and fro, through and no, of puzzling out what you think and how to express these thoughts in imaginative relation becomes key to showing how you arrive at your position. (Of course you do not include *everything*. As if you could! Every glitch you've faced; each excruciating moment of doubt. You're not aiming for the Borgesian impossibility of real-time comprehensiveness and omniscience, which can seem like soporific narcissism, after all. You want a purposefully embodied, dynamic argument, analogous to the deftness with which a fiction writer gets the character from this room to the next without a tedious charting of each blow-by-blow action.)

***

Do 'you think there are a lot of academics who genuinely don't notice how something is written?' Moi mulls. Hoping to overcome this stolidity, Moi prompts her grad students to learn courage, to shed their attachment to bland abstractions such as the ideal intellectual register. They 'need to show me where they stand,' she says. 'I want them to stop being so afraid that, in their writing, they end up sounding like robots', producing 'anemic summary' after following 'the most ingrained academic rules'. She is also unapologetic about insisting that lived 'experience' is a 'key' reference point, even though it 'has been anathema for quite a long while'. As those of us who favour autoethnographic approaches to scholarly writing know (see Murray), writers inevitably draw on their lives and positions and judgements; only, some make this self-evident and others masquerade dispassionate authority. For Moi, there 'is no point in pretending that you have a bird's-eye view. You are responsible for guiding your reader to see what *you* see' (emphasis in original).

***

And what of that fusty old codger, 'one', who still stands determined never to eschew his imperiously assumed, yet concealed, I? One (Dear One) is unwilling to concede that this pronoun has unrightly claimed pre-eminence as representative of All. I think one would do best, in one's academic writing, to avoid this remote pronominal persona. He does not exist. Nor does she, either. They are both one and the same – a relic persona from a bygone era, better left for dead, given all that they mask, all the privileged persons and cultural positions they assume as their God-given right to be and to take, in writing and de/claiming. How much more invigorating, in our research writing, when 'one' is given shape in an essay as a specific someone, a writer with particular tones and perspectives and opinions, a person who has a subjective stake in the material with which the paper is engaging, the argument the writer is making. This is far more convincing, to me (at least), than some abstracted grammatical One that assumes a superiorly ordinant place in the hierarchy of pronouns. (While I'm on that topic, here's another, related. Can we please forget about 'aforementioned' and 'hereafter' and 'our protagonist'? Even 'the former' and 'the latter' can be clunky disorientating gestures, too rote to do anything more than clumsily direct an argument's slow-moving traffic. If it's not quite accepted, yet, to write in a completely colloquial voice, at least renounce false distinctions among diction Proper and Improper; aim to forgo magisterial, even pompous 'propriety' for diction and register that get the job done, intellectually and creatively, and, in so doing, carry your argument with an authenticity far more convincing than the guise of incontrovertible certainty.)

***

And can we admit that figurative language can naturalise violence? Consider the invisible after-lives of dead metaphors. Take 'interrogation'. The go-to verb in so much scholarly writing. Kneejerk. Thoughtless. But the word sends chills. The writer's intention is generally benign, but the metaphor's backstories are torture, genocide, the abuse of power. When the goal of academic writing – the determined action – is 'interrogation', do we consider who is interrogated and who is the interrogator? Under whose illegitimate authority this brutality breaks down ideas, compelling supposed truth? What coercion is effected in order to extract meaning, to make something appear as if justified, and something else disappear as if inconsequential? What happens when we accept such linguistic-expressive violence as the discursive norm? If we stopped to question the established vocabularies of scholarly violence, would we see that any mastery so achieved is compromised, and ethically in doubt?

***

It may be a relief to find that fearlessness in academic writing need not derive from the obviously experimental; it can be developed by becoming familiar with conventions. As Moi explains, for example, she and her graduate students 'spend a lot of time co-editing individual sentences'. How old-school! But:

> It's very eye-opening for the people in the class to experience what it means to pay attention to their words, to discover what their sentence is actually saying. Every week we look at the sentence on the screen and rewrite it. At some point they realize that *this* is what it takes to make a sentence do what you want it to do, that it is really difficult but yet something one can learn. (Moi; emphasis in original)

The sentence. The prosaic building block. The sentence generally does something clear and direct and communicatively explicable, even when it proceeds, deliberately, via a purposeful roundabout. To this circuitous end, it is worth paying closer attention to the types of sentences we use in writing up our academic research. Careful variation of expression – combining sentences, phrases and clauses – can be used by a writer to carry a range of understandings and implications. If a key sentence signposts the way in which a paragraph will develop, a series of sentence fragments can embody an erratic train of thought, sometimes diverging to touch on another issue (near or far), sometimes following the eddies of poetic drift, sometimes gathering bits and pieces together towards an emphatic point that, despite grammatical incorrectness, forcefully conveys the desired idea as almost sentient. Working with writing in this way entails figuring out how to represent thought processes: Where could your argument benefit from a spare, short sentence? Could you use a tactical series of similar grammatical structures, punchy, terse, direct, before signalling a change of tack via another sentence type? Where might the writing benefit from an extended, even overly complex sentence, performing the convolutions of your struggle to engage your subject matter, and to stake your (provisional) position? And let's allow the lovely liveliness of the grammatically capricious: orthodox sentences are well and good, but the scholar can inventively bend the expectation of syntax for her purpose. Exploratory turns of broken phrase that mimic the twists and torsions of the writer's mind at work, actively performing thought, and urging a reader to do the same, these can invigorate both the writing and the reading, creating a form that actively engages, reaching innovatively beyond dutiful academic inventorying and re-citation.

> And let me say it:
> 1. the ground rises and …
> 2. a mind twists and …
> You can fill in the blanks.

In language teaching, this leaving of gaps is a form of assessment called 'close procedure'. The learner provides the correct word. It's not difficult, for some. For others, it's a challenge. Nothing is a given, in writing, even when clues are given. Writing depends not only on innovation but on patterns of prediction and expectation. Even cliché can be comforting, a familiar structuring of sense and sentiment.

Another element that academic writers could consider is the underlying figurative architecture of their papers, in which agile combinations of argument, description and account can variously push forward and create opportunities for pause, and strategic digression. Sturm (acknowledging Heilker) draws attention to the metaphors of mobility that inform essayistic prose – pointing to Virginia Woolf's 'journeying', Clifford Geertz's 'wandering', György Lukács's 'flying', Theodor Adorno's 'constellating', and William Gass's 'circling' (12-13). His point is to emphasise the power of writing as *doing* rather than merely stating or finding. I like Tim Bascom's "Picturing the Personal Essay: A Visual Guide", where he conceptualises – and renders through visually diagrammatic illustration – some of the possibilities for a writer who is keen to structure her prose using the techniques of storying, reflective meandering, (almost) full-circling, braiding, and dipping into the well. He draws on Phillip Lopate's description of the reflective essayist whirling around a subject and then homing in, 'wheeling and diving like a hawk', a looping action inconsistent with established point-first academic approaches. Understanding such differences can help us, as writers, to shift sedimented writing habits, getting us – and indeed our readers – off auto-pilot and into more active modes of consciousness. 'Picture if you can' the essay's 'profile on the page', writes Dillon,

> from a solid spate of argument or narrative to isolated promontories of text, these composing in their sum the archipelago of a work, or a body of work. The page an estuary, dotted at intervals with typographical buoys or markers. And all the currents or sediments in between: sermons, dialogues, lists and surveys, small eddies of print or whole books construed as single essays. A shoal or school made of these. Listen for the possible cadences this thing might create: orotund and authoritative; ardent and fizzing; slow and exacting to the point of pain or pleasure; halting, vulnerable, tentative; brutal and peremptory; a shuffling or amalgam of all such actions or qualities. (8)

Unlike in the traditional academic paper, the essayistic writer does not 'begin with a thesis and aim, arrow-like, at a pre-determined bull's-eye' (Bascom). Instead, 'essayists meander around their subject until arriving, often to the side of what was expected' (Bascom). 'One of the benefits of such a circling approach is that it seems more organic, just like the mind's creative process. It allows for a wider variety of perspectives – illuminating the subject from multiple angles' (Sturm). It's also exciting (despite journals' picky preferred formats) to view the page as not inherently a structure to be justified, systematically headed and sub-headed, every graf relentlessly fixed on a sagittal arc directed towards reaching the end. A page can be much more kinetic, singular, distinctive. A research writer might want to use the page as one instance in a repertoire of structural devices that carries thought and argument, asking: where could ideas be chunkily blocked (beyond block-indented quotation); where could they disaggregate into fugitive traces, leaving white space for ideas to breathe, or to tantalise, or to mimic novelised dialogue?

***

He croaks from upstairs. 'Come plug me in! My damn cell is nearly dead.'

***

I think of Richard Hugo's advice to poets about discovering how to extrapolate from the triggering subject of a poem to the actual subject. You plan to write a poem on subject x. You write this poem, with every care for craft. It's okay but, to your annoyance, it's nothing more; no matter how you chip away and polish, it remains a poem 'about x'. What now? Through a combination of deliberation and chance, waiting and re-writing and intuitive rewiring, you give the poem the space and time it needs to find its real subject, which is the haunting 'other' subject that lies buried in the body of the obvious idea that got you started. You listen to the words and lines, the 'shape' of the ideas and images. You find the musicality, a notation that combines aural, oral, even the artefactual and the auratic, however much those old notions attract derision, in some contemporary circles. You let go of overriding 'poetic mastery'. You let. You let it replay. You blood let. Illegally sublet. You let improbable ideas find their surprising conjuncture, a curious congruence that is likely to involve startling sound and visual similarities, figurative frisson and fugitive fission, the nonplus of different subject matters made proximate, more than overt arrangements of factual correlation or syntactical protocol. This can make for oddities, but it can also make for magic and animation, giving life to your writing, freeing it from deadly poetic sins such as plodding predictability and conventionalised cliché. It is a risk, when you, the poet, concede an element of creative control to the unknown; even more so, yes, when you're an academic writer borrowing poetic methods that might enable you to honour the striking, original expressive-conceptual métier of the creative texts with which you're engaging, longing to free your scholarly writing from the deadening formulae of the five-point argument progression and third-person voice we have internalised. Take the chance. Forgo the unreasonable, demanding logic of common sense, since 'sense', in its conventional meaning, can mark a dulling deficit of the senses, a deficiency of the suggestive, elusive wholeness or tangential lyrical sufficiency that, in writing, offer a plenitude that inheres beyond reason.

***

An unhoused man I happened on while walking out back, living plywood and plastic stealth in the neglected lot adjacent to our house, where water is plentiful, via the sloot. The shock of it: seeing him bedded down in the threadbare childhood quilt I'd sadly let go with the weekly rubbish collection (children grown and gone), fabric folded and enfolded like some version of a dead soldier's patriotic flag, gifted to a mourning mother. The misplaced sentiment. Sentimentality. Forgive me these ugly feelings? I remember the faded navy background of a gold-flecked sky. Perhaps there was a distant pattern to be perceived in the arrangement of the stars, but even to my invested eye those heavens seemed inscrutable. Horribly random.

***

A passage from Njabulo S. Ndebele comes to mind:

> I think that only if we attempt this pouring out of personal feeling into the public domain will a new public become possible. We cannot tell what kind of public it will be; but we do need to release more and more personal data into our public home to bring about a more real human environment: more real because it is more honest, more trusting, and more expressive. (217)

***

Not three days since his first (almost belated) visit, the rep from the medical hire company comes to collect the oxygen machine, the day after M's death. I make to hand the man the cannula. He says casually, 'Chuck it away. It's used'. And suddenly I notice the cloudy traces of misted breath, the slender line no longer pristine and clear.

But it's too soon for me to discard anything. Not when, only yesterday … I am still weighing everything up, deadened by grief. Medical waste, discards, this little lifeline is something to hold on to.

I curl the cannula carefully into a neat, tight whorl and tuck the ends under and over, trying to hold it all together.

What to do with it now? Where to put it? What to make of it?

***

Tie his cannula with millions of others. An installation of entangled plastic tubes disgorged both from the belly of the world's rapacious beast and from imagination's bottomless depths. A devastating artwork labelled 'Cannulae'. Life as death zone. A companion piece to abandoned life jackets and bloodied baby blankets and undocumented shoes.

***

Every day could be the last. A last is a foot, of sorts, a shoemaker's crafty prosthesis. A poet, trying to find her feet in a poem, and writing out of sorts, may turn to something similar, shaping and counting in shadow-sounding sonics, mutedly measuring the accentuations of metre. Even so-called innovative or experimental poets, who eschew formal prosody, might like the sound of certain feet, the footfall patterns regular, or aurality orally interrupted. Making a poem, my mind's lines still too easily fall into a juvenile habit, the lasting bardic performance of iambic pentameter, against my better judgement.

At the same time, I am weighing up precarious slips for a generous grip capable of holding my desire for an impossible many:

> say John Donne's sprung rhythm, say Leslie Scalapino's 'Language Beats', say Emily Dickinson's gnomic terseness, say

Kathleen Fraser's 'innovative necessity', and and and

say marvellous writing methods from Lyn Hejinian, Anne Carson, Harryette Mullen, Louise Glück, and and and

Where all that mismatched company gets me, I don't know. But it gets me going, and I have gotten along, and I love it. If my beginnings as a poet were footed in established traditions (no bad place to start), it's taken years to find a range of stranger angels beyond the comfortable and comforting old familiars, an extensive, heart-everlasting creative maker-scape that will be with me until the end, should life permit.

If asked, at last, a little melancholy and retrospective, if my mind still holds, will I admit an impossible ideal, the longing for some sense of Laurie Anderson, a prolific, unusually dispersed creativity winding Walter Benjamin's ideas through *Songs and Stories for Moby Dick* into Big Science, politics, pop culture and many days in the bardo?

'Bardo', in some forms of Buddhism, is a state intermediate and transitional, liminal between death and rebirth. There are said to be several bardos (do you mean 'bards', suggests Spellcheck, or maybe 'birds'?) between the pain of dying, the possibility of insight, and the space of becoming. This I cannot know except by going, going on, being *en route*, *en fuite*, until I reach The End. So for final insights, I will have to wait and see, and until then: on I go, one foot after another, sometimes pedestrian, sometimes flighty, making a soulful way. You need the right shoes for your own write working. Walking. Worn in; getting worn out. I prefer a rougher sole, a style halfway close to a reinforced ankleboot, more than slipshod slop. My laces, to boot, can be stock standard (with neat flugelbinder aglets at the end of each cord, to keep the thing from unravelling, and to make it easier to thread the end through the hole of the whole). But my laces can just as well be mismatched ribbons or fleshy ligatures, whatever works, for the purpose; even ordinary string can do the job.

***

Today, two months since he is dead, I walk again as I have come to walk every early evening since his death, in the drying vlei that staggers outside our back gate. Feeling low, eyes and heart downcast, I watch my step and pick a careful way across the baked ground, heaps mounded by the grader that an anxious municipality had summoned in winter to stem the overflowing stream. Now: dried clay, cracked. Tyre tracks wider than my height. Devastated ground heaved and halved into splayed reeds and torn tussocks. Dying lilies, sere, a season drained into giving up the ghost at this dead wits' end.

   Unearthed: a salt-glazed bottle with a chipped lip
Unused: a leg's length of discarded irrigation pipe
  Unloved: a chunked hunk of builder's rubble

Stiff, discoloured plastic crackles as I step. Flytrap 2L Coke cracked downpipe empty Energade. Broken brick. Everything seems hard, after his death. Harder. Sparse. Certainly, I have nothing to spare. My eyes are drawn. Skywise. By birds. A hoopoe, short swooping. A great trailing heron. A russet raptor upright on the spiked fence, head scanning turn. re-turn. turn. And the annual swallows, three new youngsters cutting sharp air with their parents. (For a moment, the word for such a young bird escapes me. Then a flash against the head: fledgling.)

 I am wingless. Unfeathered. Far above, untethered, hangs a remote blue mirror. If it were autumn, there would be clouds, rapidly morphing. Myriad shapes, forms, types. The comforting familiarity of scientific names: lenticular, cumulonimbus, altostratus, and the passing pleasure of whimsical pareidolia, a ruse that gifts the mind's eye a playful segue from dragon, to seal, to spectre.

 At my feet, in the grass: a single porcupine quill, striped dirty cream and brown. Always only traces, left behind, that happen in my path. Bishop's the 'art of losing', maybe. Or Dickinson: 'then the letting go'.

———————

Bibliography

Bakhtin, Mikhail. *Problems of Dostoevsky's Poetics*. University of Minnesota Press, 1997.

Bascom, Tim. "Picturing the Personal Essay: A Visual Guide." *Creative Non-Fiction Quarterly*, no. 49, Summer 2013, www.creativenonfiction.org/writing/picturing-the-personal-essay-a-visual-guide/.

Browning, Randi, Diane Freedman and Denise Stephenson. "Experimental Academic Writing." 48th *Annual Meeting of the Conference on College Composition and Communication*, 12-15 March 1997, Phoenix, AZ, www.eric.ed.gov/?id=ED416484.

Certeau, Michel de. *The Practice of Everyday Life*. University of California Press, 1984.

Dillon, Brian. *Essayism: On Form, Feeling, and Nonfiction*. New York Review Books, 2017.

Emre, Merve. "Has Academia Ruined Literary Criticism?" *The New Yorker*, 16 January 2023, www.newyorker.com/magazine/2023/01/23/has-academia-ruined-literary-criticism-professing-criticism-john-guillory.

Fitzcarraldo Editions. Publisher's Description of Dillon's *Essayism*. https://fitzcarraldoeditions.com/books/essayism.

Heilker, Paul. *The Essay: Theory and Pedagogy for an Active Form*. National Council of Teachers of English, 1996.

Hugo, Richard. *The Triggering Town: Lectures and Essays on Poetry and Writing*. W. W. Norton & Company, 2010.

Jamison, Leslie. "How To Write a Personal Essay." *Publishers Weekly*, 28 March 2014, www.publishersweekly.com/pw/by-topic/industry-news/tip-sheet/article/61591-how-to-write-a-personal-essay.html.

Kingston-Rees, Alexandra. "The Contemporary Essay / Novel Nausea / Alexandra Kingston-Reese." *ASAP Journal*. 16 May 2022, www.asapjournal.com/the-contemporary-essay-novel-nausea-alexandra-kingston-reese/#:~:text=Brian%20Dillon%20identifies%20this%20as,it%20better%20reflects%20the%20brave.

Moi, Toril. "The Speaking Subject: A Conversation with Toril Moi." Interview by Jessica Swoboda. *The Point Magazine*, 8 February 2022, thepointmag.com/dialogue/the-speaking-subject/.

Murray, Sally Ann. "Autoethnographic Life Writing: Reaching Beyond, Crossing Over." *Research Methodologies for Auto/biography Studies*, edited by Kate Douglas and Ashley Barnwell, Routledge, 2019, pp. 96-102.

Ndebele, Njabulo S. *Fine Lines from the Box: Further Thoughts About Our Country*. Umuzi, 2007.

Sturm, Sean "Terra (In)cognita: Mapping Academic Writing." *TEXT: Journal of Writing and Writing Courses*, vol. 16, no. 2, 2012, www.textjournal.com.au/oct12/sturm.htm.

Vladislavić, Ivan. *Portrait with Keys*. Umuzi, 2006.

About the Editors, Artist and Authors

Sally Ann Murray (editor and author) is Professor in the Department of English at Stellenbosch University, serving as Chair from 2015 to 2020. Her scholarly writing is known for its experimental, autoethnographic method – whether on art, literature, trans life or gardening. Murray has published queer short stories in anthologies such as *Incredible Journey* (2015) and *Hair* (2019). Her third poetry collection, *Otherwise Occupied* (2019), was nominated for a 2020 South African Literary Award, and her autobiographical novel (*Small Moving Parts* (2009)) won the 2010 M-Net Literary Award: English, and the 2010 Herman Charles Bosman Prize, among others.

Michèle Betty (editor) is the founder and director of Dryad Press. She has a BA LLB from Wits University and a master's degree in Creative Writing (*cum laude*) from the University of Cape Town. She has worked at Investec Bank Ltd, practised as an attorney at Webber Wentzel Bowens, and was poetry editor and then editor of *New Contrast Literary Journal*. Since founding Dryad Press in 2016, she has curated numerous award-winning poetry collections. Her first poetry collection, *Metaphysical Balm* (2017), was shortlisted for the 2018 Ingrid Jonker Prize. Her second, *Dark Horse* (2022), was awarded the 2023 South African Literary Award for Poetry. In 2023, for her contribution to promoting and publishing South African poetry, she was awarded the Patricia Schonstein Poetry in McGregor Award.

Gabeba Baderoon (the Foreword) is the author of three poetry collections, *The Dream in the Next Body* (2005), *A Hundred Silences* (2006) and *The History of Intimacy* (2018, 2021). She received a PhD in English from the University of Cape Town (UCT) and is Associate Professor of Women's, Gender and

Sexuality Studies, African Studies, and Comparative Literature at Penn State University, where she co-directs the African Feminist Initiative. Among her honours are the Sarah Baartman Senior Fellowship at UCT, an Extraordinary Professorship of English at Stellenbosch University, and fellowships at the African Gender Institute, the Nordic Africa Institute, Bellagio and the Stellenbosch Institute for Advanced Study. Her awards include the DaimlerChrysler Prize, the Elisabeth Eybers Poetry Prize, the University of Johannesburg Prize for South African Writing and three Best Book Awards from the National Institute for the Humanities and Social Sciences. Baderoon also wrote the monograph, *Regarding Muslims: from Slavery to Post-Apartheid* (2014), and, together with Desiree Lewis, co-edited the essay collection, *Surfacing: on Being Black and Feminist* (2021).

Henrietta Scholtz (artist) is a self-taught visual artist and curator, based at Bag Factory Artists' Studios, Fordsburg, Johannesburg. She has an English Literature degree and an honours degree in Communications Management from VEGA. Scholtz has exhibited in group shows, including the Turbine Art Fair, the National Arts Festival, Sasol New Signatures, Thami Mnyele Fine Art Awards and The Centre for the Less Good Idea's *Long Minute*. Since 2021, she has been the assistant curator of the SABC Art Collection.

On Humankind, the cover art, is a two-part meditation on what it means to be a 'self' within a body created by those who have come before. It is an archaeology of the self (both created and creative) within the time-travel of meditation and thought, influenced by the *Cradle of Humankind*. In her words:

> We are process as we live and breathe everyday within our bodies, communities and geographies. We are renewing and regenerating and decaying. From flesh to bone to dust, we continue the creative process of the physical, historical, geographical, ancestral and temporal.

Vonani Bila (author) is a poet living in Shirley Village, Limpopo, and writing in Xitsonga and English. He is founding editor of the *Timbila* poetry journal, publisher of Timbila Books and founder of Timbila Writers' Village, a rural retreat centre for writers. He has been instrumental in assisting marginalised poets reach publication, holding workshops and actively encouraging new voices. Together with Max Makisi Marhanele, he wrote *Tihlungu ta Rixaka*, a monolingual Xitsonga dictionary. He teaches in the Department of Languages and English Studies at the University of Limpopo. He holds a master's degree in Creative Writing (*cum laude*) from Rhodes University and is currently reading for a PhD in Creative Writing at Wits University. His latest poetry collection is *Bilakhulu! Longer Poems* (2015).

Phillippa Yaa de Villiers (author) lectures in Creative Writing at Wits University and is a Distinguished Alumnus of Rhodes University Journalism and Media Studies. She is a board member of the African Poetry Book Fund, worked as a television screenwriter for ten years, and comes from a theatre background. Her one-woman show, *Original Skin* (2008), toured nationally and in Germany. Her books include *Taller than Buildings* (2006), *The Everyday Wife* (2010) (recipient of the 2011 South African Literary Award) and *ice-cream headache in my bone* (2017). She was the 2014 Commonwealth Poet. Her work appears in the collections *Relations* (2023), edited by Nana Ekua Brew-Hammond, as well as *New Daughters of Africa* (2019), and *Yellow Means Stay* (2019), both edited by Margaret Busby, and in journals that include *Wasafiri, Baobab, Konch, Stanzas* and *New Coin*.

vangile gantsho (author) is a poet, healer and co-founder of impepho press. She has travelled the globe participating in literary events and festivals as an unwavering advocate for the Divine Black Feminine. gantsho is the author of two poetry collections: *Undressing in Front of the Window* (2015) and *red cotton* (2018). She holds a master's degree from the University Currently Known as Rhodes and was named one of the *Mail & Guardian's* 200 Young South Africans of 2018. gantsho is the founder of *smallgirl rising*, an international poetry-centered healing movement.

Ashraf Jamal (author) is a Senior Research Associate in the Visual Identities in Art and Design Research Centre (VIAD) at the University of Johannesburg, and a board member of the ARAK Foundation based in Doha. He has studied in the United Kingdom, Canada, the United States, South Africa, and has taught at the University of Cape Town, as well as the universities of KwaZulu-Natal, Stellenbosch, Malaya, Eastern Mediterranean and Rhodes. He has also served as editor for *Art South Africa* and *Art Africa*. His recent books include *In the World: Essays on Contemporary South African Art* (2017), *Strange Cargo: Essays on Art* (2022), and *Looking into the Mad Eye of History without Blinking* (2023). *WOW: 12 Asides on Abstraction* is forthcoming.

Liesl Jobson (author) writes from Zeekoevlei, a freshwater lake on the Cape Flats where hippopotamus once roamed. Her work appears in local and international journals and anthologies, including *The Southern Review*, *New World Writing*, *Slush Pile Magazine*, *Flash Fiction International*, *The Common*, *Lichen*, *Adanna*, *Quick Fiction*, *Schuylkill Valley Journal* and *Cutthroat Journal*. Her collection of prose poems and flash fiction, *100 Papers*, won the 2006 Ernst van Heerden Award and was translated into Italian as *Cento Strappi*. She is the author of the poetry collection *View from an Escalator* (2008), the short story collection *Ride the Tortoise* (2012), and three children's books, which were published and translated into many languages under the Book Dash banner. Jobson is a freelance bassoon and contrabassoon player and enjoys making music with various southern African orchestras.

Lliane Loots (author) is a Lecturer in the Drama and Performance Studies Programme at the University of KwaZulu-Natal (UKZN). She has a master's degree in Gender Studies, and completed her PhD in 2018 in contemporary dance/performance histories on the African continent. Loots is Artistic Director/Curator for the annual international *JOMBA! Contemporary Dance Festival* hosted by UKZN's Centre for Creative Arts. In 2003, Loots founded a professional dance company, the Flatfoot Dance Company. She has won numerous national choreographic awards and commissions and was awarded the *Chevalier des Arts et des Lettres* (Knight in the Order of Arts and Letters) by the French government in 2017 for her work (both artistic and curatorial) in the South African dance sector.

Wamuwi Mbao (author) is a literary critic and essayist. His reviews, essays and fiction appear in the *Johannesburg Review of Books*, *Africa is a Country*, and other journals. He was the recipient of a South African Literary Award in 2019 for his critical oeuvre. He teaches in the Department of English at Stellenbosch University and is the editor of *Years of Fire and Ash: South African Poems of Decolonisation* (2021), an anthology of South African struggle poetry.

Kobus Moolman (author) is Professor of Creative Writing in the Department of English Studies at the University of the Western Cape. He has published several collections of poetry and plays, as well as a collection of short stories. Moolman has won numerous national and international awards for his work, including the 2015 Glenna Luschei Prize for African Poetry. His most recent publication is a volume co-edited with Duncan Brown and Nkosinathi Sithole, *Notes from the Body: Health, Illness, Trauma* (2023).

Stephanus Muller (author) is Professor of Music and Director of the Africa Open Institute for Music, Research and Innovation (AOI) at Stellenbosch University. He holds master's degrees from Unisa, Stellenbosch and Oxford, and a DPhil from Oxford University. He has won awards for his books, *Nagmusiek* (2014) and *Sulke Vriende is Skaars* (2020), and also published the controversial *The Journey to the South* (2019), a book about university ethics and academic freedom of speech. He is a former editor of *South African Music Studies* (*SAMUS*), and published the first nine iterations of the digitally curated archive, *herri*, between 2019 and 2023.

Masande Ntshanga (author) was born in East London and has a bachelor's degree in Film and Media, an honours in English Studies, and a master's in Creative Writing from the University of Cape Town. He is the winner of the inaugural PEN International New Voices Award and is author of the novels *The Reactive* (2014) (winner of a Betty Trask Award in 2018) and *Triangulum* (2019) (nominated for the Nommo Award for Best Speculative Novel in 2019). He has also authored a collection of poetry and prose, *Native Life in the Third Millennium* (2020), published by his experimental press, Model See Media (MDL SEE).

Uhuru Portia Phalafala (author) has a PhD in English Literature and is a Senior Lecturer in the Department of English at Stellenbosch University, with teaching interests in critical race studies, material and expressive cultures, Black radical traditions, and decoloniality. She is preoccupied with the practices and poetics of be-ing, together with ancestors, the land, plants and animals, the cosmos and waters. This contemplation has thus far produced essays, a sonic documentary, poetry, and a turn to deep listening as bodied method. She is the author of *Mine Mine Mine* (2023) and *Keorapetse Kgositsile & the Black Arts Movement: Poetics of Possibility* (2024).

Annel Pieterse (author) is a Lecturer in the Drama Department at Stellenbosch University. She has a PhD in English Studies and has published articles on literature, theatre and film. She is particularly interested in emerging narrative styles across a range of media platforms. Her teaching and supervision focus on film and media studies. She has experience as a researcher, translator and script consultant in film, television and podcasting. She is the editor of *Constant Companions: South African Tales of the Supernatural*, an anthology of student writing.

Meg Vandermerwe (author) is Associate Professor in Creative Writing and English Literature at the University of the Western Cape (UWC). In 2010, she helped launch its Creative Writing degree and outreach programme (UWC CREATES), the first multilingual Creative Writing programme in South African Higher Education. She has published both academic and creative work in South Africa, the UK, the US and Vietnam, including three works of fiction – *This Place I Call Home* (2010), *Zebra Crossing* (2013) and *The Woman of the Stone Sea (2019)*. *Zebra Crossing* was selected by the *Cape Times* as one of the ten best South African books published in 2013 and was longlisted for the 2014 Sunday Times Literary Award. In 2015, it was chosen for the *Guardian* newspaper in the UK as one of the top ten books about migrants by Booker-shortlisted author Sunjeev Sahota.

Simon van Schalkwyk (author) is Senior Lecturer in the Department of English Studies at Wits University. He is currently co-editor of *Safundi: The Journal of South African and American Studies* and is the academic editor of the *Johannesburg Review of Books*, an independent literary review that publishes reviews, essays, poetry, photography and short fiction from South Africa, Africa, and beyond. His first collection of poetry, *Transcontinental Delay*, was published in 2021.

OTHER WORKS BY DRYAD PRESS

THE DRYAD PRESS LIVING POETS SERIES

earth-circuit, iyra e m maharaj
Night Transit, P. R. Anderson
Dark Horse, Michèle Betty
Star Reverse, Linda Ann Strang
Transcontinental Delay, Simon van Schalkwyk
The Mountain Behind the House, Kobus Moolman
In Praise of Hotel Rooms, Fiona Zerbst
catalien, Oliver Findlay Price
Allegories of the Everyday, Brian Walter
Otherwise Occupied, Sally Ann Murray
Landscapes of Light and Loss, Stephen Symons
An Unobtrusive Vice, Tony Ullyatt
A Private Audience, Beverly Rycroft
Metaphysical Balm, Michèle Betty

OTHER PUBLISHED WORKS

Palimpsests, Chris Mann
River Willows: Senryū from Lockdown, Tony Ullyatt
missing, Beverly Rycroft
The Coroner's Wife: Poems in Translation, Joan Hambidge
Unearthed: A Selection of the Best Poems of 2016, edited by Joan Hambidge and Michèle Betty

Available in South Africa from better bookstores nationwide, online at www.dryadpress.co.za, and internationally from African Books Collective (www.africanbookscollective.com).

www.ingramcontent.com/pod-product-compliance
Lightning Source LLC
Chambersburg PA
CBHW052047220426
43663CB00012B/2469